UNWANTED

UNWANTED

A MURDER MYSTERY
OF THE GILDED AGE

ANDREW YOUNG

WESTHOLME

Yardley

Westholme Publishing, LLC
904 Edgewood Road
Yardley, Pennsylvania 19067
Visit our Web site at www.westholmepublishing.com

First Printing June 2016
10 9 8 7 6 5 4 3 2 1
ISBN: 978-1-59416-246-6
Also available as an eBook.

Printed in the United States of America

For Teresa and P.B.

CONTENTS

PROLOGUE

On Friday, January 31, 1896, the sky over Cincinnati, Ohio, was dense with clouds. The air was thick with the smoke of thousands of fires from coal stoves and fireplaces. It was damp, but not cold enough to snow, nor warm enough to go out without a coat or cloak. Rain began to fall, and the streets were soon slick with mud and manure. Despite the conditions, the city was alive with the ring of hammers on iron, the whirl of industrial machinery, the hiss of steam engines. The alien sputter of a motorcar could occasionally be heard. Bare tree branches rattled in the parks and along parkways. The sound and smell of horses was everywhere, as was the clatter of wagons and carriages on cobblestones.

There was nothing remarkable about this day. The forty-hour workweek had not yet been established so weekends did not exist for most people. The fact that it was Friday wasn't even noted with mild significance. That night people would go to the theater, host parties, and visit saloons—to the consternation of temperance advocates—but many of them would still go to work the next day. Almost no one knew that something terrible and shocking would happen that evening. It isn't even clear that the principal parties involved knew that anything remarkable was about to occur, that a young girl would lose her life and that the story would become a national sensation, giving birth to books, songs, and legends.

The cities of Cincinnati, Covington, and Newport huddle along the banks of the Ohio River, a metropolis known as Greater Cincinnati. The largest and most prominent of the three is Cincinnati, which sits on the Ohio side of the river; Covington and Newport rest on the Kentucky side. In 1896, Cincinnati was the ninth largest city in the United States, the largest in Ohio, and second only to Chicago in the Midwest. The area had formed, millennia before, as a shallow lake. Ice ages came and went and at their whim carved basins, hills, and several rivers. The largest of these would eventually be called the "Oh-he-yo," meaning Great River in the Seneca language. The first humans to leave their mark on the land were a nameless people often referred to as the Moundbuilders. Their constructions, large earthworks, are best seen today at places like Fort Ancient and Serpent Mound in south-central Ohio. The last of these people vanished from the area at the dawn of the seventeenth century, around the time Jamestown, Virginia, was founded. Soon the region was populated by displaced Indians from the East, who were fleeing the expansion of European colonists. The colonists, now calling themselves Americans, were not long behind them.

In 1788 some settlers founded a town called "Losantiville" (a name cobbled from bits of four different languages) within a basin that was bordered on the south by the Ohio River and surrounded by steep hills in all other directions. It was part of the Old Northwest Territory, and in 1790 Governor Arthur St. Clair changed the name of the town to Cincinnati, after a Revolutionary War veterans group of which he was a member, itself named after the Roman figure Cincinnatus. In 1792 Kentucky became a state, followed by Ohio in 1803. Newport, Kentucky, was founded in 1795, while Covington, seemingly the last to seek official status, was incorporated in 1815.

Alongside this burst of sanctioned recognition, a new type of craft could be seen plying the waters of the Ohio, Licking, and Great Miami rivers: the steamboat. Water travel had always been preferred to shipping by wagon, which was slow, dangerous, and costly. A trip downriver, though posing its own unique risks, was relatively cheap, but for the same boat to go upriver required much more manpower to fight the current and was almost always not worth the effort. With the coming of the steamboat, all of this changed. Now goods flowed to and from the Greater Cincinnati area with relative ease. With progress and the money that accompanied it, the city grew.

In the 1820 U.S. census all of the big cities were in the East, save New Orleans, and all provided easy access to the Atlantic. In 1830, Cincinnati made its appearance as the eighth largest community in the country with a population of 24,831. In 1840, it was the sixth largest city, with a larger population than Brooklyn, St. Louis, and Chicago. The people of Cincinnati, including many immigrants from Germany and Ireland, old families and new, felt that something important was happening in their town.

Charles Dickens wrote in 1842 while traveling through the United States, "The inhabitants of Cincinnati are proud of their city as one of the most interesting in America, and with good reason: for beautiful and thriving as it is now, and containing, as it does, a population of fifty thousand souls, but two-and-fifty years have passed away since the ground on which it stands (bought at that time for a few dollars) was a wild wood, and its citizens were but a handful of dwellers in scattered log huts upon the river's shore."

Some people called Cincinnati the first truly American city, since it was founded and populated after the Revolutionary War. With parks, a zoo, and a great music hall, it became known to some as the "Paris of the Midwest," but to most it would always be the Queen City—Queen of the Ohio River, Queen of the West. Covington and Newport, try as they might to rise from under Cincinnati's shadow, were considered by the wider world as parts of the Queen City, if not in name.

By 1896, however, Cincinnati was on a slow decline. With the advent of the railroads and the subsequent vanishing of the steamboats, Chicago had long ago surpassed it in size and importance. In the 1890 census, Cincinnati had a population just short of 300,000, while Chicago had more than a million residents. The 1893 Chicago World's Columbian Exposition received an estimated 25 million visitors, while Cincinnati would never host anything of that magnitude. Other cities in Ohio were growing at a rapid pace; the chief of these was Cleveland, where industry and rail lines provided more incentive for business than steamboats ever could.

Yet Cincinnati and its sister cities had much to recommend them in 1896. The population was still large, despite the city's loss of status, and there was ready work in the tan yards, breweries, and factories. The iconic Procter and Gamble company, long associated with the city, was still making its popular soap in Ivorydale. There were opera houses, theaters, galleries, and all the temptations of a city at the end of the nineteenth century: gambling, prostitutes, and plenty to drink. There was boxing, horse racing, and when the weather was nice, one could catch a game of America's first professional baseball team, the Reds.

Across the river, beyond the city of Newport, lay Fort Thomas. The fort, named in honor of the Virginian-born Union general George Henry Thomas, known as the "Rock of Chickamauga," was built on a hill, often called the Highlands. It had been commissioned when it was decided that the barracks in Newport were too costly to maintain, due to continual flooding. In 1887, General Philip Sheridan, another former Union officer, ordered that 111 acres be set aside for this misleadingly nicknamed "West Point of the West." It was ready for occupation by 1890. The storied 6th Infantry Regiment currently called the fort home. The nation's eyes had recently turned toward the island of Cuba, and with a hint of war between the United States and Spain in the air, the regiment waited for orders to deploy. "Ruins of rich plantations mark the track of Cuban patriots," the *Cincinnati Enquirer* read. "Spanish press displeased with American expressions of sympathy for insurgents." The 6th would lead the charge up San Juan Hill.

The nation was on the brink of more than just war. A great debate had risen among men concerned with money, especially after the Great Panic of 1893, over whether U.S. currency should be backed by the old gold standard or "free silver." This issue, more than any other, would become the focus for the 1896 presidential campaign. The fate of the American economy seemed to hang in the balance and would produce, among other things, William Jennings Bryan's famous "Cross of Gold" speech that supported free silver and launched his nomination as the Democratic candidate for president.

The Great Panic had been a worldwide economic crisis caused by defaulted loans, first in Europe and then the United States. Thousands of businesses and farms failed. A quarter of the U.S. railroad companies went bankrupt, banks and steel mills closed, and unemployment skyrocketed; the jobless rate reached 25 percent nationally, with some states recording even higher numbers. Like the panics, depressions, and recessions that came before and after, it finally settled on the poor.

Into this storm stepped Jacob S. Coxey, a wealthy and eccentric Ohioan who owned a number of sandstone quarries. When he was forced to lay off forty workers, he felt angered that the federal government was doing nothing to aid them. He called for a march of the country's jobless to converge on Washington, D.C., on May 1, 1894, in what he believed would be a show of force, an army 500,000 men strong. He believed this army could persuade Congress to pass legislation for government-sponsored works programs. Men joined his march, leaving behind wives and children. When a group of men traveling down the Missouri River from Butte, Montana, were asked if any of them were married, one of them replied, "Lots of them, and the people of Montana are supporting their wives and children now. But what could the men do if they stayed home? There was no work and there would have been one more person to feed." Those opposed to what was called "Coxey's Army" considered them nothing more than a rabble of tramps, stealing as they went along. Those who supported the movement called it a crusade. In the end Coxey would march into Washington with only five hundred men. His demands went unmet and he was arrested for trespassing on the Capitol lawn. But Coxey's demonstration was not unique during this period. Trade unions rose and gained power. At the same time Coxey's Army was approaching Washington, thousands of workers were on strike across the country, including those at the Pullman Palace Car Company in Chicago. Reform movements began a wave of change that would lead to the Progressive Era.

Among the reform movements was the growing voice of women in the matters of government and society. Though no women were allowed to join Coxey's Army, they received help from women's organizations, particularly the Women's Christian Temperance Union, whose president, Frances Elizabeth Willard, spoke at the Chicago Exposition in 1893. "Let us not be disconcerted," she told her fellow activists, "but stand bravely by that blessed trinity of movements, Prohibition, Woman's Liberation, and Labour's uplift." Her detractors worried that she spread her organization among too many different concerns, what they derided as a "Do-Everything Policy." But all of these movements were beginning to take hold.

Dr. Stella Hunt, a lecturer at the homeopathic Pulte Medical College in Cincinnati who gave anatomy lessons to the women's class, had published a wry article on the nature of that mysterious disease known as hysteria. "Hysteria is from a Greek word meaning uterus," she wrote succinctly, "because it was reputed to have had its seat in that organ. . . . This view that hysteria is due to disorders of the womb is incorrect, for the disease exists in women in whom all functions of the uterus are healthily performed, and even in women born without a uterus." She went on to radically propose that hysteria might affect more men than women. "It is all-important," she emphasized, "that hysteria is *not* exclusively a disease of the female sex." At her home on a January 1896 evening, a small party of intimate friends and a few reporters gathered—not to hear about her medical studies in the hospitals of Paris, or to discuss her latest medical findings, or her opinions on the role of women in medicine—but for her to show off her new bicycling outfit. She happened also to be president of the Queen City Cycling Club. With careful detail the *Cincinnati Enquirer* reported that the material was of a tan covert cloth, the Norfolk jacket had a very small skirt sewed to the bottom, which was lined with silk. She wore a narrow leather belt, which was all the rage that season, and specifically designed bicycle boots. The most startling and also most practical part of the ensemble were the pants, not skirts, a pair of tan knickers, perfectly sensible for riding on a bicycle. Her cycling outfit was a sensation. Yet for some people in the city, it was going too far.

Knickerbockers were not unheard of, but this new style, not as billowy as before, proved to be troublesome. Especially in that it seemed to indicate nothing so much as a woman trying to behave like a man. This line of thinking, one can easily imagine at the time, could lead to dangerous places. Like men, women might want to vote, serve on juries or in the armed forces, go to male colleges, and work alongside men for equal pay. In the imaginations of the nation there grew a figure to be scorned or admired depending on a person's disposition, the New Woman, a term coined in 1894 by Sarah Grand. This brand-new archetype was typically educated or sought education, independent, and less interested in traditional trajectories for women, such as aspiring to an early marriage and keeping a house. The New Woman was by turns intimidating, sensual, dangerous, unpredictable, and heroic. This New Woman might just take it upon herself to leave the house and go out into the wide world, completely alone, perhaps riding a bicycle.

Frances Willard wrote in 1895 that not so long before, women wouldn't dream of going out without a male escort, "but in course of time a few women, of stronger individuality than the average, ventured to go unattended; later on, use wore off the glamour of the traditions which said that women must not go alone, and now none but an imbecile would hold herself to any such observance." In 1896 women were traveling by themselves across country or even around the world. It seemed very commonplace for a woman to board a train by herself and try to make it on her own, to find not a husband but a job in the city. It was an exciting new prospect for women of independent spirit, and yet there were also tales of women who boarded trains to find their futures and were never heard from again.

AROUND THIS TIME, Cincinnati and the rest of the country had learned of the horrors committed by a man who called himself "Dr. H. H. Holmes." As brilliantly told by Erik Larson in his bestselling *Devil in the White City*, Holmes ran a "hotel" and drugstore near the Chicago World's Columbian Exposition where he admitted to killing numerous persons, mostly young women he had hired. In December, the *Enquirer* ran a story that suggested the serial killer had been in Cincinnati. Holmes's actual number of victims remains unknown; he confessed at one point to killing twenty-seven people, but due to his seemingly inexhaustible desire for violence the true count will never be known. He would hang for his crimes in April 1896. For some this must have confirmed that it was best for women to remain at home under the protection of men. Death in the Queen City, however, was of a much more mundane nature.

In January 1896, the death count for the previous year was posted in the major newspapers as if it were the tallies of wins and losses at the horse track. Readers learned that 546 people in the Cincinnati area had died from diphtheria, 564 from typhoid fever, and a staggering 2,330 from measles. These numbers, however, were not alarming, since they were much the same as the death counts for the year before and the year before that. Measles was ubiquitous in the nineteenth century; almost every child developed the disease before they were fifteen and many died from complications. Measles was known to spread through coughing and sneezing, but nothing seemed capable of stopping outbreaks, especially among

the poor. A vaccine would not be developed until seventy
years later.

Murders, in contrast, were met with shock and dismay.
But readers couldn't quite seem to get enough of the gory
details. The more gruesome the act, the more innocent the
victim, the more people wanted to know. In 1895 the story of
Theodore Durrant traveled from San Francisco to the
Midwest. "Frisco's problem of crime," an *Enquirer* headline
of October 1895 read, "the atrocious murder of Blanche
Lamont and Minnie Williams and trial of Theo. Durrant.
The coil slowly tightening around the accused." In April
1895 two young women, both members of the Emanuel
Baptist Church, went missing within a two-week period.
The first victim, Blanche Lamont, was reported missing
three days after last being seen entering the church with
Theo Durrant, a young medical student who was superintendent of the church's Sunday school. Three hours later the
organist came to the church to practice and found Theo looking disheveled and saying he had been working on a gas leak
and found himself light-headed. When Blanche's aunt finally reported her missing, police asked Durrant if he knew
what had happened to the girl. "Perhaps she has wandered
from the moral path and gone astray," he said, telling her
aunt that he thought Blanche had been kidnapped and forced
into prostitution. He promised to rescue her.

On Good Friday Durrant and another young woman,
Minnie Williams, were seen arguing in front of the church
and then entering. Durrant arrived at a church meeting two
hours later, Minnie was nowhere to be seen. Later, some of
the women of the church gathered to decorate the pews with
flowers for Easter Sunday. They retired to a small room next
to the church's library. One of the women opened a cupboard
door, perhaps looking for a vase, but instead she discovered
the mutilated corpse of Minnie Williams. She was naked and

her underclothes were shoved in her mouth. Her wrists had been slashed so severely that the tendons as well as the arteries had been severed. She had been repeatedly stabbed in the chest with a dull knife. The coroner would conclude that Minnie had been raped after she was dead.

A thorough search of the church was conducted. The last place they looked, the belfry, was where they found the naked and mutilated body of Blanche Lamont. Durrant would be remembered forever afterward as the "Devil of the Belfry" for his choice to hide Blanche in this unused part of the church. Durrant was arrested and charged with the murders. The trial was covered in every major newspaper in the country. The defense's chief argument was that no blood was ever found on Durrant's clothes and that he did not have time to destroy any stained garments. The defense placed the guilt of the murders on the pastor of the church, but few believed their version of events. During Durrant's trial it was revealed that just prior to the murders, a young woman, another member of the church, had either come upon Durrant or been stopped by him in the library of the church—the testimony is not clear, but he was completely naked at the time. Thus the prosecutors concluded that Durrant had stripped before committing the mutilations. The jury deliberated for five minutes before returning a guilty verdict. Durrant would hang for his crimes in 1898, professing his innocence with his last breath.

IN CINCINNATI, there were concerns about the government, the economy, and the future of the region, but the dangerous stories reported in the papers such as the Holmes and Durrant cases were seemingly all from out of town. On the evening of January 31, 1896, it rained until ten o'clock. The factories had grown quiet and shops were closed, but the city was still alive with sounds of voices and music from numerous saloons. The gaslights did little to illuminate the streets that were dark with smoke and fog. A group of African American men walked toward their homes. These were the so-called "Caldwell Guards," a quasi-military group named after the current mayor of Cincinnati, John Alexander Caldwell, perhaps as a way to avoid confrontation with those who might question their activities. There is no information to suggest that they had any weapons nor were they official-ly sanctioned by the U.S. Army, but they trained in marching and combat exercises in a nearby park with the idea that they could help in some capacity if a war were to break out. Many of them, including George Jackson, captain of the guards, hoped to one day join the ranks of enlisted men.

Captain Jackson later related a story that would prove immensely important. After the drill was completed, and he was walking home, he was stopped at the corner of George and Elm streets. A white man, whom he had never seen before, approached him and his fellow soldiers and asked plainly, "Who wants to make five dollars?" It was dark and wet and George must have been tired, but he went with the man all the same; five dollars was a good sum. The man was delighted. "All I want you to do," he explained to George, "is to drive us over to Newport. I am a doctor and another physi-cian will be with me to take a very sick woman home." George agreed to do it, though there was never any evidence that he was paid the five dollars.

ONE

ILL REPUTE

SOMETIME BETWEEN SEVEN-THIRTY AND EIGHT O'CLOCK IN the morning on February 1, 1896, Jack Hewling, a fourteen-year-old boy who lived in the neighborhood of Fort Thomas with his parents, walked along Alexandria Pike and hopped a fence with the intention of cutting across a field to get to his place of employment, Colonel John Locke's (sometimes spelled Lock) fruit farm. Fort Thomas was the name of the military fort, but also had come to describe the community that surrounded the fort itself. The field that Jack crossed that morning, in fact, belonged to Colonel Locke. It was cold and foggy, making it hard to see clearly, but the rain from the day before had stopped for the time being. After walking about a hundred yards, Jack saw what he thought was a pile of clothes near some bushes that lined a disused dirt driveway. Accounts differ on what actually happened next. In some tellings Jack soon realized it was a woman lying on a bank. Knowing that this was a common spot for soldiers from nearby Fort Thomas and prostitutes to have trysts, he went to Locke's farm to find someone who might wake the woman and send her on her way.

Seeing a woman that morning was not particularly noteworthy; Jack later said that he had previously found several women in the field—presumably they had gotten drunk the night before and passed out wherever they found themselves—and had to chase off a few himself. Knowing this, the other account of that morning seems just as plausible, if not more so. Jack said that he approached the woman with the intent of waking her. As he drew closer, the fog cleared and he was able to make out more details. Her skirt was pushed up and over her head. He approached and put his hand on her dress. He pulled the skirt down, but was overcome by the sight and retched nearby. Her head was gone, her neck ended in a bloody stump. Another telling has Jack hop over the fence and go through the privet bushes and actually stumble over the woman. When he looked back he saw, to his horror, the headless body.

Regardless which story is believed, the results were the same. Hewling ran to the Locke farm and yelled for assistance. Wilbert Locke, the colonel's son, and Mike, another farm hand, hurried to the spot where the body lay. They immediately informed Colonel Locke, who went to Fort Thomas and from there telegraphed the police in Newport and told the commanding officer, Colonel Cochran, of the discovery.

The victim lay on her back on a low rise, with her legs angled up the slope, and her feet splayed. She was partly concealed under a bush. Where her head should have been was only a huge pool of blood that had soaked into the ground. Her clothes were in disarray, her skirt had been pulled up, revealing her undergarments. A bloody corset lay near the body. The upper part of her dress was torn open, as was the garment underneath, exposing her bosom. She wore no coat or cloak, which seemed curious because of the weather. The body was dry, which could only mean she had come there after it had stopped raining the night before around ten o'clock. Word spread quickly, and while the authorities made their way to the scene, interested parties (which included nearly everyone in the area) began to make their way to this corner of the Locke farm as well.

An hour after Hewling found the body, Campbell County coroner Walter S. Tingley, M.D., and Sheriff Jule Plummer along with some other officers arrived at the scene, having come from Newport. A crowd was already gathered along Alexandria Pike. The coroner and officers found one of the woman's brown kid gloves nearby and a torn piece of her dress. There was blood everywhere, on the ground and the grass around the body, and splashed up on the leaves of the bush. The victim's clothes were soaked. The investigators meticulously noted the footprints going to and from the scene. Though there were many and it was hard to determine when the footprints were made or which were associated with the crime, someone—a visitor, a reporter—concocted a possible scenario of what happened, that the newspapers would later report.

With seemingly impossible detail, from very little evidence, the footprints told their own tale, it was said, that started when a man and woman walked out into the field at a leisurely pace. There was some sort of struggle and the woman tried to flee, splashing through a puddle of mud on her way. The man caught up to her and dragged her back behind the bushes. There was a great struggle, the woman was killed, and her head removed either in a fit of savage fury or as a means to conceal her identity. The subsequent investigation would create a theory of what happened that night, but it failed to match this original "footprint story" in any detail except that the end result was that a young woman had been killed and her head removed.

Somehow, an enterprising journalist from the *Cincinnati Enquirer* was able to get a detailed account of what the victim was wearing. Along with it came some not very subtle judgments. The clothing she wore was "of the cheapest description." There was the bloody corset found near her body that was originally all white and probably new. The shoes, the unnamed observer decided, were the only thing about the victim that did not speak of poverty. They were a pair of black cloth-topped dress shoes size 3 1/2. Over these the woman wore rubber galoshes. She wore a dark blue flannel skirt and black garters with plated buckles. Under all of this she wore "gray suit of union underwear," which is the kind of undergarment later associated with old country men with a flap in the rear held up by buttons. Both for the times and the time of year this was a sensible article of clothing. Her green dress was a "wrapper," that is, a common work dress or housedress. "It was such a dress as a woman of the lower class would wear indoors, and, covered with a cloak, on the street," the *Enquirer* reporter explained. "She undoubtedly wore a cloak, which the murderer wrapped her head in when he carried it away." Women of lower classes often had only wrappers and no formal dresses, which was not so bad since wrappers are generally regarded as the more comfortable of the two.

While the footprints and clothing seemed to tell their own stories, Coroner Tingley, fittingly, focused more on the condition of the body and the blood evidence at the scene. He was forty-nine years old, having served as a state representative, a minister, and a physician. He had a wife named Harriet, and one daughter, Georgia, who had passed away fourteen years earlier. If she had survived she would have been nineteen years old, a young woman much like the victim that lay before him. He was a Republican and had been elected to the position of coroner in November 1894, as part of a wave of Republican wins in Campbell County. One of the only Democrats to keep his position was Tingley's companion at the crime scene, Sheriff Plummer. The region had been dismayed by the success of the Republicans in a southern state, but this was northern Kentucky and this shift in power further demonstrated the pull of Cincinnati on its neighbors across the river. Tingley proved to be a fine coroner.

Though this was far from his first case, it was probably his most gruesome. He must have known, as he looked at the horrible scene, that he would be called upon to remember every detail of that morning. Summoning himself, he took careful notice of the most horrifying detail. "On viewing the stump of the neck," he later recalled, "I found an irregular cut on the back, and upon turning it over found a smooth cut. The incision was as though a clean disarticulation had been attempted."

He noted the disheveled clothes, as if someone were searching for something on the girl's person. He searched the body as well as he could in the cold and damp bushes. He wondered if there were any other marks of violence, but he only found three. "Across (the) fingers of the left hand were cuts. The first finger just a slight cut. Two other fingers were cut deeply. They were apparently clean cut."

He determined that the wounds appeared recent. They were most likely delivered the night before by a keenly sharp knife. The head, as many people had already noted, was nowhere to be found. Tingley concluded that the killer must have taken it with him, adding to the belief that the head had been severed from the body as a means to elude identification.

He knew the answer he needed to determine before all else: the cause of death. Seeing the blood clots near the neck, the blood in the grass, the stains on her clothing, he took

what he knew of the human body and the cuts on her hand
and the missing head and made his preliminary determina-
tion, which would remain his working theory for the rest of
the investigation. He had come to the conclusion that the
decapitation was done and the murder was committed with
the same stroke. "I think the artery was severed while the
heart was still beating," he said.

Despite the widespread presence of blood at the scene,
Tingley questioned if it was actually *enough* blood. At the
inquest on February 11, he was asked to take into "consideration the amount of blood on the ground and the arrangement of her clothing, do you think that the woman was killed
where found?" Tingley replied with confidence, "It did not
seem so to me. There was not enough blood on the ground to
lead me to that conclusion."

At the scene of the crime, Tingley finished his initial study
and allowed the body to be taken to Newport and kept at
White's Funeral Home, which acted as a mortuary. There is
no indication that Coroner Tingley or Sheriff Plummer
remained at the scene much longer than that. The crowd that
had gathered was large by this time. Most stayed on the road,
but some, dismissing any scruples if they had any, hopped the
fence and began to rummage about the field.

In 1896 there was no fear of contaminating a crime scene,
except with regards to footprints, which had already been
noted. There was no gathering of fingerprints, not even from
the corset that had been "marked by bloody fingers." Sir
Francis Galton had published his landmark book
Fingerprints in 1892, but using fingerprints as a means of
identification was not yet an established procedure, despite
the fact that in Mark Twain's 1883 memoir, *Life on the
Mississippi*, a murderer was found by his unique fingerprint.
Cincinnati police employed what was called the "Bertillon
system" to identify criminals. This unique system was created by Alphonse Bertillon in France in 1879, and had been

adopted in the United States in 1887, first in Illinois. Bertillon's system used specific body measurements and two photographs, one from the side and one from the front, to identify criminals. (The photographs would be the basis for the modern mug shot.) The body measurements and photographs were used instead of a name because criminals often gave false names when arrested. The system was designed to catch repeat offenders, not to solve crimes. But Cincinnati's Bertillon system was quite different. The Cincinnati police appeared only to take measurements of the head of a suspect, and thus were able—in their judgment— to determine just what kind of criminal they had on their hands. It was a practice much more closely related to the pseudo-science of phrenology.

The curiosity seekers near Fort Thomas were allowed to approach the scene freely. At some point the residents of the Locke farm began to provide refreshments. The people gathered began to collect souvenirs. They pulled branches off the bushes, pulled grass from the ground, some people even brought shovels and buckets, digging up the soil and carrying it off, finding when they did that the blood had soaked the ground several inches. They took anything with blood and they were able to find blood all around the scene. Whether they were well-meaning amateur sleuths or bloodthirsty profit-seekers is unknown. They took their souvenirs and left, while more people gathered to take their place, possibly purchasing leaves and branches from the collectors on their way out.

"There is almost nothing to go on as far as the efforts to identify the victim and get some clew to the murderer are concerned," the *Cincinnati Enquirer* reported. "It is believed that she is a woman of the town who has been living in one of the resorts of Cincinnati, as many of these women frequent the neighborhood of the military post." ("Clew" was once the preferred spelling on both sides of the Atlantic and originated from the term for a ball of thread, which one might use to find the way out of a maze.) The only clue, if it could be considered that, was the speculation that the woman had been a prostitute.

It was not a wholly absurd assumption. There was nothing about the body that indicated this was a woman from the growing middle class or high society. The finest thing she wore were her curiously small shoes and even those did not indicate wealth, just that they were nice shoes. There was no obvious reason why a woman of good character would be out in a farm field after ten o'clock in the evening, they reasoned. As Jack Hewling explained, this was a common place to find "women of low moral character" or "women of the town," which were polite ways to describe prostitutes. They were fond of the soldiers at the fort and by all accounts the soldiers were fond of them.

PROSTITUTION IN THE LATE nineteenth century was big business. Some have argued that it provided the most economic freedom and the best wages for women who had little in the way of employment opportunities, and the prime example is invariably the successful madam who owned property and gained her own wealth in a time when few women achieved this level of independence. For others, it was a different economy, such as a single mother, widowed or whose husband had left her, where prostitution became the only option. Food was so scarce during the depression that followed the Panic of 1893 that mothers turned to prostitution just to obtain sustenance for their children. These were not New Women, educated and active, they were women who made choices out of desperation.

At the same time there were stories of women and girls forced into prostitution. Reformers called it the new slavery and denounced it. It was an evil institution, which did nothing but destroy the family and the community. The pimp was a slave master, and his prostitutes were helpless victims. Much like the argument for or against Prohibition or the debate over free silver against the gold standard, each side was fervent and had ready examples, but neither could claim a complete hold on the truth. It is hard to determine the day-to-day life of a prostitute in late nineteenth-century urban America, because no one appears to have asked them or obtained specifics on their condition. This would come later.

Prostitution had long been considered a necessary vice in American society, but by the end of the nineteenth century attitudes were changing. In previous decades, prostitution was relegated to particular districts in most cities. For instance, there was a "tenderloin" district centered around George Street in Cincinnati where bordellos could carry on their business without much interference from the police. This did not mean prostitutes were always free from prosecution; for example, under the *Enquirer* headline of "Local Brevities," an African American prostitute name Martha Turner was sent to the workhouse, not for her occupation, but for drunkenness. She received an additional fine for calling the arresting officer a "vile name." The reactions to prostitution were varied. In some cases girls were "reclaimed" by the police and were sent to institutions such as the Home for the Friendless or the House of the Good Shepherd, without formally being charged for a crime. At other times prostitutes had to be registered with the police, a process that involved a lecture from the chief on appropriate behavior. Prostitution would not become illegal in Cincinnati until the beginning of the twentieth century, but reformers had been working to criminalize it for some time. They did not think prostitution was an inevitable part of society, but instead argued that the creation of vice districts only encouraged prostitution by giving it a sense of legitimacy.

In the early 1890s an evangelical man named H. G. Petersen, a printer by trade, rented the lower portion of a house at 151 George Street with the expressed intention of reclaiming fallen women. The upstairs of the same house and an adjoining apartment had long been used by prostitutes. So, every night, in the very heart of the vice district, Petersen held meetings encouraging women to abandon their sinful employment and return to the path of righteousness. He prayed with the women and was known throughout the neighborhood as an enthusiastic reformer; however, his attentions were focused on saving the women one at a time, not on changing the opinions of the wider public or seeking political action. In the long run, he effected very little lasting change.

Possibly the largest organization against prostitution at the time was, not surprisingly, the Women's Christian Temperance Union with their "Do-Everything Policy." By 1896 there were over two hundred thousand members, with chapters in every major city. They organized letter campaigns, wrote petitions, and published extensively. At the last annual meeting of the WCTU in October 1895 in Baltimore, its president, Frances Willard, was the keynote speaker. She spoke on many issues: equal suffrage without distinction of sex, opposition to landlords and tenements, prohibition of alcohol, money issued only by the federal government, and a commendation to New York City police superintendent Theodore Roosevelt; but her main theme was one of purity.

Frances Willard, born in 1839 and raised in Wisconsin and Illinois, resigned as dean of women at Northwestern University in 1874 to become the corresponding secretary of the newly formed WCTU. In 1879 she became president of the organization and continued in that capacity until her death in 1898. Susan B. Anthony once introduced her to a U.S. Senate Committee as a "general with an army of

250,000." Willard once said that the WCTU worked "to make the whole world *homelike*." This may seem like a benign sentiment, but Willard's view was far reaching. She demanded equal access to work for men and women, and equal pay to go with it. The WCTU denounced rich corporations for not creating safe working environments. She argued for municipal ownership of utilities and unions for women workers, and worked to set up shelters for ex-prostitutes to give those unfortunate women a path out of their sinful employment. Willard declared herself a Christian socialist.

Regardless of the morality of prostitution or how it should be addressed through social programs, it was a dangerous enterprise. Going off alone with strange men to engage in sex was an exceptionally risky endeavor, even if someone, somehow, didn't know the horrors of the Whitechapel murders that had gripped Londoners in 1888–1891. Medical experts had become well aware of the way in which venereal disease spread, noting several cases where a married man met with a prostitute, contracted the disease, and gave it to his wife. If his wife became pregnant, the disease could be passed on to the child. This was clear evidence, reformers were quick to point out, that prostitution could literally destroy a family.

Another danger to the prostitute was unwanted pregnancy. Women often became prostitutes due to financial troubles; it would be an economic burden to conceive a child with a customer. Due to the mores of the time, it is not generally known how prostitutes exercised "reproductive control." In 1883 it was reported in Indiana that a young woman, like the other women in her brothel, douched with a mixture of water and carbolic acid. Though this could obviously cause irritation and "nervous symptoms," she concluded that it stopped pregnancies and helped to fight off venereal disease. This was all very controversial and spoke to the double-mindedness of the times, that prostitution was tolerated in many places, yet the thought that a woman might be able to practice birth control was a threat to society and would lead to wantonness. Condoms were available, but there is no clear evidence on how often they were used. There is more evidence that when faced with an unwanted pregnancy, prostitutes turned to illegal abortions. Some aging prostitutes in the late nineteenth century performed abortions, demonstrating that they had some previous experience with the methods.

Disease and unwanted pregnancies, however, were arguably not the most frightening thing about being a prostitute. The woman found in Col. Locke's field, people reasoned, obviously went off with a client, probably a soldier, hoping to make some quick money, but instead she found herself in the grips of a monster, a demon like H. H. Holmes or Theo Durrant, who killed her in cold blood, took off her head with skill, and then kept it as a kind of souvenir.

WHEN THE CINCINNATI POLICE DEPARTMENT finally got word of the murder that Saturday morning, they sent two of their best: Detectives Cal Crim and John McDermott. David Calvin Crim and had come to Cincinnati from Maryland when he was fifteen years old. He had worked as a bootblack then a desk clerk at the Brighton Hotel. In 1886, he joined the Cincinnati Police Department that was being reorganized under the new chief Phillip Deitsch because, he said, "a fireman's hours were too long." He quickly worked his way up the department's hierarchy and became a detective, working in the vice squad. When he and his partner were called to be part of the Fort Thomas investigation he was thirty-two years old. In a later photograph, one can see the young man, the soft features, the unassuming expression, the intelligent eyes. He does not strike the viewer as a hard man, but instead as an easy friend, with a clean straw hat pushed back a little on his head. Jack McDermott was new to the position and had previously been a clerk with the water works. An article on McDermott said, "He combines intelligence with a rare amount of energy." He was married and had three children.

When the two men arrived on the scene they found chaos. One report indicates that soldiers from Fort Thomas were enlisted to provide a barricade around the scene, but it is unclear how long this barricade stayed in place, how effective it was, or when the soldiers were allowed to disperse. Some of Crim's later statements indicate when he got to the scene, the barricade was gone. However other reports indicate that someone had telephoned Newport, Covington, and Cincinnati police departments at the same time and that Plummer, Tingley, Crim, and McDermott had all been at the scene at the same time and within the barricade set up by the soldiers.

The souvenir-hunters had gathered everything they could, though Detective Crim was able to pocket a few blood-stained leaves from a nearby bush. Ladies in fine dresses stood away from the sight where the body had been but glanced discreetly in that direction so that they might catch something horrific from the corner of their eyes. The bush under which the body was found had been stripped bare, and the branches were taken, leaving only a few empty stalks. Despite the efforts of the souvenir-hunters, there was still some blood evidence left. The detectives found blood as high as six feet on leaves above where the body had been. As one writer put it, "Upon the under and the top sides of the leaves of the privet bushes, to the height of over seven feet, drops of blood were found which sparkled in the morning sun like drops of dew."

That Saturday, the afternoon papers gave the first account of what was being called "the Fort Thomas mystery." Many businesses and factories closed early on Saturday and so peo-

ple began to go out and gather in any place connected to the
tragedy. Locke was forced to station men around his property to keep away relic hunters. People flocked to the White &
Company funeral home in Newport where the body was
being kept.

THIS GRUESOME SCENE and the intense interest in it spoke to
the timelessness of humanity's fascination with murder, from
Greek tragedies to the stories that filled the daily papers. Still
this might seem odd for the times. Late nineteenth-century
America brimmed with optimism, a harbinger of the bright
future of the next century. America was gaining wealth at an
amazing rate. Despite the fact that many thousands of poor
and jobless were still suffering because of the recent depression, the wealthy were getting richer and many were joining
their ranks every year. The number of millionaires went
from twenty in 1840 to several thousand by 1896. New mar-
vels were being created at what must have seemed a dizzying
rate. The telegraph had been long established, but now came
the telephone and its ability to carry the human voice. The
light bulb, or incandescent lamp, could safely light streets
and homes. The typewriter, adding machine, and fountain
pen transformed businesses. The Kodak camera gave pho-
tography to the middle class. The automatic dishwasher
reduced kitchen drudgery. Skyscrapers rose in cities across the
country, and with them, elevators and escalators. Even small
things like safety pins and paper clips were marvelous in their
simplicity and practicality. Some must have thought this was
the beginning of a new age of wonder and prosperity.

The most popular music of the time was anything but
melancholy or dark. John Philip Sousa, former leader of the
U.S. Marine Band, had formed a marching band in 1892.
They toured the country almost continuously. Sousa became

known as the "March King" and his music embodied just
what the audiences of the late nineteenth century were looking for: patriotic, masculine, forceful, yet simple compositions. Sousa's pieces were never long, never complicated. He
favored standards, formulas. To use a favorite phrase of the
time, it made the listener want to shout through a massive
grin, "bully!" In 1896, on a return home from a European
vacation, Sousa would compose his most famous piece, "The
Stars and Stripes Forever," which he would debut in
Philadelphia the next year. In April 1895 Sousa and his band
had played in Cincinnati at the beautiful music hall. The
papers raved, "The concert by Sousa's band last night, in
Music Hall, was again a convincing illustration of the mag-
netic influence upon the public of a popular conductor, a popular band, and a popular programme. Mr. Sousa is principal-
ly known by his marches, and as conductor of the Marine
Band, he gained a reputation by catering to the tastes of the
masses of the American people second to no other conductor
in this country." His songs were "swinging" and "vivacious"
with plenty of "vim" and "snap" and especially "dignity."
This was not music for dwelling on the macabre side of life.

There was another type of music beginning to find its way
into the lexicon of the American songbook. The first time it
appears in the *Cincinnati Enquirer* it is completely innocuous.
It is an advertisement, under an ad for muslin underwear
and above another ad for side combs, for a music book selling for twenty-three cents called *Ben Harney's Ragtime
Instructor*. Ragtime was apparently discovered by the general
public at the World's Columbian Exposition in Chicago in
1893. The chief figure in the genre, Scott Joplin, a sometimes
itinerant pianist, cornetist, and composer, was on hand to see
this very early marriage of traditional European piano music
"ragged" to the tempo of African music. Ragtime was jovial,
brimming with energy. Some early recordings, closer to the

time of Joplin's compositions, seem manic. The players, though much more controlled than later jazz impresarios, sped through the music, as if the goal were to see the thing finished as quickly as possible.

Ragtime was born in the brothels and bars of American cities in the Midwest and South. A music that seemed ready made for the rowdy crowds of the 1890s, it would later become the stock music of saloons in Western films. While Sousa was taking his band on whirlwind tours via train and playing in the grandest venues in the nation, Scott Joplin was playing in churches, whorehouses, dance halls, and by the banks of the Mississippi. He was not on a tour, he had no "programme"; he was traveling and playing when and where he could. Joplin's greatest hit, "Maple Leaf Rag," might have been written as early as 1896, although it wasn't published until 1899. It would become the gold standard of the ragtime genre. The song, like all ragtime songs, is still at its core a march, but its syncopation reveals a complexity not found in Sousa's work. The primary social difference was this: you could, and were encouraged, to dance to ragtime; there was no dancing at a Sousa concert. After a few years, ragtime had sealed its popularity when preachers were denouncing it as "obscene."

America was picking up its collective tempo, and there was an air of progress, but the nation was not so blinded by the promise of tomorrow to forget the horrors of the past. In 1896 there were plenty of people who remembered the carnage of the Civil War, and many of the men who came home with missing limbs—some having also lost something deep within their souls—still could be seen in communities across the country. *Frankenstein*, first published in 1818, remained a popular tale, describing a being created from discarded bits and pieces of corpses. A headless girl found on a foggy winter morning would always attract attention, cause readers to pause. Detective Crim stood in the cold, among the people milling about, and tried to piece together this seemingly hopeless mystery, and unbeknownst to him there was someone else close by doing the same thing.

TWO

OUTRAGE

I T BEGAN TO RAIN AGAIN ON THE AFTERNOON OF SATURDAY, February 1, 1896. Much of what remained after the public had scoured the scene, was quietly washed away. Detective Crim later described his observations on coming to the scene, "I was notified by the Chief of Detectives, Hazen, to report to Newport and assist in clearing the mystery of the crime. With Detective McDermott and Sheriff Plummer I went to where the body was found, and came to the conclusion that she was murdered there."

Crim didn't know of Coroner Tingley's assessment then, nor later under oath. He explained: "There was so much blood on the ground that it led me to this belief, and I also found blood high on the surrounding bushes, which I believed to have been caused by the blood spurting from the neck. I found blood on all the underside of the leaves, showing that the course of blood was upward, as though the body was on the ground when the throat was cut." Though they differed on the location of the murder, Crim and Tingley both agreed the woman met her end by a knife wound to the throat.

A large crowd was beginning to gather outside White & Company, the Newport undertaker's establishment. One report called it a "black mass of humanity." They craned their necks and jostled with one another in the cold rain to get a glimpse of the body, but anyone trying to get a look at the remains was disappointed, as officers stationed at White's door had orders to refuse anyone admission unless they were genuinely looking for a missing girl or woman and might be able to identify the remains. Rumors began to swirl around this newborn crime. Any girl or woman who hadn't been seen since the night before became the victim. Any man acting suspiciously became the murderer.

One of those allowed to view the body was Green Palmer, who lived not far from where the body was found. He believed the body might be that of his niece, Fannie Palmer. She had two moles on the back of her left hand, he explained, and upon seeing the moles on the victim's hand, he identified the body as that of his niece. He then broke down, crying uncontrollably. The man seemed completely certain, and some of the police gathered at White's were sure then that they knew, at least, who the dead woman was. Their relief proved short-lived, however, when about an hour later a Lieutenant Smith returned to state that he had located Fannie alive and well right there in Newport. It would become just the first in a long line of false trails. Those officially involved in the investigation would develop a healthy skepticism, but the average person seemed happy to believe and spread any rumor they came upon. The newspapers printed every theory, any half-formed stories that hinted at solving the case, almost all of them unfounded.

Why White & Company undertakers and embalmers was selected to house the body is not readily apparent. Located at No. 9 East Fourth Street in Newport, it was on a block of narrow, tall buildings mostly devoted to offices. There was a drugstore nearby and residences not too distant. That afternoon, however, it was as if a foreign dignitary had decided to visit this river city and take a respite at this unassuming undertaker's establishment, as a curious crowd pressed against its door and windows. Inside, Coroner Tingley was able to conduct a more thorough examination of the body; it was not an official post-mortem, but he did determine that the woman had not been "outraged."

To be "outraged" was often a euphemism for rape. As H. L. Mencken quipped, the early nineteenth century was a "golden age of euphemism." By 1896, things might have gotten a little better; it was acceptable to say the word "pants," for instance, and even that most delicate of words "leg" instead of the once preferred "nether limb." We have already touched upon the reluctance of newspapers to use the term prostitute, but instead relying on "women of ill repute" or "women of the town" or simply "certain women." Rape was hardly ever mentioned and it was often stated that a victim had been "seduced" by the perpetrator. It became difficult to tell the difference between an actual seduction and a case of rape.

How Tingley determined that the victim had not been raped is not clear. Given the reluctance of the time to speak plainly on such matters, it isn't altogether clear what exactly he meant by "outraged." Perhaps he was referring to evidence that the body was not sexually molested after death. If it was specifically rape that Tingley was referring to, it was also unclear what exactly that entailed. At the end of the nineteenth century rape was not clearly defined. For decades many doctors expressed the opinion that a healthy, adult woman could not actually be raped. At the same time judges often discounted the opinions of doctors in cases of alleged rape, not believing that they could be authorities on the subject. By the 1880s common law in the United States held that sexual intercourse with any female under the age of consent was rape, though that age differed by location. In Kentucky the age of consent appears to have been twelve years of age.

The *General Statutes of Kentucky* published in 1887 defined rape as sexual intercourse with someone under twelve years of age or carnal knowledge of a female over the age of twelve "against her will or consent, or by force, or whilst she is insensible." The person who commits this crime "shall be guilty of rape, and punished by confinement in the penitentiary not less than ten nor more than twenty years, or by death, in the discretion of the jury." This shows that someone convicted of rape could face harsh punishment, but it was not always easy to prove that rape was committed. In order to successfully bring a case of rape against an assailant, the victim would need to have an unblemished record of chastity. The victim needed to prove that she had offered as much resistance as she possibly could, otherwise it was assumed the victim, on some level, was allowing the act to take place and so was consenting. She had been seduced or coerced, but not actually forced.

This was only true when the victim and the assailant were both white. If the victim was black, she had little chance of bringing a case against her attacker. From studies of the time, it appears there is no clear evidence of a black rape victim bringing a successful trial against a white attacker. If the victim was white and the assailant was black, the situation was very different. Juries readily convicted black men of rape, although the accused, rightly or wrongly, could be lynched before ever seeing the inside of a courtroom, particularly in the South.

In 1888, Mrs. J. C. Underwood of Elyria, Ohio, accused William Offett of raping her in her kitchen while her husband was away. Offett denied the charge and claimed he had been invited there by Mrs. Underwood. As he was a black man and she was a white woman (a minister's wife no less), his word was worthless before the jury. Lucky for him, he was in the North where he was less likely to be lynched. Regardless, the jury found him guilty and sentenced him to fifteen years. After Offett had been in prison for four years, Mrs. Underwood, feeling her own guilt, confessed the truth to her husband. She had met Offett at the post office and he had carried some bundles home for her. "He had a strange fascination for me," she explained. She invited him to call on her, which he did several times and each time they were intimate. "Why I did so I do not know, but that I did is true," she told her husband. "I did not care after the first time. In fact I could not have resisted, and had no desire to resist." When asked why she had lied, she said, "I had several reasons. One was the neighbors saw the fellow here, another was, I was afraid I had contracted a loathsome disease, and still another was that I feared I might give birth to a Negro baby. I hoped to save my reputation by telling you a deliberate lie." Offett was freed and the Underwoods were soon divorced. Six years later, in 1896, in cases in which the alleged perpetrator was black and the victim was a chaste white woman, guilty verdicts were still handed down swiftly.

Race relations were at their bleakest since the Civil War. On June 7, 1892, Homer Plessy, a thirty-year-old Creole with "one eighth African blood," sat in a whites-only car on a Louisiana train. This was not happenstance. Plessy was acting on the behalf of a black civil rights organization, which thought he would be the best test case since he could easily pass as a white man. The rail company had been forewarned that Plessy would be there and that he would identify himself as black. Plessy was immediately arrested. The case would make it to the Supreme Court, which would hear the arguments and rule in the spring of 1896. In its famous *Plessy vs. Ferguson* ruling, the court would uphold the "separate but equal" laws of the South and thus began sanctioned segregation.

In his dissenting opinion, Justice John Marshall Harlan conceded that the white race was superior, "but in view of the Constitution, in the eye of the law, there is in this country no superior, dominant, ruling class of citizens. There is no caste here. Our Constitution is color-blind, and neither knows nor tolerates classes among citizens. In respect of civil rights, all citizens are equal before the law. The humblest is the peer of the most powerful." These words would be ignored well into the coming century.

On January 29, 1896, one Cincinnati paper reported a tale from West Virginia. Alex Jones, who was described simply as a "negro desperado," boarded a train while drunk and became loud and quarrelsome. When an attempt was made to subdue him, he pulled two revolvers and began firing inside the train car, which was filled with passengers. Jones shot and killed a postmaster, wounded a conductor, and shot a black miner through the right breast which was "probably fatal." Jones was arrested and put in jail. He was then placed on another train to be transported for trial, but the train was stopped by a mob of one hundred men, who took Jones, shot him repeatedly, and strung him up in a tree in the town of Hemphill. A note was pinned on his chest that read, "This deed was done for the purpose of example and warning to negroes; so beware."

If the story is true, Jones was undoubtedly guilty of murder and by the law of the time he should have died for his crime, but his punishment was meted out extralegally. This was true for much of the experience of blacks and other minorities in the 1890s. The law dictated equal rights and equal treatment, but society had not caught up with the law. In the late nineteenth century society bent the law backward so that blacks were second-class citizens.

The catchphrase of segregation was "separate but equal"; in practice, however, it was never equal. In the papers blacks were often "brutes" and bent on the destruction of peace and order, lacking any sign of virtue. In *Race Traits and Tendencies of the American Negro* published in 1896, statistician Frederick Ludwig Hoffman, who worked for the Prudential Insurance Company, wrote with all the authority of what he considered sound evidence, "Until the Negro learns to respect life, property, and chastity, the criminal tendencies will increase." He was addressing what many considered the "negro rape problem"; that is, that African American men were more likely to commit rape. No one considered that the public might have had a collective bias that more easily defined rape when the perpetrator was black, but when the perpetrator was white, the victim had to prove she was not complicit.

However, in some cases, late nineteenth-century attitudes were changing about the definition of rape. Some argued that sexual assault did not require that the victim be under-age, out of her senses, or held down by a group of men. These progressive thinkers argued that the race of the victim or the assailant did not matter. As Charles Gilbert Chaddock, the noted neurologist who is believed to have coined the term "bisexual," wrote in 1894, "The old question whether it is possible for a single man to force a woman of good physical development, while in full possession of her sense, to submit to coitus, is quite besides the mark in cases of actual rape. Under such circumstances, capable of successfully resisting the sexual approach of a man, her failure to do so would be no evidence that she had not offered all the resistance possible to her at the time." People began to entertain the idea that a woman could be raped not just by physical force but also by the threat of violence.

As Coroner Tingley examined the unnamed victim's underclothes, he found that they were intact, not torn or cut, and they remained on her body, thus he could have easily believed that there was no reason to think she had been raped, but it is hard to say anything with certainty, other than his statement that she had not been "outraged." Elsewhere the investigation continued.

As the day progressed, Colonel Melville Cochran, at Fort Thomas, was beginning to find support for something he already believed was true. There appeared to be nothing in the fort or anything concerning the soldiers stationed there that implicated them in this heinous deed. All the soldiers were accounted for. Their possessions had been searched and no evidence was found.

Cochran had been in his current position for over five years, as commander of the 6th Infantry Regiment. Besides Company A at Fort Wood and Company E stationed at the Newport Barracks, the rest of the companies were stationed in the Highlands. The 6th Infantry was in its eighty-eighth year of existence. They served in the War of 1812, the Mexican War, the battles with the Seminoles in Florida, and the Civil War; they built the first fort west of the Missouri River and founded the earliest settlement in Nebraska. Behind Colonel Cochran stood the ghosts of all the previous commanders of the regiment. He might have wondered if they watched now, as soldiers were searched and the grounds checked for any sign of a connection to this terrible crime.

Unlike Coroner Tingley, Detective Crim, and Sheriff Plummer, Cochran was hoping that no evidence would be found, nothing to tie his men with that headless body in that forlorn field. He might have worried that someone involved in the search would come across a bloody cloak, a knife, or even the poor girl's head. If he did have those concerns, he never expressed them to the press. He assured everyone he could that morning that his men had nothing to do with the murder, and he would prove to be right.

A new story was developing among people who had been near Fort Thomas the night before. They had seen a man "tall, powerful, and fairly well dressed" in the company of a woman who was "slight and young enough to be good looking." The couple had stepped off a Fort Thomas trolley car at about eleven o'clock and, perhaps, stopped at one of the bars in the row of buildings opposite the fort. They then walked off into the night. Nothing more could be discerned about the couple, they apparently didn't speak directly to anyone and there was nothing particular about them that caused anyone to give them a second thought until the next morning. The man did not appear to be keeping the woman against her will. This fit well with the theory that the victim had been a woman of ill repute and that she had not been raped. The portrait of the killer was beginning to take shape—he was a man of cold-blooded intentions, like H. H. Holmes and Theo Durrant; he was not in a frenzy from drunkenness, he gave off no signs of being deranged. He lured the woman into that field under the pretensions of prostitution, but his purpose was much more sinister than that.

In the crowd standing outside White's funeral parlor, a man named Chapman Gaskins was overheard to say that he knew just who the dead woman was and who had killed her. The police immediately took him into custody. After "threats and persuasion" were applied he stated that he had seen the victim near Fort Thomas the night before, in the company of a man he knew. He refused to give the name of the man, only saying that he was in the business of selling rugs and curtains. He was brought before Sheriff Plummer, who instructed

him to tell the truth or else he would be arrested for con-
tempt. Gaskins then asked to have a private word with the
sheriff, which they did, and Gaskins was quietly let go and
never heard from again. No one divulged what Gaskins had
said, but it must have been an admission that caused the
investigators to disregard his earlier statements.

Even though the discovery of the body caused a great stir
in the Greater Cincinnati area, other large and small events
were dutifully recorded in Saturday's paper. It was the last
day of the fifteen-year-career of John Van Luenen, superintendent of the Covington, Newport, and Cincinnati Street
Railway Company. He would be surprised at the end of his
shift when his employees gave him an engraved gold watch.
The night before in Lawrenceburg, Indiana, just downriver
from Cincinnati, there was a great train wreck; the bodies
pulled from the wreckage were all tramps, homeless wander-
ers. The papers seemed little concerned with the dead men,
but did report that "the loss to the railroad company by the
destruction of rolling stock will doubtless be very large."
There were four weddings in Covington that Saturday; one
of the couples, it was noted, was black, so it can be assumed
then that the other couples were white. At this time, interracial marriage was illegal in Kentucky, punishable by ten to
twenty years in prison. As in the case of Homer Plessy, it was
not always clear who was white and who was black. In 1885,
for example, Calvin Ruff, a white man, proposed to Libby
Lightburn, a mulatto, in Louisville. They secretly traveled
across the Ohio River to New Albany, Indiana. Interracial
marriages were illegal in Indiana as well, but Ruff was able
to get the marriage license claiming that he was a "colored
man."

Despite prevailing white attitudes toward blacks, especially black men, that they were prone to assaulting white
women, that they were violent and brutal, there is no evi-

dence to suggest anyone suspected that the murder committed near Fort Thomas was done by a person of color. The
answer to this might be simple. The assumption from the
beginning was that the victim went willingly with the killer
into the field. Even if she were a prostitute, the victim was
white, and would not have gone off alone with a black man
for any reason. White prostitutes giving attention to black
men could face punishment. Those who claimed they saw
the couple the night before all agreed it was a white couple.
If it had been an interracial couple, it can be assumed, they
would have drawn more attention and there is every reason
to believe they would never have been allowed to go off
alone. If there was anything to suggest that a black man was
the killer, then a lynch mob might already have been forming
that Saturday afternoon or evening. There were mobs, but
none of them displayed any sign of violence. There was simply not enough information to act upon, and what information was being provided proved to be spurious. As the
Louisville Courier-Journal reported, "A hundred different
clews to the murder and beheading of a woman near Fort
Thomas on Friday night are floating today. Many of them
have been traced to a worthless origin."

No one knows exactly where information of a "worthless
origin" came from. The Cincinnati chief of police, Phillip
Deitsch, for example, was told that the murdered woman
was one Mary Riggle. It was said Mary lived in the neighborhood of George and John streets, in the Tenderloin district. A
reporter and an officer Palmer canvassed the area but were
unable to find anyone who knew someone called Mary
Riggle. They did turn up the fact that a prostitute, what the
paper called an "inmate at a resort," named Mamie Beaver
was known to frequent Fort Thomas and was last seen
Friday afternoon. When a description was given of Mamie,
·however, it was determined she was not likely the victim.

That Saturday afternoon after the body was found, John Locke was interviewed by Chief Deitsch concerning the discovery of the body on his land. Locke was not able to provide any further information, but he expressed his opinion that the head had been taken strictly to stifle identification. Chief Deitsch agreed to keep detectives Crim and McDermott on the case indefinitely, and returned to his office.

ON WEST NINTH STREET in Cincinnati, a man named Scott Jackson, a dental student, was contemplating what to do that evening. Scott, who was known to his friends as "Dusty," had a stylish blond mustache and dimples on his chin and cheeks. His eyes were described as violet-blue. Despite a high forehead that might have been a receding hairline, he was generally considered to be quite handsome and social. He never appeared to have a hard time finding company. Earlier he had gone to his barber, Fred Albin, for a shave. At some point he decided to go to the theater and perhaps to one of his favorite haunts, Wallingford's Saloon. According to various reports he had with him a black leather valise, a hand satchel about fifteen inches long. Albin later stated that Jackson had the valise when he had stopped by that same day. It is not known when Scott Jackson heard of the horrific discovery near Fort Thomas, but it seems likely that it was sometime that Saturday. One can imagine him picking up an afternoon edition of one of the many city papers or being told the story by an acquaintance. At the time, no one had any reason to think Dusty Jackson was connected in any way to that headless corpse across the river.

THREE

BLOODHOUNDS

A T AROUND SIX O'CLOCK THAT SATURDAY EVENING, A YOUNG
man named Arthur Clark arrived at Cincinnati's
Grand Central Station with three dogs. He had traveled almost ninety miles from Seymour, Indiana, which lies
sixty or so miles south of Indianapolis. The dogs, who
belonged to Arthur's father, were named Jack, Wheeler, and
Stonewall. They had, according to Arthur, successfully assisted in the capture and imprisonment of at least twenty criminals. The press captured the moment of Arthur's arrival and
a likeness of the dogs appeared in the *Enquirer* the next day.
Arthur, the dogs, and a small party then traveled to Newport
where the dogs were allowed to get the scent of some of the
victim's clothes. They then went to the scene of the murder
where Sheriff Plummer met them and provided the corset
and a sleeve from the undergarment to provide a scent for the
dogs. Having heard that the scene had been tread on by what

was believed to be thousands of people by that evening, Clark expressed doubt that the dogs would be of much use. But he would try.

Bloodhounds, or any dogs used to track humans, had a long and storied past. One early mention can be found in *The Brus*, the epic Scottish poem about the legendary King Robert the Bruce. The poem, believed to have been written at the end of the fourteenth century, describes a period in which the hero is in flight and being pursued by a "slouth-hund," a tracking dog native to Scotland. To avoid detection Robert crossed a stream in order to stop the trail of scent. The Scottish slouth-hound, from which we get the word sleuth, however, appears to have been a different breed from what we know as bloodhounds, which have unclear origins. Arthur Clark's dogs were long of leg and had the familiar floppy ears and sagging jowls associated with the modern bloodhound. In John Caius' 1570 book *De Canibus Britannicis* or *Of English Dogs*, the bloodhound is mentioned as being used to a large extent in the borderlands between Scotland and England first to hunt down stray cattle and then to hunt down "pestilent persons"—that is, cattle thieves. Bloodhounds continued to be used to uncover rustlers and thieves, but their first official use in attempting to track a murderer was in the Jack the Ripper case in the late 1880s. The experiment was a failure, but from that time the use of bloodhounds became more commonplace in law enforcement.

That Saturday the light had faded and lanterns were brought out to help the party follow the hounds. Noses to the ground, the hounds searched back and forth. Eventually they set out cross country. The party came upon the remains of a homestead and found the opening to a dry cistern that was covered by a rock placed on top of a board. Some keen-eyed observer picked out a bloody handprint on the rock and it was then believed the killer must have stopped and considered throwing the head in the well, but since it was relatively shallow and dry, he moved on. The dogs finally stopped at the edge of the Covington Reservoir, which despite the name was not in the city of Covington but in the neighborhood near Fort Thomas. The reservoir was the largest of three located in Fort Thomas. It was five hundred yards long, three hundred yards wide, and forty feet deep. When the hounds stopped at the side of the lake, Arthur pointed toward the water and said, "You will find the head there," despite his earlier reservations about the dogs' ability to catch a scent. It was surmised that the killer had thrown the head into the reservoir, where it would be found if the man-made lake were drained. Preparations were made to begin the long and costly process of draining the reservoir.

The investigators were confident that they were on the trail of their man and they had no doubt that it was, in fact, a man who had committed this crime. It was not that they thought a woman incapable of murder, however the brutality of the crime spoke of a man. Women killers, it is often noted, seem to prefer poison as a means to dispatch their victims and it is very rare indeed for a woman to mutilate her victim, let alone remove the head. Take, for instance, the case of Lizzie Halliday, who was on trial in upstate New York in the summer of 1894. She was said to have killed at least five people, though some believed the total was much higher. She had various husbands, many of whom died mysteriously. It was believed she tried to poison at least one. Her last husband, Paul Halliday, went missing, though Lizzie said he was away on business. A search of their home revealed the bodies of two women, who had been shot with a revolver. Paul was eventually found under the floorboards. Lizzie was immediately arrested and put in the Sullivan County jail. While there she refused to eat and lashed out against her captors. She tried to strangle the sheriff's wife and managed to set her own bedclothes on fire. She tried to hang herself at one point and then cut herself with broken glass. Dubbed "the worst woman on earth," she was sentenced to execution but the sentence was commuted and she was sent to the Matteawan Hospital for the Criminally Insane. While there she continued to attack her caretakers. In 1906, she murdered again, this time a nurse. Lizzie stabbed the woman over two hundred times. Despite all her terrible acts Lizzie never appeared to mutilate her victims for pleasure, to help dispose of the bodies, or to discourage identification. Thus, it seemed perfectly reasonable to the people of Greater Cincinnati that their newest killer was a man, since even "the worst woman on earth" seemed disinterested in decapitating a victim. It was also assumed that a woman did not have the strength and endurance to behead someone. Perhaps this was a false assumption, but it appears to have been held by everyone involved in the Fort Thomas case. This was not to say that women could not commit murder, even disregarding the particular case of Lizzie Halliday.

As Sheriff Plummer continued his investigation, a murder trial was under way in Terre Haute, Indiana. Bloodhounds were not used in the case, but footprints proved to be an important clue, and the accused murderers were a man and two women. The victim was a young woman, Clara Shanks, whose body had been found in a large pool of water near her home. She had left her house the evening before, upset over an altercation with her neighbors in which she was accused of being familiar with the husband of her neighbor. A postmortem was conducted in which it was believed that the girl had taken her own life, but then this conclusion was overruled by another postmortem which decided she had died at the hands of persons unknown. The neighboring family was immediately suspected. Daniel Keller, his wife Nannie (who had accused Clara), and Daniel's sister Maggie were all arrested, while their house was searched. Some blood spots were discovered and a pair of Daniel's pants was found to have bloodstains as well. By February 1896 they were on trial, and the heart of the matter seemed to lie in the question of whether murder had been committed at all or if the first postmortem had been correct and Clara had taken her own life.

The case rested on injury done to Clara Shanks's body, thus pointing to murder. The evidence, however, was circumstantial. The supposed blood spots were explained away as red paint. After a chemist testified that he had analyzed the spots and found them to be mammalian blood, he was forced to admit he could not prove it was human blood, but might have been from any number of other animals. The experts who testified that Clara had met with violence were likewise forced to admit that her fractured neck, skull, and teeth might have come from some other means. The prosecution's story seemed unclear. By the charges it appeared they held that all three Kellers had killed Clara by beating her to death. The weapons, however, were never found. Nor was it fully explained what led Clara to the Kellers' house and how exactly she met her end. The only other evidence provided was the presence of a man's footprint near where Clara's body was found, but this was never linked directly to Daniel. Nothing linked the women to the crime. By mid-February, while the Cincinnati area was engrossed in the tragedy at Fort Thomas, the Kellers would be found not guilty. It would never be known for certain whether Clara Shanks took her own life or whether a family got away with murder.

The investigators in Fort Thomas were keen to get as many clues as possible, which is why they had brought in the bloodhounds. In an effort to get to the bottom of the mystery they drained the Covington Reservoir. Even here a crowd began to gather. They stood in the dark and in the cold rain to watch the waters recede, at a mind- and body-numbing pace. The sluices had been opened at eleven o'clock at night, and by five o'clock the next morning the water had barely dropped.

On Sunday morning, February 2, the decision was made to drag the reservoir. By then the papers had all printed tales of the body and details of the investigation, and this led to an increase in the number of onlookers. Four men came to do the actual work; William H. Brownfield, his brother Arthur, Will Frommel, and Charles Sterritt. They came with a wagon carrying a large net that was weighted down with sinkers. The net was 120 yards long. Two of the men climbed aboard a boat, the *Trixie*, and pulled the net behind them, the other men stayed ashore and fed the net out. The net was then pulled in, bringing in a catch of a few fish and several stones. The process was repeated seven times with nothing to show. Two more men came and dragged the reservoir with fifty large, so-called "buffalo" hooks, all to no avail. By Sunday night it was generally decided that the head would not be found in the reservoir. A nearby pond was dragged, but this too produced no results. The crowd, standing in the dwindling light, having braved cold wind and rains, finally lost their curiosity and dispersed. All that remained was a guard of Highlands police who stood vigil around the emptying reservoir to stop anyone from going into the freezing water and mud.

The draining of such a source of water was not a light decision. For one thing it meant the displacement of some 32 million gallons of water, which were diverted into a stream near Alexandria Pike, turning it into a raging torrent. The cost of pumping the water into the reservoir was estimated at $1,300, not a small sum in 1896. The Covington Waterworks Trustees, who oversaw the reservoirs in the area, had agreed immediately to drain the lake when the dogs had stopped there. For them it must have seemed a small amount to lose in the hopes of identifying the victim and getting that much closer to finding the brutal killer.

Bloodhounds are amazing animals, but it might have been wiser for Arthur Clark to stick with his initial assessment. It was very likely the overrun condition of the scene caused the hounds to be confused and catch a scent that did not lead to the head or any other clue. Despite the investigators' hopes, bloodhounds are not perfect. They were given the scent of the victim's clothes, but it is impossible to know if that was the scent they followed to the reservoir. In the previous month, in West Virginia, a "black fiend" who had attacked an eleven-year-old girl with a croquet mallet was able to evade the pursuit of a hound by presumably doubling back on his own trail. The suspect, Jim Sherman, was later captured and identified by his victim, who had survived, and put behind bars.

Clark claimed his bloodhounds had tracked down at least twenty men, but those stories don't appear to have made it to Cincinnati. Of course, bloodhounds were by no means seen as unsuccessful. In October 1895 a squad of bloodhounds was acquired to track down the murderer of one Mrs. Bell in rural Texas. The hounds tracked the suspected killer to a small shed where those investigating the crime found a black man named Henry asleep. Henry was arrested, apparently solely from the evidence of the hounds stopping at his home, and was taken away only to be stopped by a mob of 200 people who had somehow gotten word of the arrest. The mob took Henry and, after a short kangaroo court, decided he should be sentenced to death by fire. Henry was eventually taken to the center of the nearby town and fastened to an iron post on a scaffold, around him was kindling, wood, and coal oil. Mr. Bell, the husband of the victim, lit the first match and the fire was set. Henry cried for mercy, but was ignored, it would take him almost an hour to die. Those involved in his death felt justified because he had confessed to the crime he died for, but that confession must be cast in doubt considering the circumstances under which it was gained. The governor of Texas denounced the killing and in Austin it was reported by the *New York Times* that "the act is condemned here."

Back at the reservoir, those standing in the freezing rain were witness to what was left after the water was drained away; mainly mud, fish, and rocks. In 1873, the city of Cincinnati released an authorized report that indicated that the water being pulled from the Ohio River was unsanitary. More than twenty years later, the water was still being pumped from the river, fed into these reservoirs, and then distributed to the public for consumption completely unfiltered. However, plans would soon be finalized by the Cincinnati Water Works to create a massive water pumping station that featured the area's first sand filtration system. The year before, in 1895, a Captain Hawkesworth was employed to inspect the Cincinnati water supply and make a recommendation on how to improve the condition of the water. His paper proposed the sand filtration method that would be adopted and which had already been perfected in London. The filter beds would consist of fifteen to thirty inches of fine sand, resting on top of a bed of gravel that increased in size as the water descended. This method, it was claimed, would take the current water, "which sometimes presents the appearance of soup, containing two to three hundreds grains, and even much more per gallon of slimy and clayey matter, so that sediment will appear in a few seconds even in a spoonful at some stages of the supply," and turn it into water that was "perfectly clear, free from soot, and absolutely fit to drink." Hawkesworth cautioned that while

some authorities advised boiling water to get rid of the
pathogens, his own research indicated that some microbes
could withstand boiling for over three hours and were
immune to the introduction of chemicals into the water.
Despite Hawkesworth's assertions, the scientific community
would eventually learn that boiling water and adding chemicals to kill virus and bacteria is much more effective than the
sort of filtration system that Cincinnati adopted. The new
pumping station, which was placed in the nearby town of
California, Ohio, would possess the tallest steam engines ever
built, or so it was claimed.

In the late 1880s, Louis Pasteur had fully demonstrated his
germ theory to science, but as is often the case, the public was
slow to catch on. As early as 1855 it was known, to at least one
bright British researcher named Dr. John Snow, that cholera
was spread through contaminated water, but in 1896 cities
were only just beginning to address the need to clean water
and even then it was more an effort to rid the water of "tur-
bidity" or cloudiness and not to destroy pathogens. This was
addressed by the adoption of slow sand filtration, such as that
used at the station in California. It would not be until 1908,
in Jersey City, New Jersey, that disease in water supplies was
dealt a death blow by the introduction of chlorine; it would
take further decades before a solution was found at a national level.

THE PEOPLE OF Greater Cincinnati might not have been
overly concerned with what was in their water, but they were
concerned with the details of the murder investigation. On
Vine Street, in Cincinnati, Joe Vetters, a security guard at the
Atlantic Gardens concert hall, told reporters he felt certain
that the dead girl was a young woman who frequented the
venue, usually well dressed and accompanied by a soldier

from the fort. He only knew her as Mollie, but said that she had not been around for several days and that two months previously "she got into some trouble over there, and, as a result, was locked up in the Newport jail." It should come as no surprise that this would prove to be a false trail, though the whereabouts of Mollie were never apparently reported.

By Saturday evening, while Arthur Clark and his dogs were following the trail to the reservoir, the police on both sides of the river were being flooded with leads in the case, but they had learned to become very selective, not putting too much credence in some of the tales. For instance, it was reported that a tall man carrying a large butcher knife had gotten onto an electric car in Cincinnati. When he got off at Dempsey Street, the conductor asked him what he was going to do with the knife.

"I'm going to kill the [we can only assume he said something like 'son of a bitch' since the paper edited out his words] who cut my sister's head off across the river."

The conductor replied, "Do you know who did it?"

"Yes," the unnamed man replied, "he betrayed and then killed her."

The man then walked off in the direction of some railroad tracks. The exchange was reported to the police.

Theories about the Fort Thomas case were sprouting everywhere; rumors seemed inexhaustible. Every half hour, it seemed, the missing head was reported to be found. It was said that a man, covered in blood, had been arrested in Newport. A soldier supposedly had committed suicide and left a note saying that he was guilty of the crime. None of these stories turned out to be true. Detective Cal Crim, acting on a tip, went to the offices of the Associated Charities because someone there was supposed to have information on the case. All he found was that the superintendent, like just about everyone else in the city, had a theory about what happened Friday night, but he lacked any hard evidence. Sunday morning a man came to the Central Police Station in Cincinnati asking whether the victim had India ink stains on her arms, as he believed he might know who she was. He was informed that there were no such marks on her arms. Police combed the area around Dempsey Street trying to find the knife-wielding man who claimed the victim was his sister, but they found nothing. They concluded that he must have been simply looking for attention.

SINCE THE DISCOVERY OF THE BODY, the public's mind was pre-occupied with the idea of murder. The papers tried to provide every scrap of information connected to the case, whether relevant or not, but there was only so much to print. The *Enquirer*, fearing the results of the investigation given the lack of hard evidence and the seemingly countless false leads, reported other unsolved cases from recent memory. Two years earlier, Mary Eckhart, a woman from Dayton, Ohio, was found strangled with a bed sheet in an apartment near Seventh and Walnut streets. The police quickly arrested her sweetheart, a man named Hildebrand, but were unable to find any evidence to implicate him and soon released him. Though many theories were advanced, no one was ever found guilty of the crime. The *Enquirer* put forward the idea that Mary had actually been the victim of a serial killer who became known as the "Denver Strangler." According to the paper, murders in New York, Denver, and Victoria, British Columbia, all bore the hallmarks of this "human monster." The strangler used two knots, one loose and one extremely tight. The victims were typically killed in apartments on the first floor, adjacent to an empty apartment, which suggested the killer's method of entering the homes to commit his crimes. Unfortunately, it appears no one ever put an identity to the "Denver Strangler."

Other recent unsolved deaths recalled by the paper were many and varied. A man named Doolittle was found shot in the head, but he was unable to provide any details on who shot him before he succumbed to his injury after a few days. Suicide was considered, but it was officially set down as an unsolved murder, despite the fact that he had recently secured a life insurance policy for himself and it was known that he was deeply in debt. In another case, a young girl named Emma was found dead in a lumberyard, which had become a makeshift playground for her and her young friends. There were signs on her body to indicate she had been in a struggle before being killed, and word came out that there might have been evidence that she was raped as well. Her body was found under a pile of lumber, yet the police and the coroner inexplicably ruled the death a suicide. Her attacker was never found. Five years earlier a man had been bludgeoned and shot to death on the street; the motive and culprits were never tracked down. A watchman named Lewis was shot to death in a train yard, but no one ever found out who did it or why.

One case that had made headlines a few years earlier would remain in the public's imagination for generations, overshadowing almost every other murder case in America. It began on a hot August day in 1892 when the bodies of Andrew and Abby Borden were found in their home in Fall River, Massachusetts. Both had been attacked with an ax, and Andrew's face was "hacked to pieces" and "beyond recognition," as the local *Fall River Herald* reported. Initially the assumption was made that the killer must have been a tall intruder, due to the direction of the blows and the viciousness of the attacks, but as investigators looked more closely they discovered, to everyone's shock, that the most likely suspect was Andrew's daughter, Lizzie. She was put on trial but eventually acquitted.

Part of the continuing fascination with the Lizzie Borden
case is the controversy over the evidence. Historians and
amateur sleuths have pored over the documents related to the
case and come up with a spectrum of theories, some more
plausible than others. At the heart of the story is the unnerv-
ing fact that murder cases are often never black and white,
and even something that might seem so simple at first glance
turns out to be a mess of contradictions and guesswork.
Every conviction, we are told, must clear the bar of reasonable doubt, yet what is reasonable to one person is not so to
another. Tantalizing clues surfaced in the Borden case.
Andrew's body was warm when they found him, while his
wife's body was cold. This indicated not just that Abby was
killed some time before Andrew, but that Andrew had not
been dead very long when he was discovered. There were
other people around the house that day in addition to Lizzie;
Maggie Sullivan, the maid, and a worker who had come by
at some point asking for payment from Andrew but was
refused. Lizzie's story of that day did not add up to investigators, and yet the murder weapon was never located and crucial blood evidence was never found. No one was ever found
guilty of the crime, and so the mystery remained.

"Everything that tells of the Borden murder(s) is yet
intensely interesting," the *Enquirer* reported, probably
pulling the article from another paper. "Even the graves of
the murdered pair are constantly visited by people from all
parts of the world. A beautiful monument was recently
placed there by the sisters. It is one of the most beautiful and
costly structures in the cemetery."

Eventually rumors of ghosts in the Borden house were
spread, and a song was written in which Lizzie "gave her
mother forty whacks, and when she'd seen what she had
done, she gave her father forty-one." The rhyme gets the
number of strikes wrong and also calls Abby Lizzie's moth-

er, when she was in fact her stepmother, but it is a catchy song and has endured to this day.

Like the Borden case, Cincinnati's latest murder was a compelling mystery, but unlike the Borden case, the authorities did not know the identity of the victim, and that became the primary focus of the investigators.

FOUR

TRAMPS

SOMETIME ON FEBRUARY 3, TWO DAYS AFTER THE BODY WAS found, a Mrs. Hart was led into the office of Cincinnati's chief of police, Phillip Deitsch. Mrs. Hart was middle-aged, and she wept quietly as she explained to the chief that she had gone to Newport, viewed the body, and identified it as that of her daughter, Ellen Markland. Ellen had married Emory "Red" Markland and by him had four children, the oldest of whom was ten. The marriage was not a happy one, and in December 1895, the children were placed in the Children's Home at the request of the parents. On New Year's Eve, Ellen had returned to her parents' house and explained that she and her husband had separated. Mrs. Hart pleaded with her daughter to rent a room, get a job, and take care of her children, but Ellen refused and left. That was the last time Mrs. Hart had seen her daughter.

Emil Eschler, who was acquainted with Ellen, said that after leaving her parents' house, she went to work as a maid at the Burnet House hotel under the name Ella Gold, but left after less than a week of employment. She was then seen at the infamous Atlantic Garden saloon with another woman, talking to a soldier and another man. The soldier and the other man, for some reason, came to blows, and in the confusion Ellen simply disappeared. This story is what prompted Mrs. Hart to examine the body. Her daughter had been born with crooked legs, she explained, and they had healed in a particular way. Mrs. Hart was convinced that the legs of the body were the same as the legs of her daughter. This is what led her to Chief Deitsch's office.

The one snag in her claim was that Ellen was dark–haired, but the little bit of hair evidence that was found on and near the body indicated light blond hair. It is not known how long poor Mrs. Hart remained convinced that the body was that of her daughter or how long she thought her daughter was missing, but in 1903 a short article appeared in the Cincinnati papers declaring that an "Ella" Markland was finally divorcing "Emery" Markland, father of her four children, for "gross neglect, failure to provide, and habitual drunkenness." She asked that she be awarded the custody of the children.

Another story crept up concerning the murder. This time it took place at the train station in Brent, Kentucky, which lay on the Ohio River east of Fort Thomas. The night operator, Howard Shaw, believed that he had a run-in with the murderer after the deed had been committed. He told his story to a reporter, who claimed to print it just as Shaw had recounted it. "I remember Friday night well," he said.

> It was pitch black and the rain fell unceasingly up to about 10 o'clock. I was busy with messages during the early part of the evening, and nothing unusual occurred to attract my attention. The first section of No. 80, a freight train, arrived here at 1:16 a.m., east-

bound, and left four minutes later. It was about 2 o'clock when my dog, who always keeps the night watch with me, began to whine and scratch at the door as though he wanted to get out. He is a shepherd dog (Jack, I called him), and very keen of scent. All of a sudden he began to bark loudly. At the same instant the bloodhound at Nick Miller's house on the hill, began to bay in a vicious manner. I silenced Jack, after an instant, and then strained every nerve to listen. In a second or two I heard the steady footfall of a man up there on the [Alexandria] pike. It gradually approached closer, sounding louder as it came. Then I heard the steps descending the path to the station. The man walked across the corner of the platform, but instead of keeping it, preferred to take to the track, as I think now, with a view to getting as far as possible from the light shining out of the station window.

This struck me as being very suspicious. There are frequently tramps about here who congregate at the water tank, just above the station, where the trains usually stop. Whenever they pass they always look in the station window to see the clock and speak to me. This man did not do so. I glanced out of the window, and could barely discern the form of a man as he was disappearing in the gloom, west on the track. Probably a quarter of an hour later I was looking out of the window and saw a bright light on the river bank, about an eighth of a mile in the direction the mysterious stranger had taken. It grew larger by degrees, and I finally saw that it was a fire. It burned probably for an hour and then died away. At 4:19 a.m. the second section of No. 80 arrived at the station, and left eight minutes later. This train was also east-bound. It is my firm belief that the mysterious stranger, knowing about the train, that he boarded it and went away. You know that a bloodhound can scent blood at a great distance. If this stranger was the murderer, he had blood on his clothes, and that would have accounted for the racket made by the bloodhound and my dog. I have often heard that bloodhound howl, but his howl has never before been so significant and unusual as it was that morning, and so impressed me at the time.

The location of the fire was found, but only a few charred sticks remained. The eastbound freight train that the stranger was believed to have boarded could have led the man to any number of destinations given the possibility that he jumped trains at various stations along the way. It was a compelling story but, like all of the other stories that circled the body, it lacked substance. The story did draw the attention to a kind of person that society preferred to forget: the only man who could be expected to be near a train station late at night was a tramp.

On Monday night came the electrifying news that two men were being held in Ludlow, Kentucky, under suspicion of a connection to the Fort Thomas case. The story by now was spreading outside the Greater Cincinnati area. The *Louisville Courier-Journal* reported on the two men: "At midnight to-night the principal development in the tragic mystery of the Kentucky Highlands is the holding of two suspects in Ludlow, Ky., jail. Both are tramps. George Hanrohan, the principal, was caught washing a bloody shirt sleeve in a spring. His companion, George Morgan, is held as a witness. . . . Both say they were tramping to Lexington, Ky., in search of employment. Both say they spent last Thursday and Friday nights in the station-house at Hamilton, O. The belief is that they will not be held long."

To tramp simply means to walk, usually heavily. In the late nineteenth century a tramp was a vagrant who traveled around looking for work and begging. There was reason for the public to entertain the idea that a tramp might be guilty of the horrible crime. The general opinion was that tramps were an unsavory group, prone to committing crimes. Though they might be of any race, the attitude toward tramps was not dissimilar to the prejudice against the black population in general. In 1886 a paper was presented at the National Conference of Charities and Corrections which gave the results of a survey conducted of charitable societies, public officials, and philanthropists on what were the causes of the tramp. Some of the reasons given were drink, lack of employment, ignorance, tobacco, strikes, worthlessness, immigration, aggregation of capital in manufactures, social-istic ideas, overpopulation, loss of manhood, lack of trade, hospitality of jails, uncomfortable homes, specialization of labor, Chinese immigration, and the devil. Tramps, it was explained, were exclusively men, perhaps stemming from the fact that men were the primary workers at the time. In addi-tion, many were Civil War veterans who had "tramped" to battles and now hitched rides on the same railroads that had transported them during the war. Women fell into other cat-egories and were apparently not prone to the wandering spir-it of the tramp.

In 1896 there was nothing particularly romantic about tramps. They were either hard luck drifters or angry rabble; they were a social problem that lacked a solution. The idea that a tramp might have killed and beheaded the young woman in Fort Thomas must have been inviting, given the belief in their criminality or, as some insisted, that they were products of the devil. It is not clear from the article why the two held in Ludlow were expected to be released. The obsta-cles to believing that either of these men committed the crime were the witnesses who said they saw a well-dressed man in the company of a young woman that Friday night, but it is not known how seriously these accounts were taken. These witnesses did not see the murder, but a couple strolling in Fort Thomas, which was not an uncommon sight. There was nothing to suggest these stories formed a definitive link between the mysterious couple and the body at the funeral home in Newport. The reason that the tramps in Ludlow were not held longer is now lost, so it remains open to speculation. George Hanrohan's bloody sleeve might have been from anything, considering the dangers of the life of a vagrant. Like so much else about the case, there was nothing concrete connecting them to the murder.

This did not mean that a tramp could not have been the killer. As Professor Francis Wayland of Yale explained in 1877, just when the word "tramp" began to become commonplace in the United States: "As we utter the word 'tramp,' there arises straightaway before us the spectacle of a lazy, shiftless, sauntering or swaggering, ill-conditioned, irreclaimable, incorrigible, cowardly, utterly depraved savage." The tramp was, for people like Wayland, a force of destruction and evil. "He will outrage an unprotected female, or rob a defenseless child, or burn an isolated barn, or girdle fruit trees, or wreck a railway train, or set fire to a railway bridge, or murder a cripple, or pilfer an umbrella, with equal indifference, if reasonably sure of equal impunity."

Many places instituted laws against vagrancy, making tramps criminals by default. The most common solution was forced labor, "whether they liked it or not." In 1889 a story from Anderson, Indiana, was printed which described how, when faced with a group of tramps invading their town, "a gang of about 30 men, armed with poles and barrel staves . . . and led by the town Marshall, went to the station and formed a gauntlet along the railroad. Through these lines of men the tramps were forced to run, their speed being accelerated by heavy blows well laid on by the men. . . . It has been nearly three years since tramps bothered Anderson, it being the custom here to run them through the gauntlet into the river. Citizens generally approve the course." In this way communities pushed the tramp problem elsewhere, thus forcing tramps to wander from place to place. Yet, it is certain that most efforts to solve the issue only made it worse. No one kept track of just how many tramps there were on average each year, but one estimate in the mid-1890s placed the number at around three million men during the worst periods of unemployment; this out of a population of only forty million at the time. Like the unemployed of any other time, it appeared that when jobs were available, people, for the most part, worked. A life of homeless wandering, threatened with forced labor, jail time, and physical violence, was not appealing. There was a certain troublesome thought that bubbled up now and again in this largely Christian society. As Lafcadio Hearn, the famous reporter who wrote for many years for the *Cincinnati Enquirer*, put it, "We scarcely dare to make the suggestion, but is it not true, nevertheless, that in our day some people would call *Him* a tramp." In other words, if Jesus were to appear in America in the late nineteenth century, he might have easily been run out of town or forced into hard labor.

This does not mean that all tramps were innocent. In fact, papers often had a tendency to label someone as a tramp if they engaged in criminal activity whether or not there was clear evidence that the man was unemployed and/or homeless. The idea to provide tramps with work, not forced labor, but meaningful paid work, was not seriously entertained and was not particularly feasible at the time. The permanent question was: Who would provide these jobs and, more important, who would pay for them? The solution was simply to harass and annoy the tramp until he moved on to another place, thus perpetuating his nomadic existence.

Some did feel pity or kinship with these sad figures of poverty. Perhaps through keen observation or simply by understanding the nature of such things, some saw that every tramp's story was different. While some might be lazy or criminal by nature, others were men who lost their livelihood through misfortune and were unable to catch a break. These people must have felt sorry for the rough treatment that tramps often received. They might have delighted in the story that came out of Lawrenceburg, Indiana, in December 1895. It seemed that three men came upon a tramp and decided to have some fun with him. They produced stout switches and told the tramp to dance.

"The fellow complained that his feet were sore and he could not dance without music. 'We will furnish the music,' said his tormentors, as one of them produced a mouth harp and began blowing a lively tune. 'Now dance or take a switching,' commanded the other two, as they raised their heavy switches. Instead of instant compliance, as expected, the fun-makers were startled by the sight of a big revolver, which the tramp suddenly presented, and, with a sardonic grin upon his grizzled and desperate countenance, cooly cocked his weapon, and covering the trembling trio, shouted, 'Now you dance, damn you!'" The would-be tormentors were forced to dance for an hour before a passing farmer broke up the scene and the "grinning tramp bade them good-by, and walked away triumphant."

While the story hints at the desperation of the tramp, indicating that he might be on the edge of madness, the ending of the story shows a calm and collected man who had balanced the scales. The tormentors were themselves tormented and, presumably, they learned something from the experience. The tramp is undoubtedly the hero of this tale. He is not the savage, lazy, foul-tempered character ruled by evil forces, at least not in that moment that he walks away from those young men with a smile on his face.

Some proposed that the state or federal government take a hand in solving the tramp problem. This was, after all, the purpose of the Coxey Army of 1894. However, like Coxey's Army, all these attempts were met with failure. It would be almost forty years before the government would assume responsibility for employment in the U.S. and even that was often seen as too much involvement. Logic ensured that business owners would not hire more persons than they needed. The immediate solution of simply giving tramps jobs was unattainable, though the status quo didn't seem to be working either.

The problem, it appeared, lay with the tramps themselves. They were a contradiction: jobless yet able-bodied men. The initial reaction was to exclude them from any relief that might be offered through municipal governments and charities. They were not among the "deserving" poor, which included (depending on who was speaking) the very young, the very old, the sick or otherwise disabled, and widows. The general opinion that jobs were plentiful and all a man had to do was to be willing to work had to be reevaluated after the depression of 1893, when America, in effect, discovered massive unemployment for the first time. In that year the American Federation of Labor argued for relief to its members who had lost their jobs. At a convention the union said, "When the private employer cannot or will not give work, the municipality, state, or nation must." In response state and federal agencies did nothing. Some cities tried various programs, most notably Mayor Hazen Pingree of Detroit, who offered small plots of land, seeds, and advice to poor families so that they could grow their own produce. These "potato patches" became briefly popular and spread to other cities, but the programs were extremely limited and effected no real change.

Charities, long the only source of relief for Americans in need, found themselves unprepared for the strain of economic panic and depressions throughout this period. They, for all intents, ignored tramps and other able-bodied poor. They did what they had always done, but it was not enough to solve the problem of the growing numbers of poor. A Massachusetts commission on unemployment eventually had this to say: "The ordinary charitable institution as now constituted is not in touch with industrial conditions. . . . They are so well accustomed to deal with the degraded or particularly unfortunate class that they necessarily lose a certain sort of tact and generous discrimination which is needed in dealing with men and women, who, under ordinary conditions, are steady wage-earners. . . . The inquisitorial and repellant attitude assumed by those who apparently regard the chief duty of a relief body to detect imposition reflects unfortunately upon the work of a relief association as a whole."

In September 1895, the *Washington Star* printed a story that was at once certainly fictional and also an example of the concerns of the time. It told of a "very seedy and disreputable tramp" who found his way to the back door of a mansion. He knocked on the door and the lady of the house answered. The tramp bowed to the woman and asked a favor, "I'd like for you to tell me if you think I am in your presence as a common tramp seeking nourishment in the shape of a pie?" She responded that she did not think this, but that he was a common tramp seeking anything he could get with the hope that it might be a nickel, "so that you might get beer with it." The tramp then explained that he was not a common tramp, in fact, he was not a tramp at all. He was "a dreadful example of what the people of this great and glorious country of ours is coming to if the silver men have their way in politics and flood the country with free silver. In me, lady, you see what all the people will look like inside of a year from the time the silver flood is turned on."

The tramp discovers, much to his disappointment, that he has called upon a house of "free silver people" and consequently has the door shut in his face without anything to show for it. "By gum!," the tramp says to himself, "that's what a man gets for talking politics to a woman. Politics is something that can't be made to fit the female mind under no circumstance."

It is clear that the public generally feared tramps or thought them a nuisance, even while they might be depicted as mostly harmless. On the other hand, there is no clear evidence for why the public felt that tramps were a problem that needed to be solved. There were times, perhaps, when they were too numerous to ignore. While there were plenty of stories of tramps harassing people or even being violent, they did not appear likely any more to be violent than a working-class person. In 1892–93 J. J. McCook, a sociologist at Trinity College in Connecticut, conducted a survey of 1,349 tramps. The surveys were administered by police officers and so it can be assumed that it was not the most rigorously conducted "tramp census." In addition, it was a very small sampling of a population that numbered in the millions. Still the results were interesting:

Fifty-seven percent said that they had a trade or profession while 41 percent were unskilled laborers. Fifty-six percent were native born; this dismissed the impression some held that tramps were all immigrants. Also contradicting some widely held beliefs, 90 percent were literate. Eighty-three percent said they went into the life of tramping because they were out of work. Only 11 percent admitted to having been inmates in almshouses. Sixty-seven percent were decidedly not teetotalers, which would explain why 39 percent had been convicted of drunkenness. Twenty-seven percent said they worked for their food, yet 38 percent said they paid for their food. While 20 percent said they begged, 9 percent said they worked and begged. Of all the men that answered the questions, 90 percent were unmarried. Except for the fact that some of them begged, these numbers were not all that different from what was known of the working class at the time.

Despite these results, the general public viewed tramps and the working class as completely separate. Tramps were vagrants, and their presence alone was a sign of trouble. They might engage in petty theft, they might steal an entire train engine, they might incite a riot among otherwise lawful workers; they would rape, murder, and destroy. Why the two tramps in Ludlow were not held for more questioning will remain a mystery. There must have been something to convince the authorities of their innocence. Those two tramps, like so many other characters in this investigation, faded into obscurity after their brief brush with infamy.

By Sunday, February 2, the papers were devoting whole sections to the crime. The *Cincinnati Enquirer* put all of its coverage at the end of the paper, perhaps hoping people would read through the whole edition just to get to the latest stories about the murder. The next day the flood of reports intensified. The reservoir had been fully drained. Countless false leads had been followed to no conclusion. One headline seemed to sum up the general feeling of the public and the investigation. It read simply, "Baffled."

There were, however, a few leads that still seemed promising.

FIVE

MARRIAGE

Mrs. Anna Burkhardt came to police headquarters with what she believed to be information that would identify the dead woman. Her story started two years earlier, in April 1894, with the wedding of Dr. Conrad Kettner to Miss Frances Engelhardt. Dr. Kettner had traveled to Cincinnati from South Dakota, answering an advertisement, and pledged himself to Miss Engelhardt after a short courtship. Miss Engelhardt had stayed with Mrs. Burkhardt for a time, but even after she found accommodations elsewhere, Frances still visited the Burkhardts and sometimes stayed the night. Mrs. Burkhardt's daughter had been a witness at Kettner and Engelhardt's wedding. The couple frequented Fort Thomas immediately after their marriage. Mrs. Burkhardt harbored doubts about this German-born doctor from South Dakota and she told Frances to be careful. Frances responded by pulling her marriage certificate from inside a pocket in her corset and explaining that she would never part with it, but keep it always near her. Ten days after the ceremony, Mrs. Burkhardt explained, the couple disappeared.

A few months passed. A special dispatch from Mitchell, South Dakota, appeared in the paper explaining that a few years earlier, a Dr. J. C. Kettner had come to Mitchell with his wife from New York City and established a thriving practice there. After a few months, Kettner left for a medical gathering in Chicago. That was the last his wife had heard from him until she received a letter for her husband from F. W. Reiber, president of the German Veterans' League of North America, in which Reiber discussed the possibility of opening a chapter in Cincinnati, and also congratulating Dr. Kettner on his recent marriage in that city. Mrs. Kettner was understandably surprised. It also seems that she procured a copy of a Cincinnati German paper which announced her husband's marriage to Miss Engelhardt. Mrs. Kettner then sued for divorce, as well as pursuing her husband on a charge of bigamy.

The theory that the body was that of Frances Engelhardt was promising. She was from Cincinnati and had been known to visit Fort Thomas. She was caught in the middle of a love triangle and traveling with a desperate man. Most important was the detail that she kept her marriage certificate in her corset, perhaps explaining why the body in Fort Thomas had been searched and the corset taken off and thrown aside. Dr. Kettner, the theory went, then removed her head, something he had probably learned in medical school, and disappeared before authorities could track him down.

Of course there were a few problems with this theory. First, there was no evidence that the couple had been in Cincinnati or Fort Thomas on the night of the murder. Next, the reason for murder seemed questionable, though not impossible. Dr. Kettner, fearing being caught as a bigamist, was destroying the evidence, mainly the marriage certificate and the person of Frances Engelhardt. The law in Kentucky stated that someone guilty of bigamy could face three to nine years in prison. Depending on where Dr. Kettner would be tried, he faced years in prison. This might be enough reason to murder Frances and take off her head, but it seemed unlikely. Of course, as with previous leads, it would turn out that Dr. Kettner was not the killer and Frances was not the victim. It is hard to determine, but it seems that Dr. Kettner was never even brought up on charges of bigamy.

In 1910, a John C. Kettner, forty-three, was in the census in Leola, in the county of McPherson in South Dakota with a wife Margrette, twenty-nine, and two young daughters. In 1914 this same Dr. J. C. Kettner is listed as the superintendent for the McPherson County Board of Health in the Biennial Report of South Dakota's Board of Health. The early reports on Dr. Kettner's bigamy did not give the name of his first wife, so we have no way of knowing if she was Margrette or if Dr. Kettner had divorced both of his previous wives and then settled with Margrette afterward. There is little doubt that the Dr. John C. Kettner of 1910 and the Dr. Conrad Kettner of the 1890s were one and the same. Both were the same age, both born in Germany, both connected to South Dakota, and both doctors. How he avoided bigamy charges remains unknown. There is a tantalizing clue in the 1900 census of a Conrad and Frances Kettner living in Grand Rapids, Michigan. Their date of marriage is given as 1894, which fits nicely. The logical solution then is that Dr. Kettner was able to divorce his first wife and stayed with Frances for several years before he married Margrette. In 1908 there is a Frances Kettner who married one Charles Wersch, the bride's father's last name is given as "Engelke . . . ," the rest of the name being lost between the pages of the register. If this is Frances Engelhardt, then we must assume she and Kettner divorced, she stayed in Michigan, while he went back to South Dakota. So goes the story of Dr. Kettner and Frances Engelhardt.

Obviously, Engelhardt was not the victim found in Fort Thomas, but this did provide a new element to the mystery. It offered the possibility that the victim was not a prostitute, but just a young, innocent woman led into that field only to be butchered. The story of Dr. Kettner suggests that the victim may have been a wife and the killer her husband. Everyone knew that this was possible. Husbands killed wives and wives murdered husbands; it was the sometimes fatal truth of familiar love. Marriage in 1896 was, like much else, multifaceted. There were certain things expected in every marriage and then there was the reality.

Early in the nineteenth century, Americans (excluding slaves who were technically not allowed to marry) had an understanding about what marriage was. Marriage combined a man and woman into a single identity, as husband and wife. Marriage was permanent and nonnegotiable. At least, this was the understanding. Throughout the nineteenth century, legal separations occurred, with agreements being drawn up and signed between husband and wife so that both could live separately, though there were always legal bonds connecting them. For instance, collectors could often pursue a husband for debt a wife had incurred even if they were separated. Legal divorces were granted in some states, usually if a spouse demonstrated neglect, adultery, abandonment, or some other cruelty, and the number of states who granted legal divorces grew following the Civil War, though some states still did not allow legal divorces until well into the twentieth century.

The Monday after the Fort Thomas murder, the *Enquirer* published a brief notice:

Death of a Good Woman. Mrs. Moses Hull, the ven-
erable mother of Deputy County Clerk Lum Hull,
died yesterday at her home in Independence. Mrs.
Hull was a pioneer resident of Kenton County, a
Christian woman of charitable disposition, loved and
esteemed by a wide circle of acquaintances. She will
be buried tomorrow morning at 10 o'clock.

It does not tell us much, but it gives an outline of what a
"good woman" was to the *Enquirer* and its readers. She was
married and a mother of at least one successful child. She was
Christian, charitable, and had a wide circle of friends.
Christian here is meant not just as a description of her faith,
but of her character. Nothing in the little block of text indicates that she had ever divorced, had illegitimate children,
had an affair, had an abortion, consorted with blacks, or was
ever involved in criminal activity. Of course, there is nothing
to say that she didn't do some of those things. But those are
just the sorts of things that would not indicate a "good
woman."

At the time, marriage was deemed to be a natural progres-
sion of humanity. All girls would grow up to be wives.
Marriage, this official merger of two identities, should produce happiness and offspring. However both parties in a
marriage often sought to control the products of the union.
The control of reproduction was a complicated affair. The
attainment of happiness within marriage was often just as
elusive.

Despite the legal and societal expectations of marriage, it
was becoming a more fluid institution in the late nineteenth
century. People moved frequently, often for work. A husband might go to find work in a distant city, or go to work
the mines, or he might enlist as a soldier; he could very easily present himself as single, divorced, or widowed. The wife,
and possibly children, were thus abandoned at home and left

to fend for themselves. While divorce could be allowed on the grounds of desertion, divorce laws required the parties to go through formal procedures, such as a requirement that both the husband and wife sign the proper forms. This could be exceptionally hard when a wife could not locate her husband, as in the case of Mrs. Kettner in her attempt to find her bigamist husband to secure a divorce.

Most of what is known about marriage, divorce, bigamy, and desertion would be a mystery if it were not for the Pension Bureau records. Due to laws passed in 1886 and later in the 1890s, widows of Union Civil War veterans could claim a pension no matter when or how their husband died. A widow could receive up to twelve dollars a month, so the motivation to make a pension claim was great for working-class families. In order to get a pension, a widow had to have proof of marriage to a veteran, but this proved difficult for some poor whites, American Indians, and African Americans who were married in their customs or private ceremonies, but did not have an official marriage certificate. Thus the Pension Bureau had to devise various ways to determine a lawful marriage. These methods were sometimes criticized as too liberal and thus encouraged fraud, but the bureau as a whole was concerned with giving the aid that was genuinely needed, while their investigators hunted down any cases of possible wrongdoing. Of particular note are the cases of "contesting widows"; that is, where two or more widows claim the pension for a single veteran. Eighteen percent of the pension applications indicate some sort of family desertion. Following the Civil War, there was a major increase in tramps, as some former soldiers could not readjust to civilian life and chose a life on the road instead. Other reasons that a husband might leave his family, perhaps take on a new name, and remarry are many and varied. Sometimes it was financial troubles that first led them to leave the home, or perhaps they

were simply unhappy. Perhaps something terrible had driv-
en them away. As California miners sang:

> *Oh, what was your name in the States?*
> *Was it Thompson or Johnson or Bates*
> *Did you murder your wife*
> *And flee for your life*
> *Say, what was your name in the States?*

Given that the Fort Thomas victim was still unidentified,
the chance that she was married was very real. As the song
implies, if perhaps partially in a morbid jest, it was not
unheard of for a husband to kill his wife and flee to an area
where he was unknown. The papers of the late nineteenth
century were full of accounts of spouse homicide. In June
1895, a barber, Charles J. Uhl, appeared to have poisoned his
wife and mother-in-law in order to collect on life insurance
policies he had taken out on them. Uhl, however, denied the
charges, claiming only that "the spirits" had foretold his
wife's death and that was it. Earlier in the year a New Jersey
man, Peter Cassidy, brutally kicked and attacked his wife,
sending her to the hospital where it was presumed that she
would die. They were estranged and she had come to visit
their young boy. In September 1895 in New York City, a
drunken cart driver named Philip Ryan came home to his
apartment in "Mixed-Ale Row," and found his wife and children preparing for supper. He must have been unhappy with
the proposed dinner because he reportedly claimed there
was, "nothin' ter eat again," and then allegedly exclaimed,
"I'll teach yer some talkin'." He then began to beat her
around the house. The neighbors heard, but did not bother to
interfere. The wife, Margaret, found herself near an open
window. A neighbor heard her cry out, "Don't kill me, Phil!"
She was pushed from the window and fell six stories to her
death. A policeman close by was informed of the situation,

but when he caught up to Phil Ryan, the man simply said, "I didn't do it!" As Ryan was walked to the police station, a crowd began to gather, shouting threats and encouraging each other to "lynch him!" Ryan made it safely to the station, where he was arrested.

The people of Greater Cincinnati, however, were no closer to identifying the victim or arresting her killer. As a February 5 headline read: "MYSTERY May Enfold Forever. The Story of This Ghastly Crime. Ft. Thomas Tragedy Is No Nearer Solution." No one knew, that part of the solution lay just a few blocks away from White's Funeral Home, at a shoe store.

Louis D. Poock, a shoe dealer, had heard of the discovery of the headless woman on Saturday morning when the body was first found. A nephew of John Locke had called upon Poock and gave him what details he could. Poock was successful and respected, a Mason and highly regarded member of the United Brethren Church. He had worked for sixteen years selling shoes and in 1893, when the rest of the country was plunged into a depression, Poock opened his Newport shoe store. Poock was thirty-five at the time of the murder. His portrait shows a respectable man, with a thick, neatly trimmed beard and earnest eyes. His parents had emigrated from Germany and settled in Dayton, Ohio, where Louis was born in 1861. In the book he would later write recounting his involvement in the case, he never indicates anything of his past, beyond his career as a shoe salesman, nor whether he was married or had children.

On the Sunday after the body was found, Poock's curiosity over the mystery got the better of him and he went to White's Funeral Home, or the "morgue" as he called it. He was well known and on good terms with the officers guarding the door and so was readily admitted. He came to the room where the body lay. There were only a few people in the room, among them an old man who was there to see if the body might belong to his daughter. The body was covered and they pulled back the covering, but the old man could give no assurance that the body belonged to his daughter. Almost at the same moment an officer entered to give the good news that the old man's daughter had been found alive. Poock next walked up and uncovered the body.

He later wrote, "After taking a passing glance at the body, I stepped to where the neck was covered up, and there my attention was attracted to the way in which the body had been decapitated. There being a splendid light, I noticed that the head had been severed from the body by a remarkably smooth incision. Not a jag had been left that would have caused an expert surgeon to blush." Like Coroner Tingley, Poock, though an untrained eye, agreed that the cuts seemed surgical and exact. Poock explained that he did not see a single irregular edge, nothing but a smooth disarticulation.

In a small room adjacent to where the body lay, the personal effects of the victim were displayed. The clothing found on the body was hanging from a clothesline. The dress and underclothes were completely stained with blood. He examined the corset, hoping to find a maker's mark, but none was apparent. Sitting upon a windowsill were the shoes the victim had worn. Poock was immediately drawn to these. "Picking them up, I noticed that they were very short and extremely narrow, and that they were shoes of a quality that were considered very good. They were what shoe dealers call a 'western made' shoe. By this term is meant that the shoes were made west of the Allegheny mountains, and had the appearance of having been made by some manufacturer in Cincinnati, Ohio, or that vicinity."

He recognized that the shoes were a size 3 and wondered if a woman of the dimensions of the body lying in the other room would wear such small and narrow shoes. When he went back into the room where the body lay, he was in luck because another shoe dealer, whose shop was next to the morgue, was in the room examining the body. Poock asked him if he would not mind getting a measuring stick from his store, and the gentleman obliged. When the man returned, they determined that the woman could wear a size 2 or 3 shoe. "Her feet were petite, webbed between the toes, without corn or bunion. A very dainty foot, indeed. After making my examination, I returned to my home, it being the noon hour, and gave myself up to a deep reverie."

SIX

CHILDREN

O N MONDAY, FEBRUARY 3, 1896, A POSTMORTEM WAS conducted on the body. Coroner Walter Tingley presided with consultation from other doctors: Charles T. Phythian, J. O. Jenkins, F. W. Fishbach, John L. Phythian, and Dr. Robert Carothers, who performed the operation. It was done at White's funeral parlor, in the same room L. D. Poock had seen the body. They found the woman to be young and healthy; there was nothing to indicate that she was a prostitute and everything that pointed to a more genteel way of life. But the main revelation was that she was pregnant when she was killed. This gave tantalizing indication of a motive. When the examination was completed, Dr. Carothers gave the following statement to the press:

> I am satisfied that the girl was not outraged. The
> man had reason to kill her, and the result of the post-
> mortem shows it. I judge it was premeditated and

cold-blooded murder. The girl, in my opinion, was from the country and was comparatively innocent. She was brought to Cincinnati to submit to a criminal operation. Once here she was taken to Fort Thomas and murdered. Her head was taken away, horrible as it may seem, merely to prevent the identification of her body. Yes it would be very easy for a man to cut a woman's head off with a knife, even if he had no knowledge of anatomy. I could cut off a woman's head with a small penknife and it wouldn't take long to do it.

The "criminal operation" he refers to is an abortion, but he fails to provide any reason why he thinks she came to Cincinnati for that purpose. His nonchalant attitude toward decapitation seems questionable as well. There were conflicting reports as to whether the cuts at the throat were clean or jagged, but everyone seemed to agree that the cuts at the back of the neck and the separation of the vertebrae were done with a steady hand. It does not seem reasonable to think that the average person would know that the easiest way to sever a head would be to cut from both sides, front and back. This would seem to indicate at least a passing familiarity with anatomy, in contrast to Dr. Carothers's assertion. Perhaps it is true that anyone can cut a head from a body with a knife, but not everyone would perform the deed the same way as it was done in Fort Thomas. The question that Dr. Carothers words did not address was this: Did the killer skillfully remove the head or was it the work of an amateur?

After determining that the pregnancy was four to five months along, the doctors removed the fetus, put it in alcohol, and sent it to A. F. Goetze's pharmacy, for reasons never fully explained. They took the woman's stomach and sent the contents to Dr. W. H. Crane of the Medical College of Ohio for examination.

Dr. Carothers spoke with the authority of the community when he pronounced that the girl was "comparatively innocent," despite the appearance that she was pregnant—possibly out of wedlock, since they did not find a wedding band on her finger. She was presumed to be a country girl, drawn to the city by a cold-blooded murderer. That the victim was soon to be a mother, that the killer, in fact, stopped two lives with his violent act, added more tragedy to the crime.

In the public's mind an archetype was beginning to form. The innocent, almost virginal, country girl is seduced by a man, a demon in disguise, who is her utter ruin and destruction. She is Little Red Riding Hood and he is the wolf, or to pull from George du Maurier's bestselling novel of the time, *Trilby*, he was her Svengali, she the helpless victim in the clutches of a monster.

Dr. Carother's assessment that she had come to the city to abort the pregnancy, that the fetus was unwanted, must have factored into the public's opinion of the victim, but since she was the victim of such a horrendous crime, they were willing to suspend judgment for the time being. The killer might have tried to force the abortion on her. The connection between mother and child was as sacred in America in the late nineteenth century as any other time in human experience. As Henry Clay Trumbull wrote in his *Hints on Child-Training* in 1893, "In estimating the agencies which combine for child-shaping through child-training, the power of a mother's love cannot be overestimated. There is no human love like a mother's love. There is no human tenderness like a mother's tenderness. And there is no such time for a mother's impressive display of her love and tenderness toward her child as in the child's earliest years of his life. The time neglected, and no future can make good the loss to either mother or child."

Trumbull's words echoed the general mores of the time for social purity. Abortion and unwanted pregnancies did not fit within the agendas being pushed by the various social reformers. Official attitudes toward abortion and contraception were clear; they were illegal. Yet, there was still demand among the public. "Sanitary Syringes" especially "adapted to married women" were advertised. Reproductive advice was given under headlines of "On Sterility" and "Conditions Unfavorable to Pregnancy." It is hardly surprising then that the majority of newspaper reports of the postmortem seem to skim over the possibility that the victim herself was looking for an abortion, especially so advanced in her pregnancy. "It is well demonstrated," the *Enquirer* reported, "that the victim of this most awful murder was a young and trusting girl, whose only offense was having loved too well." The article only vaguely suggests that the victim was to be a mother and does not even mention that she might have been seeking an abortion.

Had the pregnancy been wanted, which it might have at least to the victim, the girl might have herself consulted Trumbull's book on "child-training," or any one of the many books on child rearing. Compared to other texts of the time, Trumbull is quite specific in his approach to parenting. He explains, "Child-training includes the directing and controlling and shaping of a child's feelings and thoughts and words and ways in every sphere of his life-course, from his birth to the close of his childhood." It is only through complete control that a child can be "trained" properly.

Take, for instance, James Compton Burnett's 1895 treatise dealing with "delicate, backward, puny, and stunted children." At first the work seems revolutionary, discussing these various maladies of children as being treatable with medicine, but a brief examination reveals Burnett's methods. For children deemed to be too small, he recommends rubbing them down with salad oil as opposed to cod liver oil, which has a disagreeable smell. For a child that didn't have the use of her lower limbs, he prescribed *thuja* and *arsenicum*, common homeopathic cures. Over time the child, who presented swelling on her back, began to seemingly improve. The swelling subsided and when Burnett saw the child ten years later, she had full use of her limbs and was being seen for a stutter. As a side note seemingly without context, Burnett assures his readers that the New Woman only belongs in novels, not in nature. Burnett's treatments, based on medicine of the era, may seem questionable and his anecdotal evidence hardly stands the test of time; but that he sought to help any of these afflicted children is commendable. However, based on his statements, it is clear that these were not poor children he was treating. The child of poverty and the poor mother had fewer options.

Social reformer and journalist Jacob Riis, in his follow-up to *How The Other Half Lives*, titled *The Children of the Poor*, puts it clearly: "The problem of the children, is the problem of the state. As we mould the children of the toiling masses in our cities, so we shape the destiny of the State which they will rule in turn, taking the reins from our hands." The Fort Thomas victim was possibly faced with a child out of wedlock, and the likelihood she would end up in poverty would have been very real unless she came from a wealthy family. Still, she would have been shamed. She might have been forced to the city, anyway, to find work, becoming one of the toiling masses. Instead, according to Dr. Carothers, she was coming to the city for an abortion, though he declined to provide his reasoning for believing that. Given that abortion was illegal and cost money that some people did not have, it was not always an option for unwanted pregnancies. In the late nineteenth century, there were plenty of reasons to want to avoid pregnancies.

For the poor, once a child was born, there were considerable obstacles to raising the child to adulthood. Disease was common, and like much else there were two classes of health care: the wealthy could take their children to doctors, specialists, and clinics; the poor had few or no options. The problem was left mostly to the cities to solve on their own. Many had health boards that assigned doctors to specific city wards, though there were often not enough doctors for the numbers of patients they needed to treat. Vaccinations were known and used, but many false ailments were associated with them and people remained skeptical. Poor children, left on their own, proved to be a problem for cities. Some found work, but many turned to petty crime and general loitering, which is not at all surprising in the time before playgrounds or areas set aside for children's recreation. Thus, these children posed a possible threat to upper-class people going about their business in the city. Riis saw relief for these children as a means to deal with the threat they posed. "Philanthropy we call it sometimes with patronizing airs," he commented. "Better call it self-defense."

By the 1890s the problem was becoming increasingly evident. Organizations and campaigns were born to "save the children," a battle cry that seemed to bring together more reformers than any other cause of the time. It coincided with a shift in the understanding of children as more than simply small adults, to seeing childhood as a series of phases (much of the thinking borrowed from Darwinism) that represented the evolution of man. Children lost their economic value, but instead gained a kind of emotional value that was deemed priceless. Children who were unwanted or could not be cared for were no longer put in institutions that had proved unable to produce well-balanced adults, but instead were put into foster care. Decades before, a family could adopt a child because they needed more labor at home, but this no longer became an accepted reason. Couples who had a desire to have a child now looked for babies, for whom they would pay handsomely, rather than older, stronger children. Societies

for the Prevention of Cruelty to Children and Children Aid
Societies were created, sometimes combining with organizations opposed to cruelty to animals.

The efforts to save the children struck at the heart of a
debate over what was called "poor relief" in the late nineteenth century. The charity societies of earlier generations
were unable to deal with the widespread unemployment and
poverty that plagued the growing population of the United
States. A younger, more liberal generation felt the responsibility should fall on the government—city, state, and federal,
to provide relief to those in need. The older generations were
hesitant to look to the government and thought the best
approach was to keep the aid in the hands of private institutions. Children in need were caught in the middle of the
debate, the results were mixed, and have continued into the
twenty-first century.

For women like our victim, who faced having a child out
of wedlock and would need to work to support herself and
her child, it was not always possible to find relief. Unwanted
children were not safe even after they were born. In the
1870s, people began to speak of "baby farming," which on
one hand appeared to be an early form of day care that specialized in infants; however, closer scrutiny led to rumors
that these enterprises were in the business of infanticide. The
women who baby farmed were generally poor, and by and
large, ran legal establishments from their homes where they
took care of several children. This allowed single women to
work while their children were being looked after.
Sometimes the arrangement was just for the day, sometimes
the children stayed longer. In the most extreme cases, the
children never made it out of the baby farms alive. Residents
in one Philadelphia neighborhood reported a baby farm that
had eight children die in as many weeks, the tiny coffins regularly being carted away.

In 1883 a report from the Pennsylvania Society to Protect Children from Cruelty stated clearly: "The inadequate provisions existing in this City for the care of infants belonging either to the very poor or the degraded classes, is the occasion of much suffering and cruelty towards children and of fearful temptation to the crimes of desertion and infanticide on the part of those who are by nature or complication of circumstances charged with their care."

Baby farms could be found in every major U.S. city, including Cincinnati. In a dingy back room in a tenement house on Central Avenue, an old woman named Mrs. Murray cared for infants of single mothers. At any given time Mrs. Murray had seven children in her care, cramped in her single room with three cribs on the bottom floor. When asked for information about the mothers of the children she was watching, she would give no names and would say only that they had gone away, in some cases to New York. The mothers came from Dayton, Louisville, and other areas; only one, according to Mrs. Murray, was a child from Cincinnati. Within a space of two weeks, John Hauser, the Overseer of the Poor for the Third District, was called upon to bury three children from Mrs. Murray's home. An investigation found she had been feeding the children bad milk and in some cases a mixture of starch and water. No formal charges were brought against Mrs. Murray, only a warning that she must close her baby farm or face punishment, so she shut down her business.

For children who survived infancy, an attempt to provide for their education became paramount. In 1836 the U.S. government granted large sums of money to each state in order to build a common public school system. New York, the most populous state, received $2,750,000; Kentucky, by comparison, received $1,433,757. At the time, however, states were engaged in massive structural improvements and often used

the federal school funds for other projects. The budget for
Kentucky schools was quickly reduced to $1,000,000 and
then to $850,000. Despite cuts to the budgets, states soon set
up the basic outline of the public school system. Taxes were
levied, schoolhouses built, and certificates given to approved
schoolteachers. In 1896, the superintendent of Kentucky's
education system was "Billy Jeff" Davidson, described as a
Methodist raised in a "typical backwoods home not far
removed from the good old colonial times." Judging from the
complaints of the individual county superintendents, the
chief problem in Kentucky appeared to be a lack of interest
in school, on the part of not just children, but their parents as
well.

For children that chose to go to school, the quality of education offered varied. In Cincinnati, for instance, where
German immigrants wanted to retain their heritage, students
could take class half a day in English and the other half in
German. This became known as the "Cincinnati Plan."
While German immigrants to Cincinnati did not all share
the same opinions and beliefs, the one binding element was
their common language that they wished to pass along to
their children through the public school system. However,
this kind of local action appeared to undermine the idea of a
common school education in America. But the reality, people
quickly discovered, was that an equal education for every
child was virtually impossible. Private schools had long been
a haven for children of wealthy families. Given the reliance
on community contributions, it was clear that poorer communities would have poorer schools, while more affluent
areas had more numerous and better options.

For the Fort Thomas victim, had she been able to give
birth, and had the child survived infancy, her child would
have attended school, but there was little chance that that
child would have had access to a quality education, particu-

larly if she remained a single parent. In 1889, the Ohio
General Assembly made school attendance mandatory and
gave authorization to truant officers to make certain children
were going to school. By law, then, every child in Ohio
should have been going to a school of some kind, but delinquents were a seemingly intractable problem for cities such
as Cincinnati. Like every other major city in the country,
Cincinnati was divided, not with clearly visible markers, but
by a kind of invisible map within the population's collective
consciousness. The city, and this included Covington and
Newport across the river, had a business district in its center.
This heavy traffic area was the focal point of most of the business of the city. Here you found banks, printers, headquarters
for large companies, insurance companies, and the like.
Tramps and beggars were here as well, but so were the police,
directing traffic and trying to maintain order. Outside of this
central location were the residential areas. These, to people of
the time, were of two types: tenements and suburbs. One
strived to have a home in the suburbs, not the distant suburbs
of today, but neighborhoods that were often just a short trolley ride from the downtown. Most precious of all was own-
ing a house on the surrounding hills; the higher elevation
provided fresher atmosphere and was far removed from the
city and its "bad airs."

The tenements, often referred to as the slums, were considered an eyesore, but from them came much of the labor
that kept the city running. Here too were found the worst
saloons and all of the city's brothels. Yet, because automobiles
were not very common, cities were still more compact than
the urban sprawl of today. Because of this, a person could
walk just a few blocks down Central Avenue and see fine
Italianate houses belonging to prominent families, and then
just a little bit farther, one could find a row of brothels and
saloons that rang with voices and ragtime music into the dim

hours of the morning. Children who grew up in the squalor, if they survived, were expected to become manual laborers, criminals, roughs, or prostitutes. If they were black or immigrants from certain undesirable countries, there were no other options. But even if they were white and natural-born Americans, if they grew up in the slums, their prospects were bleak. It is not surprising that many of them chose not to go to school and took their chances of being caught by the truant officer.

Despite the problems with the tenements and the general attitudes toward the children who grew up there, most of these children did attend school. As a matter of fact, many cities were faced with not a lack of attendance, but with too many students and not enough schools. Regardless, there were delinquents, usually boys, who the authorities believed loitered on street corners and engaged in criminal activity. This was one of the factors that led to the birth of state reform schools for boys, but those schools were not very successful and instead compulsory education for all children seemed to be the answer. There was segregation in schools from the beginning, and not only by race. School districts often followed economic indicators, and so children from tenements did not often find themselves in a school with children from the suburbs.

For those who could, the solution seemed simple: move away from the tenements to cleaner and healthier conditions. As one woman put it, "To the Anglo-Saxon race, life in great cities cannot be a healthy and natural mode of existence. The fresh air and clear sunlight, the green foliage and God's blue sky are dear to the heart of this people, who cannot become reconciled to the idea of bringing up their children in hot, dusty, smoky, germ-producing tenements and streets." She seemed to assume non-Anglo-Saxons had no desire for fresh air and clear sunlight, and that anyone who stayed in the tenements simply had to reconcile themselves to the condition.

~

WITH THE GENERAL SUCCESS of the public education system, the demand for higher education grew, and the latter half of the nineteenth century saw the foundation of colleges and universities through endowments from the ultra-wealthy: Cornell, Vanderbilt, Johns Hopkins, Stanford to name a few, as well as the University of Chicago, established by a gift from John D. Rockefeller. In addition, schools for law, medicine, and other professions were established. During this period there was a rash of one specific kind of school: the proprietary dental school.

Medical schools were reluctant to take on the extra expense of training dental students, and dental schools opposed being simply a subset of larger schools. Although the American Dental Association had been established in 1859, in the late nineteenth century there were self-proclaimed dentists who had little or no professional education. In an effort to organize and improve dental care, states enacted regulations that required that dentists be certified, but did not require any standard examinations. Dental schools by and large were not regulated and many were dubious, to say the least. By the turn of the twentieth century, states had cracked down and most of these diploma mills were out of business.

The more respectable dental schools were affiliated with established universities. The Ohio College of Dental Surgery, which had been founded in 1845, was the second private dental college in the world. A progressive institution, it graduated its first woman dentist in 1866. In 1887, the school became part of the University of Cincinnati.

In 1896, the Ohio College of Dental Surgery had two particular students who also happened to be roommates: Alonzo Walling and Scott "Dusty" Jackson. They had been acquaintances in Indianapolis, and having renewed their friendship in Cincinnati, they shared a room at a boardinghouse. This arrangement required them to eat all their meals out. On Monday, February 3, 1896, around eight o'clock, while the city was reading that the Fort Thomas victim had been pregnant at the time of her murder and that the medical examiner believed she had come to the city to seek an abortion, Jackson went to a saloon on Ninth and Central Avenue. As he got up to leave, he asked the barkeeper, John Kugel, to keep his bag safe for him. It was a leather valise, the same one he had had when he went to the barber on Saturday.

Meanwhile, Louis Poock was struggling with a way to connect those dainty cloth-topped shoes with the name of the victim.

SEVEN

THE SHOES

WHILE DR. CAROTHERS SEEMED TO BELIEVE ANYONE with a knife and a few minutes could have severed the head of the victim from the body, Louis Poock was convinced it had taken a skilled hand to produce the cuts he had seen on the body. He explained, "The body had been decapitated without leaving even a portion of the skin with a ragged edge. The articulation of the vertebrae was separated to an exact nicety, a feat which, to perform, would have required the skill of an expert surgeon." Obviously Carothers had more experience to back up his claim, but there is the chance that, knowing his statement might be used later in court, he was hedging his bets, if, for instance, the accused happened not to be a skilled surgeon.

Yet, Poock's expertise lay in a more specific area. The shoes, he reasoned, were the link in the chain to identifying the poor girl. He felt certain that if he could ascertain who made the shoes, who sold them, where, and when, he would find the girl's name. The shoes, in his opinion, were of an uncommon type. He would later relate, "It is a fact that if a thousand women, each weighing from one hundred and twenty to one hundred and thirty pounds, were to come into a store to be fitted with shoes, it is barely probable that not more than three of them could wear a shoe as short and narrow as these were. Again, they were cloth-topped, button shoes. The sale of cloth-top, button shoes is very limited."

The numbers found on the shoes, 22, 11, 62458, were in fact a code called the "French system," which would give the size and last (the form used to shape the shoe) as long as someone had the key. The "22" stood for size "3" and "11" for last B. The code "62458" was the stock number given by the manufacturer. The French system was adopted by shoe dealers so that patrons could be fitted with shoes without knowing what size they were really purchasing, apparently a sacrifice to the vanity of the fashionable.

Poock, now armed with an idea of how to track down the girl's name, approached Sheriff Plummer and put his theory to the officer. Plummer was doubtful; he still believed the head might be found and the girl thus identified. Poock told him that he hoped the sheriff was right, but that he, himself, did not believe the head would be found and that the only chance to solve this crime was to look at the shoes. They went to the morgue and examined the shoes again. Poock picked up the rubber overshoe the girl had worn and explained that these types of rubbers were not sold in that area; she had come from some distance away.

Plummer was convinced. Poock remembered that the sheriff told him, "I am still of the opinion that we will be able to find the head, but I must acknowledge that your explanation is clear and reasonable and I am so impressed with it that I wish you would do this particular kindness for me, because of your fitness and understanding in this particular branch of trade, and go ahead with it according to your theory and keep me posted from time to time of your progress."

Plummer gave Poock one of the shoes and one of the over-shoes to take with him.

On the morning of Monday, February 3, before the post-mortem and while dental student "Dusty" Jackson was still presumably sticking close to his valise, Poock was in the offices of one of Cincinnati's largest shoe manufacturers attempting to ascertain if the shoe had been made anywhere in the city. The superintendent informed him that the shoes could not have possibly been made there, because all twenty shoe factories in Cincinnati did their inseaming in a particular way and it did not match the shoe that Poock held. Poock, daunted but not discouraged, went to another factory and was told the same thing. Nonetheless the superintendent was sure the shoes were made "in the west," meaning they were not made on the East Coast.

Leaving the second factory Poock ran into an acquaintance of his, a shoe salesman from Philadelphia who specialized in children's shoes. Poock showed him the cloth-topped shoe and wondered if he might know the maker. The salesman could not be sure, but he believed that a company named Drew, Selby, & Co., of Portsmouth, Ohio, used the same style of top-face stitching as the shoe from Fort Thomas. Poock was delighted.

With this lead, Poock next went to the Palace Hotel to visit another acquaintance, Mr. Hume, local salesman for Drew, Selby, & Co. Upon inspecting the shoe, Mr. Hume declared that he believed his company had been the manufacturer. The stitching and the French system markings matched those used by the company he represented. However, Hume was sure he had never sold this style of shoe from his store. Poock was not at all surprised, since he was

already convinced that the overshoe was from somewhere
else. In fact, almost all the investigators were now beginning
to believe the girl was not from the city. He clothes and her
general appearance suggested country life.

On his way back to Newport, Poock tried to make a long
distance phone call to Drew, Selby, & Co. but was unable to
connect—not surprisingly, since it was such new technolo-
gy—and he realized that someone would need to travel the
one hundred miles to Portsmouth, Ohio, to determine if the
shoes did, in fact, come from there. Poock had kept his store
closed that Monday morning and seemed unconcerned to
leave his business unattended for the afternoon as well. His
hope was that the shoes in question had been damaged in
some way, and as a result had been given to one of the female
employees of the factory. This would make it easy to identify
the victim, had that particular employee gone missing. A
quick trip to Portsmouth should be able to wrap the mystery
up nicely, or at least that was Poock's wish.

Once back in Newport, Poock went to the sheriff's office
to explain what he had found. When he arrived, however, he
was informed that Sheriff Plummer and detectives Crim and
McDermott had gone to Ludlow, Kentucky, to follow up on
a clue, and were not expected back for some time. The
deputy sheriff suggested that Poock go to Campbell County
judge Norval Bennett because he, too, was familiar with the
case. Poock went to see the judge and quickly relayed everything that had occurred since he had viewed the body and
spoken with the sheriff. Judge Bennett advised Poock to continue his investigation and to go ahead with his proposed trip
to Portsmouth. Poock was able to catch the noon train and
arrived at three in Portsmouth, where he went directly to the
Drew, Selby, and Co. offices.

The factory was a massive five-story brick and glass building. Illustrations of the time show a structure that would eas-

ily cover a city block. The company was formed by a merger between Irving Drew and George Selby in 1879. Before Selby had come along, Drew's operation exclusively manufactured hand-sewn shoes; it was a successful, but small business. Selby brought machines that could form and stitch one hundred pairs of shoes a day. As a result, the business expanded exponentially. Portsmouth was not a random location; in some circles it was known as "the Shoe Capital of the World," a title that dated to 1850, when Robert Bell opened a shoe factory there, which later became the nationally known Portsmouth Shoe Manufacturing Company. By 1896, Drew, Selby, and Co. was the largest operation in the city. Yet the shoe business proved complicated, and in 1906, Drew and Selby would split and reestablish their own companies. The Irving Drew Company, which would later become Drew Shoes, remains in business today.

Poock found the offices extremely well organized and the employees there happy to help him in his investigation. It soon became apparent that Poock's hopes of the shoes having been given to an employee were in vain. He recounted what he learned: "In April 1895, Drew, Selby, & Co's traveling man received from Louis & Hayes, of Greencastle, Indiana, an order for ten dozen pairs of ladies' shoes of different styles and lasts. This order was to be made for the fall, and to be shipped about September 1st. When this dozen pairs of shoes were made, they were given the factory stock number for this particular lot; namely, number '62458.'" He also learned that a pair of shoes, size three, was included in the order. Stock numbers were never repeated, so it proved that there was only one pair of shoes in the world of that kind marked "22, 11, 62458." Poock immediately telegraphed Judge Bennett, as the shoe factory conveniently contained its own telegraph office:

Portsmouth, Ohio, Feb., 3, 1896
Judge N. L. Bennett,
Newport, Ky.
    Absolutely the shoes sold at Greencastle, Indiana.
Louis & Hayes, of that place, got bill from them Sept.
3rd last. They got but one pair size 3, of that particu-
lar style and that pair was on her feet.
L. D. Poock

Poock was ready to travel back to Newport that instant
and perhaps even then to go on to Greencastle, but his hopes
were dashed when he learned there were no trains leaving
for Cincinnati or Newport until three the next morning.
Feeling anxious that his message might not reach the judge,
he sent an identical telegram to Sheriff Plummer. Tired from
the day's work and wanting to be able to catch the early
morning train, Poock got a room and retired for the night.

HAD THIS MURDER OCCURRED decades before, Poock would not
have been able to connect the singular shoes with the order
sent to Greencastle. The Industrial Revolution had slowly
taken over the manufacture of shoes as it had other products.
Where once the various parts of a shoe had to be cut and fashioned and then sewn together by one or a few people working in a small shop, pieces were now cut in large quantities
and sold in bulk. This created more options and many more
styles of shoes, for both men and women. Thanks to industri-
alization, women of the middle class, not just the wealthy,
now had a wide variety of shoes from which to choose.
Following the Civil War, women's shoe fashion favored
toward higher and higher heels, some as high as six inches.
Boots and cloth-topped shoes, such as those worn by the victim, had been popular since the 1870s. Many were laced, but
some were secured by buttons or belts. Usually they were of
dark, neutral colors, such as black and brown. In the summer

women might wear white canvas or suede shoes. In the 1890s
yellow shoes were all the rage for a short time. For certain
special occasions, women wore ivory or white satin shoes.

Women's fashion, and not just shoes, was undergoing a
transformation at the end of the nineteenth century. One of
the most well-known health advocates of the 1890s, Dr. J. H.
Kellogg (inventor of Corn Flakes cereal), developed a "dress
system" for women that was meant to be "practical, healthful
and artistic." He completely did away with the corset and
focused on alleviating the pressure on women's hips and
shoulders inflicted by previous fashions. For undergarments
he suggested a union suit, the same worn by the victim
(though he would have frowned upon her corset). Another
dress system, developed by Annie Jenness Miller, closely mir-
rored Kellogg's and focused on providing more practical and
comfortable dress for women. Other similar dress systems
soon followed.

The motivation for these new garments was mainly out of
a concern for women's health, but there was an aesthetic element as well. People of artful inclination pointed to the universal beauty in the draping folds of classic sculptures of god-
desses and compared it to the distorted picture of a heavily
corseted woman. The old fashion, they argued, was warping
what nature had already perfected.

The leaders of the women's rights movement, however,
did not feel fashion was an appropriate topic for them to
address. Surely they applauded any effort to make women
healthier and more comfortable, but given the obstacles they
faced it is little wonder that they did not want to distract the
public with arguments about undergarments while they
were trying to win equality with men. Much like the obsta-
cles faced by any second-class group in any society, they had
to strike a careful balance if they were to gain any victories.
They could not fall into the stereotypical roles that were

expected of them, but at the same time they needed to show that they could fulfill their expected duties, as well as the new opportunities they were asking for. In other words, they needed to show that they could handle the freedoms that equal rights entailed. Therefore, it was imperative to those for and against women's equality, that young women remain chaste. Young, unmarried women should not have sex.

However, it was apparent, despite the closed-lipped attitudes of the time, that young unmarried women were, in fact, having sex. The victim's pregnancy is a prime example. It was believed that Theo Durrant, the Demon of the Belfry, lured his two victims away to have sex inside a church. Of course it is hard to determine how much sex young people were having. Perhaps not surprisingly, those most concerned with the purity of the country believed the problem to be epidemic. One of the causes, they claimed, was women's dresses, which, because the hems were too high, allowed for a brief, titillating view of the ankle or calf if the woman leaned over in a particular way.

Another problem was obscene literature that could be found at almost every train station and corner shop. The Women's Christian Temperance Union created a department dedicated to the suppression of indecent literature in 1883. Other problems, of course, were saloons, dance halls, and— most particularly—alcohol.

Yet, while alcohol remained the most prevalent intoxicant by a wide margin, the late nineteenth century was filled with a wide array of drugs. In a time before prescriptions and government regulations, one could simply go to the nearest druggist and buy a variety of narcotics. The Civil War had seen widespread use of morphine to dull the pain of battlefield injuries, and soldiers who returned home often brought an addiction with them. Before the nineteenth century, drugs like cocaine and opium could only be found in their natural

state, such a coca leaves which were chewed. Modern manufacturing processes led to these drugs being refined and
reduced to powders, tinctures, and the like; the development
of the hypodermic syringe also led to faster and more powerful effects. Morphine seemed, at first, a miracle drug because
it could erase the most severe pain. Cocaine was a common
ingredient in cough drops and children's medications.

The U.S. government, backed by the Constitution, firmly
believed that it was up to the states to control and regulate
medicine and drugs. The states largely ignored the problem
for most of the nineteenth century. Poets and artists seemed
to be fueled by opium and its derivative laudanum, an alco-
holic drink containing morphine. Headaches and toothaches
dissolved, mothers were more patient, and fathers less prone
to anger. Drugs, like women's clothing, were swayed by fashion and cultural attitudes. Smoking opium was frowned
upon because it was connected to Chinese immigrants. By
contrast, smoking opium in China was looked down upon
because it was viewed as a tool of Western domination.
Likewise marijuana would often be associated with immigrants from Mexico and cocaine with blacks.

It did not take long for people to see the dangers of drugs
like morphine. As early as 1818, a paper described the dangers of prolonged use of the drug and the effects of withdrawal. By the end of the century, certain locations were
beginning to place restrictions on morphine usage and began
to require a prescription from a physician. Cocaine use, however, remained largely unchecked. Most famously, it could be
found in Coca-Cola from 1891 until 1906. It had been touted
as a cure for morphine addiction after its discovery in
Germany in 1859. Perhaps just as famously, Sigmund Freud
experimented heavily with the drug in the hopes of finding a
therapeutic use for it. In 1895, while high on cocaine, Freud
performed a surgery in which the patient almost died. It was

said he never used the drug again. Around the same time cocaine was found to have wonderful applications as a local anesthetic, specifically for eye, nose, and throat surgeries.

Like many of the other drugs of the time, cocaine was thought to have a multitude of effective puposes. One suggestion, given by an unknown source, was that a large amount of cocaine could result in a miscarriage: just the sort of thing that might help a young unmarried woman in a delicate situation or a young man needing a way out of a compromising position. When the contents of the stomach of the Fort Thomas victim were examined by the Medical College of Ohio, the results were sent to Coroner Tingley: she had consumed a large quantity of cocaine.

EIGHT

GREENCASTLE

LOUIS POOCK CAUGHT THE 3 A.M. TRAIN OUT OF Portsmouth, Ohio, and arrived at Newport, Kentucky, around 7 o'clock in the morning. A quick glance at the morning papers revealed that reporters must have been following his every step because the previous day's adventures were clearly printed on the page. Poock was surprised to read about his trip to Portsmouth because he thought Sheriff Plummer had indicated that he wanted to keep Poock's mission something of a secret. He found out that his messages had been received, and that the sheriff and detectives Crim and McDermott had left at 2 A.M. As he stood in Newport, they were reaching their destination in Greencastle, Indiana.

The main attraction in Greencastle, then as now, is DePauw University. Greencastle (sometimes written early on as Green Castle) was not an obvious site for a school in 1837, being then little more than a frontier town. But the

Methodists who were to found the school were persuaded by the $25,000 the community raised for them. Originally Indiana Asbury University, the name changed in the 1870s after a large donation from Washington C. DePauw, a Methodist philanthropist who had made his fortune in investments in grain, steel, glass, and government supplies, and who was often regarded as one of the wealthiest men in Indiana. Notably, the school admitted women in 1867 and became home to the nation's first sorority, Kappa Alpha Theta. The college featured a liberal education with history, classics, and a school of music. Greencastle, likewise, benefitted from a growing center of higher learning, becoming the quaint college town of collective imaginations. It remained a rural Indiana community, despite the grandeur of the school.

Upon arriving in town, Plummer, Crim, and McDermott retired for some needed rest as they were wayworn. They picked up their investigation later that Tuesday afternoon, February 4. Their first stop was the Louis & Hayes shoe store. The day before, the *Greencastle Banner and Times* ran a short article entitled "That Murder Case," which related briefly the discovery of the body and the fact that it had been learned that the shoes she wore were marked as having been sold at Louis and Hayes, one of the most well-known shoe dealers in Greencastle. An inquiry by the paper into the sale of such shoes to Louis and Hayes found out "that they sold two pairs of such shoes here, that they can trace by their books, one to a student and the other to a domestic. These two people are here and alive and have their shoes. The shoes were evidently sold to some traveling woman, as the style is a popular one and quite a number of pairs of them have been sold." The sheriff and two detectives found the Louis & Hayes staff exceedingly helpful and were immediately shown the sales books. The books, however, proved to be something of a puzzle. The three officers and a number of clerks pored over the records but could find no trace of the size 3 shoes from Drew, Selby, and Co. that had been delivered the previous fall. They could not determine who bought the shoes or even when they left the store. Exhausted from searching, they decided to take a break.

It must have been at this time, as no other time seems plausible, that the sheriff and the detectives decided to canvas the town for any information concerning any missing girls. They had with them some of the clothes, including the wrapper dress, that the victim had been wearing. They spoke with several people, but almost all were of the conclusion that no one from Greencastle could be caught up in a murder. At some point Sheriff Plummer decided to go back to the shoe store and go over the books another time. After hours of searching he happened upon the exact entry he was looking for:

> Nov. 18, 1895. Pearl Bryan, ladies cloth-top button, size 3, "B" last. Cost $1.85 for $2.50

One of the clerks then remembered selling the shoes to Miss Bryan and also that she had been with her sister, Mrs. Mary Stanley, a widow. Mary Stanley lived with her parents, after having moved from Topeka, Kansas, presumably when her husband died. Thirty-three years old, she ran a clothing store in town, and had a new line of corsets, with samples ready for display. Despite the rumors of the New Woman ridding herself of corsets, Greencastle had little to worry about. Mary Stanley might have been a better example of the New Woman than what was found in magazines and newspapers. She had known loss, struggled, and had persevered. Once, her parents left Mary in charge of the house while they were away to visit her ill sister. At the time she perhaps had given her youngest sister, Pearl, more freedom than was right, but that had been months ago. Her parents returned, the ailing sister having passed away. Mary surely mourned, but she did not close her shop; she was there practically every day until night.

At roughly the same time Plummer had discovered the sales entry, one or both of the detectives had struck up a conversation with A. W. Early, the manager of the Western Union Telegraph office in Greencastle. He heard them speak of a young woman and Cincinnati, and it reminded him of something. He had become friends with a man named Will Wood, a student at DePauw, and Will had taken to showing Mr. Early his letters. In one of the letters a friend of Will's named Scott Jackson spoke of a relationship with Will's cousin, Pearl Bryan.

Early told them, "I remember one from Scott Jackson, a young man from Greencastle, who is in Cincinnati attending dental college. In this letter Jackson confided to his chum, Will Wood, that he—Jackson—and Pearl Bryan had been too intimate, that she had loved not wisely, but too well, and as a result he had betrayed her, that Pearl would soon be a mother, and asked Wood's help in the matter."

What sort of help, they wondered.

"He quoted recipes calculated to prevent evil results of their indiscretion, and asked Wood to get them and give them to Pearl. . . . These drugs did not have the desired effect."

He told the detectives that Jackson had then asked Wood to send Pearl to Cincinnati so that she could have an abortion. She had told her parents she was going to Indianapolis to visit friends.

At some point, though it is never stated, the detectives and Plummer met up again and shared their discoveries. The timeline of events is confused because one source might mention Early's story, but fail to include the record found at the shoe store; while another source mentions the record but not

Early's conversation. When, exactly, Plummer found the entry in the sales book and when Early related what he knew is unclear, though the implication is that both occurred sometime during the afternoon or evening of Tuesday, February 4.

Regardless, the investigators were sure—at last—that they had found their victim. The shoes matched, and if Early's story was true, then Pearl Bryan was pregnant and desperate, and had gone to Cincinnati. The obvious suspect was the lover, Scott "Dusty" Jackson. There was also some connection then between the affair and Will Wood, Pearl's cousin and Jackson's friend. They must have discussed the matter thoroughly and debated how best to handle the situation. They learned that Pearl came from a large farming family, one of the most respected in Putnam County. If they left that moment, they would get to the house after midnight. They decided it was better not to wait.

Earlier that Tuesday, the Cincinnati papers related events as quickly as they could. It was not hard for the papers to get news of events in Greencastle, since they had sent reporters to tail the sheriff and detectives. Frank Crawford from the *Tribune*, C. E. Lambertson from the *Post*, and Theodore Mitchell from the *Enquirer* had all arrived by the same train as the officers. They wrote of the victim, "a young woman whose only crime was to love too well." The man who had seduced her must be either the murderer or the instigator of the killing. They mentioned briefly that two lives were lost, but they did not belabor the death of the fetus. "It was also learned that the shoes worn by the murdered girl were purchased at a store in Greencastle, Ind.," the *Enquirer* related. "The trade-mark they bore was stamped only upon the shoes of a special order which was shipped to a retailer in the Indiana town. Sheriff Plummer, of Newport, and Detectives Crim and McDermott are satisfied that the girl came from the neighborhood of Greencastle." Under the title "Poock's

Discoveries," the paper related in detail Louis Poock's adventures in tracking the shoes to Greencastle.

Greencastle was not unaware of the presence of the sheriff, detectives, and Cincinnati newspaper men. The *Greencastle Banner and Times* reported on their arrival Tuesday, stating that "the Cincinnati papers telegraphed their correspondents here that there was a story afloat that a woman was missing from this city, but the people here know of no one who is suddenly missing." Rumors circulated relating to a Mrs. Kesterson, who had eloped some time before, but these reports had provided little fruit.

No one suspected that it could have been Pearl Bryan. She had, after all, said she was going to Indianapolis, not Cincinnati, to see friends. If she had hidden her pregnancy, as she most likely had done, no one would have guessed she was the girl. It seemed that only Scott Jackson and Will Wood knew, and Mr. Early, the telegraph office manager.

There is no record of the journey out to the Bryan farm early that Wednesday morning. We can assume it was cold, being early February. There must have been tension and apprehension. The investigators had solid evidence that they had found their victim, but they had been down dead end trails before. If this was the right girl, then they were on a terrible mission, to tell her family that she had been brutally murdered, far from home. That she was most likely with a man she trusted and loved, who had betrayed her and shamed her. She had been discarded in a farmer's field, under some bushes, her head removed and missing.

Sheriff Plummer, Crim, McDermott, and most likely some newspapermen, arrived at the Bryan house around two o'clock in the morning. The knocked firmly on the door and dogs barked in return. The house was roused. Pearl's father and mother came to the door, as did Pearl's sister Mary and her brothers Fred and Frank. First the parents were asked if they had a daughter named Pearl. They responded that they did and that she had left a week ago to visit friends in Indianapolis. As delicately as possible, the officers explained the reason for their visit and the trail that had led them to the Bryans' farm.

The dress, the corset, one of the shoes, and other items were shown to Mrs. Bryan and Mary. They recognized them immediately.

"My Pearl, my Pearl!" Mrs. Bryan exclaimed as she began to cry.

Mary Stanley pointed to the corset and said it had come from her shop; it was a sample and that was why it had no identification. The family wept and consoled each other. The police asked if Pearl had any remarkable features, such as on her feet. Mary said she had webbed toes. "My God, it is Pearl! We used to tease her about that when she was little."

If the officers had any doubts, they were now dispelled. Pearl was their girl. As soon as they returned to town, Crim composed a telegram:

> Greencastle, Ind. February 5, 1896
>
> Philip Deitsch, Superintendent of Police, Cincinnati, Ohio: Arrest and charge with murder of Pearl Bryan, one Scott Jackson, student at Dental College, about 24 years old, 5 feet 7 to 8 inches, weighs about 136 pounds, blonde, nearly sandy mustache, light complexion, may have beard of about six months growth, effeminate in appearance.
>
> Positive identification of clothing by family. Arrest if in Cincinnati, William Wood, friend of Jackson. Charge as accomplice. About 20 years, 5 feet 11 inches, light blonde hair, smooth face, rather slender, weighs 165 pounds. We go from here to South Bend after Wood as he left here for that place.
>
> Crim, McDermott, and Plummer.

That Wednesday morning, a $25 reward was posted to be paid "by Louis & Hayes to anyone having bought at their store at any time between September 19th, 1895 and January 31sr, 1896, a pair of ladies cloth top, kid, button shoes, size 22-11, stock number on lining 62458. Price $2.50." Obviously the ad had been placed before it became known that Pearl was the victim.

The *Greencastle Banner and Times* waited until Saturday to divulge the identity of the victim. The papers in Cincinnati did not print the identification of the body until a few days later as well. Perhaps it was simply a matter of when the information reached the papers and when the papers went to print; however, it did buy the investigators some time.

As in many of the communities involved in the case, this would be the sensation and horror of Greencastle for some time. Their distance from the murder must have had a psychological effect on the citizens. The killing had not happened there, the murderer was not among them. Regardless, this was the most sensational news to come out of Greencastle since its founding.

PERHAPS THE MOST NOTABLE EVENT to happen in Greencastle up this point was the devastating fire of 1874. Spreading out from its source at C. J. Kimble & Son's Mill on the east side, the fire began to consume large portions of the city. Local leaders realized the folly of failing to organize a fire department. The fire burned out of control until dawn, though a fire engine was brought from Indianapolis and volunteers arrived from other parts of the state to help. Half the business district was destroyed and twenty-three families lost their homes. In total the damages were estimated at $250,000. Five months later, when another fire broke out, the damage was only $43,000 thanks to the newly created fire department.

The most notorious crime to happen anywhere near Greencastle had occurred twenty-eight years before Pearl Bryan's murder, and almost fifty miles to the northeast, in Indianapolis. In that case, the victims had been a married couple, and the suspects had been two men and—most improbable to the public—a seemingly respectable grocer's wife.

On September 12, 1868, a farmer's boy discovered two dead bodies on the banks of the White River, about three miles north of Indianapolis proper. The remains were determined to be those of Jacob and Nancy Young. Jacob had been shot in the head with a double barrel shotgun, which lay close to his body. Nancy's body was partially burned. At first assumptions were that it was a murder-suicide, Jacob perhaps finding that his wife had not been faithful to him. But the postmortem revealed that Nancy had died by a pistol shot to the head as well as a blow from a blunt object, such as a rock. Though the circumstances were never fully explained, it was believed her body might have been burned by her dress catching fire from the pistol's discharge. At first glance the Youngs seemed reputable members of Indianapolis society, but a closer examination revealed that they were heavily involved in questionable financial practices.

Indianapolis, though it did not boast the population and attractions of Cincinnati at the time, was something of a boomtown, lying on the rail lines that connected north to south and east to west. This made it a perfect location to sell get-rich-quick schemes, investment plans that were the precursors to Ponzi schemes, and cash loans with unimaginably high interest rates. After careful research and investigation it soon became apparent that the Youngs were part of a group who were making large sums of money in this way, some of it skirting the law, but much of it clearly illegal. However, the justice system largely ignored these scams—until Jacob's and Nancy's bodies were found.

There were a large number of players, but signs began to suggest that the possible mastermind behind these dealings was an unassuming grocer's wife named Nancy Clem. It would later be said that Mrs. Clem held the entire state's finances in her hands and that she could enter any bank in the city and make a withdrawal of any amount she chose. There were several suggestions as to how the Youngs had gotten on the wrong side of Mrs. Clem. They owed her a large sum of money that they refused to pay; Jacob refused to leave his wife for Mrs. Clem; and so on. Like much in the case, the specifics were never fully revealed.

The prosecution's theory was that Mrs. Clem lured the Youngs out of the city and then Mrs. Clem's brother and a confederate fell on the couple, shooting Jacob in the face with the shotgun and shooting Nancy from behind with the pistol. When Nancy showed signs of life, she was bludgeoned with a rock. The presence of a woman's heeled footprint near the bodies showed that Mrs. Clem was there, they argued. To confuse matters, Mrs. Clem's brother left a confession and then killed himself in his jail cell, contending that his sister was in no way involved. Some suggested that he had actually been killed by his cellmate, the supposed confederate in the murders.

Nancy Clem sat through four separate trials. The attorneys pored over bank statements, though Mrs. Clem never kept a bank account. There were enticing details which showed that on the same day Mrs. Clem's physician withdrew a specific amount, Jacob Young would in turn deposit the exact same amount into his own account. Mrs. Clem's "sewing girl" testified that Mrs. Clem offered her two hundred dollars if she would tell the authorities that she was at home on the afternoon of the murders, even though she was absent. Mrs. Clem's husband, the grocer, had never met Jacob Young, and he did not even know his wife was acquainted with the man until after the bodies were discovered. In spite of this it was found that Nancy Clem and Jacob Young visited each other's houses several times a week.

Four times she was found guilty and sentenced to life in prison. However, the venue for her fifth appeal trial was changed to another county and the jurors in this county did not agree with the previous verdicts and found her innocent. The state determined that it had spent too much time and money on trying to convict this woman and so gave up the fight. At the time Pearl Bryan's body was discovered, Nancy Clem was an old woman living a quiet life. She steadfastly maintained her innocence, though she did spend four years in prison for crimes linked to her financial dealings.

In later years, there was some indication that Mrs. Clem possessed special knowledge about some of the wealthiest men in Indianapolis. It was noted that many leading families suffered hardship upon her arrest for the murders. She would divorce the grocer, but leave behind an only son. He would later claim that there was more to the murders than the papers stated, and that his mother had sealed her lips in order to protect prominent men and their families. He couldn't elaborate any more on the subject, saying that she only spoke of it once and "then she only said that if she had acted honestly at the time other people's children and not her own would have suffered." She would die of natural causes in the summer of 1897.

The Clem case and the Pearl Bryan murder were completely disconnected by time, distance, and circumstance; but similarities remained. The players are all seemingly respectable citizens, gentlemen and ladies at first glance. Yet, like every case in which someone takes another's life, there is betrayal and that essential moment, the point when the killer or killers makes the clear decision that the best option, the only option, is to murder another human being.

Part of the search now for the investigators was to determine when that moment occurred and what led up to it. The
postmortem and hints dropped by Mr. Early's statements
pointed clearly to the moment that Pearl Bryan's path parted
from the bliss of youth. It must have been when she recognized the signs that she was with child. It now rested on the
shoulders of Plummer, Crim, and McDermott to determine
who the father was and if it was his work that had led Pearl
to such a gruesome end.

NINE

AN ILLEGAL OPERATION

Perhaps it was the cocaine found in her stomach, though this news wasn't related until later (and there is also reason to believe this was given to her as a means to kill her and not to force a miscarriage). Perhaps there were lacerations or markings within the uterus or around the vagina; we'll never know. Perhaps it was simply a wild theory, but there would later prove to be plenty of evidence to support it. We will never know why Dr. Carothers announced after the postmortem, and Coroner Tingley would later support this deduction, that Pearl Bryan had come to Cincinnati seeking an "illegal operation," that is, an abortion.

A. W. Early, the Western Union manager in Greencastle and close friend of Will Wood, told the investigators that Wood had showed him many letters from Scott Jackson,

> one letter, I remember was in answer to one in which Wood had written to Jackson, informing him that

Pearl Bryan was showing the effects of her indiscretion and intimacy with Jackson, and telling him that
the recipes sent by him had been furnished by Wood.
Jackson regretted that his recipes had failed but said
something must be done and suggested that the girl
be sent to Cincinnati, stating that he could arrange to
have an abortion performed on her. Wood told me
afterward that Pearl had gone to Cincinnati to have a
criminal operation performed, and had told her parents she was going to Indianapolis to visit friends. She
had money with her, sufficient to cover any expenses
she might incur in such an undertaking.

Abortion, the termination of a pregnancy before birth, has
a long history in the United States. Though abortion was illegal, it was not particularly surprising that Pearl had sought
out such a solution. This did not mean, however, that abortion was accepted or viewed lightly by society. As far back as
1742 there is record of Amasa Sessions apparently convincing
his pregnant lover, Sarah Grosvenor, to "take the trade," or
take an abortive drug, and when that didn't work he hired a
local physician to perform an abortion. Sarah did not survive
the operation, and Sessions and the physician were charged
with "highhanded misdemeanor," but only the physician
stood trial, though he fled before he could be punished.

In Puritan society, abortion was a serious offense; however,
convictions for abortion were rare, only one every few
decades. The evidence is too scarce to get a clear picture of
abortion in the eighteenth and early nineteenth centuries.
For the most part, it seemed that parents welcomed any children they could have despite the dangers of childbearing. Yet
there were times when children became an economic burden
on the parents and repeated, close pregnancies often took an
excessive toll on the mother and family. All the while, there
were children born out of wedlock that were often unwanted.

Cases in which a pregnancy was clearly unwanted and a miscarriage occurred may be an indication of a possible termination, but due to the reluctance of people of the time to speak of such things, there is no way to know.

By 1850, however, things had changed. Reproductive control had become commercialized. Women began to gain more independence in their choices of contraception and abortion. This led to national campaigns of "social purity"— usually comprised of middle-class white men and women— who sought to restore the public good, not unlike the progressive and temperance movements that would rise up in the ensuing decades. The campaigns proved very successful and soon state laws were created to make abortion a very serious crime. Some states made abortions at any stage in the pregnancy illegal, those prosecuted faced charges of second-degree murder and manslaughter. Some states made exceptions if the abortion was done to save the mother's life.

Previously abortions had usually been misdemeanors, not felonies, and only then after "quickening" or when motion was apparent in the fetus. This yardstick was still used in many trials, and juries were often hesitant to convict if the abortion had taken place "pre-quickening." By 1888, state laws varied greatly on the subject of abortion. In some states, like New York, the laws were harsh and very clear. However, perhaps ironically, five states including Kentucky had passed no clear laws on abortion. The general rule was that abortions were nationally illegal and so this drove the practice underground—making them expensive and exceptionally more dangerous.

In 1873, Congress passed what came to be known as the Comstock law, named for its main proponent and a crusader for purity, Anthony Comstock, a United States postal inspector. The purpose of the law was to tighten loopholes that allowed interstate trade in obscene literature and material. The law defined obscene material in a number of ways,

including "any article whatever for the prevention of concep-
tion, or for causing unlawful abortion." States used the law as
a model as well, so that soon it became a serious offense to
offer anything that might prevent or terminate a pregnancy
in any way, regardless of the circumstances. In some states it
even became a criminal offense to talk about abortions.
There were some exceptions, but in many cases a doctor was
not even permitted to discuss contraception or abortion, in
any way, with his patient, even if he was warning against it.

As shown by the story of Pearl Bryan, this did not stop
abortions from happening. The working theory was that
Pearl was alive when her throat was cut, the first cut that
would lead to her decapitation. Scott Jackson and Will Wood
were not wanted in connection with an attempted abortion,
but with the first-degree murder of Pearl Bryan. However,
A. W. Early's recollection of the telegraphs and letters he had
read had indicated that Jackson would arrange for an abortion and this suggests that an "abortionist" might have been
consulted.

Due to the legal implications, abortionists were inherently
shadowy figures. A woman going in for an abortion had no
idea what to expect and was, quite literally, putting her life in
the hands of strangers. The most well-known abortionists
operated out of New York City, and the most famous of them
was Ann Lohman, more often called Madame Restell. She
was an English immigrant who at first tried her hand as a
seamstress, however she moved on to being a midwife, and
this led to her foray into the world of family planning. It was
said that Madame Restell's clients were among the most
prominent women in the city, and that many lived in fear
that she would divulge their names, though she never did.
She committed suicide after having been deceived by
Anthony Comstock, who had her arrested after she provided
abortion pills for his wife at his pleading.

At the beginning of the 1800s the fertility rate for the average American woman was seven children, and by the end of the century this had dropped to four children. What exactly contributed to this change is impossible to say, but it at the very least indicates that the Comstock law and similar legislation, as well has the harsh punishments for abortions and using contraception, did not succeed in their intended goal. Much like Prohibition would prove in the next century, people continued on much as they had, only now with the associated dangers of criminality attached to the activities. Unlike the assumptions of part of the population, the presence of practitioners such as Madam Restell shows that social impurity was not confined to the lower classes. Also, it is worth noting that in this period, abortions were much more common among married couples than among the unwed.

A. W. Early had described "recipes" that Jackson had suggested that would lead to an abortion. Due to the Comstock law, no one could directly publish or sell anything that could be construed as instructions or products that could abort a pregnancy. So it is impossible to know just what Jackson's recipes were and what effect, if any, they might have had. Some of the advice for unwanted pregnancies was simply to partake in activities that were believed to induce a miscarriage: long walks, climbing of any kind, or rigorous carriage or wagon rides. In this way a woman might easily claim ignorance, even though she might have engaged in the activity with the hopes of ending a pregnancy.

Abortive drugs, or abortifacients, were varied and were often ancient in origin. There were prescriptions that had more to do with magic than medicine, such as rubbing certain areas with the dried skin of a snake or carrying certain stones. There were drugs derived from Sabina, saffron, mace, and rue that were said to expel an unwanted fetus. Other drugs came from known poisons and were said to kill the fetus and then the body would naturally expel it. There was the well-known use of pennyroyal tea, a very old prescription. As global trade expanded, herbal abortifacients became commonplace. Until the Comstock law, women could easily purchase these through the mail, prompted by advertisements in the newspapers. Even after Comstock, companies still advertised, but the ads were purposely vague and only indicated that the product was a "married woman's helper" or some other euphemism. Exotic plants were presented as guaranteed abortives, while miracle drugs like cocaine, laudanum, and the like were said to help as well.

Abortion procedures, however, were harder to come by, especially after the campaigns for social purity toward the end of the nineteenth century. An abortion by a well-regarded practitioner might cost as much as $500, a sum that only the upper class could afford. Despite what A. W. Early had said about Pearl Bryan bringing money with her to Cincinnati, it seems unlikely that she had such a large sum with her. A less reputable abortionist might charge as little as $5, but one must wonder what such an operation entailed and how dangerous it might be. An abortion done in secrecy, conducted by someone with little to no skill, could be a recipe for the eventual death of the mother, probably after a long, agonizing battle with infection.

PEARL BRYAN, upon realizing she was pregnant, must have felt a sudden overwhelming burden fall upon her shoulders. After the Bryan family identified the clothing as belonging to Pearl and suggested the investigators talk with Scott Jackson—as they were coming to accept the fact that they had lost their youngest daughter in such a terrible way—they recalled now that the usually lively and happy Pearl had been despondent at times. It was not enough to alarm the family or for them to notice she might need some sort of help, but looking back, they realized she must have been thinking of the child that was growing inside her and of the man who would be the father. They said that she had showed no interest in social gatherings and had not sought the company of young people, as she usually did.

They could not say what she was distracted by exactly, as she confided in none of them. It will never be known, despite the implications given by others, whether she truly wanted to keep the child or not. We will not know if she loved Scott Jackson and wanted to marry him, or if she felt much the same as he and wanted to be rid of the affair and the unhappy accident. The family told Plummer, Crim, and McDermott that Pearl had met Scott through Pearl's second cousin, Will Wood. They found out, also, that Will Wood had been with Pearl when she departed for Cincinnati and that he had taken a train not long after her to South Bend, Indiana. It is no wonder that they firmly suspected Wood to be involved in the affair and that if Pearl had confided in anyone, it must have been him. Since Jackson and Wood seemed so close as well, they also reasoned Jackson must have confided in Wood, too. Early's recollection of the letter all but proved this theory. So while the Cincinnati police would hunt down Jackson, Sheriff Plummer and detectives Crim and McDermott would be on the trail of Will Wood.

THE DAY BEFORE, Tuesday, February 4, Scott Jackson had gone into one of his favorite Cincinnati restaurants. As he came in, a newsboy shoved a paper at him. "More news about the murder," he explained. Jackson bought a copy and read the article that described Poock's adventures in verifying that the shoes had gone to Greencastle, Indiana, and that they were singular shoes that should easily be traced. Just then, his classmate and roommate Alonzo Walling entered in a hurry and sat down next to him. Walling had in his hand a copy of the same paper. They shared an intense stare, then glanced around the room, but said nothing. A moment went by until Jackson, who perhaps could hold his thoughts inside no longer, uttered, "Damn the shoes."

They went back to their rooms, where they had suitcases filled with women's clothing. Methodically they removed the clothes, a little at a time, and disposed of them, mainly by throwing them into the Ohio River. Jackson grabbed the valise and brought it with him to the bridge, but he did not throw it in; instead, he brought it back with him. It is not known if he threw whatever was in the valise into the river or not. Other bundles of clothing were thrown into the sewers via catch basins. They went to sleep that night, exhausted from their efforts.

In the morning the police chief Phillip Deitsch found the telegram from Crim on his desk and immediately sent out officers to apprehend Scott Jackson. Officers in civilian dress stood outside Jackson's rooming house on Ninth Street and waited. Jackson had got up early that day and taken another bundle, this one of muddy, blood-stained men's pants, and put them in Walling's locker at the Dental College. The detectives had to wait until nine o'clock at night when they spotted Jackson as he walked by the boardinghouse, looked up at it, and then began to walk on. One of the detectives quickly approached him and said, "Hello, Dusty."

Jackson stopped in his tracks.

"Yes, what is it?" he asked.

"You are Scott Jackson, are you not?"

"Yes sir; that is my name," Jackson said (later reports said there was a tremble in his voice).

"Then you are my prisoner," the detective said and formally arrested him. He did not carry cuffs, and Jackson went willingly.

In short order Jackson was taken to Chief Deitsch's office. Since the arrival of the telegram, the police station had been bustling with anticipation of the news of Jackson's capture. There was always the fear that he had been too quick, smart, or lucky and had fled the city already. As soon as the news came in that Jackson was in custody, several people gathered for a chance to see him, to view what the monster looked like. Perhaps to their surprise he appeared to be a normal, good-looking young man, though he looked small and of low spirits to them. The prisoner was taken to the mayor's office and sat before a desk; gathered in the office were the chief, Cincinnati mayor John Caldwell, several police officers and detectives, and several representatives of the press.

The police chief conducted most of the interview.

"What is your name?" he asked the prisoner.

"Scott Jackson," the man replied.

"You are also known as Dusty?"

"Yes, sometimes."

The reporters noted that Jackson seemed exceptionally nervous and his answers were strained and forced.

"Where is your home?" Deitsch asked.

"My home is in Greencastle, Indiana," Jackson replied.

"Do you know Pearl Bryan?"

"I do," he said.

"Where did you see her last?"

Scott Jackson thought for a moment, "It was during the holidays, I think January 2nd."

"Have you seen her since?"

"I have not," Scott Jackson said.

TEN

PEARL AND SCOTT

Pearl's father, Alexander Bryan, was born about 1825 in Kentucky and moved with his family to Greencastle. Before Pearl's death it was recorded that he owned about a thousand acres outside the city and was well known as a cattle and real estate dealer. In a short biography of one of his sons-in-law, he is mentioned as a "gentleman of considerable reputation" in the state of Indiana. Pearl's mother, Susan (though she might have gone by Jane), was from Indiana and by all accounts was a dutiful and loving wife and mother.

As of the 1880 census, they had eight children living with them: Ella, Marion, Mary, Anta, Fred, Jennie, Pearl, and Alexander. A daughter, Belle, had married Elijah Yates ten years earlier and was presumably living in Kansas with him. The records are not completely clear, but they indicate that another married daughter, Flora, would die the year after the census. Marion would follow the year after that. Jennie

would die in 1885 and Anta in 1892, though which daughter
was supposed to have died while Mary Stanley and Pearl
remained at the house, around the time Pearl was with Scott
Jackson, is not clear. This might have been Anta, but then her
passing should have been three years later, which is entirely
possible. Equally possible is that the story was confused and
Anta did die in 1892, while Pearl didn't meet Scott Jackson
until 1895. Regardless, the Bryans obviously knew grief and
loss. The oldest son was James, who was out of the house by
1880; little is known of him.

They were, by all accounts, the model of a well-to-do rural
family, and Pearl was their charming, youngest daughter.
Reports written later often say that Pearl was the youngest of
twelve children; however, records from the time indicate she
had a younger brother, Alexander, who may have gone by
Frank. It would seem he was one of the brothers mentioned,
along with Fred, who were present when the sheriff and
detectives brought Pearl's bloody clothes to the Bryan farm.

Pearl was born in 1873; she was twenty-two years old
when her life was taken. She graduated from the Greencastle
high school, as the general consensus is that her father
encouraged education for both his sons and daughters and
that she was a student in good standing. She was believed by
the community to be a pure and chaste girl, not a New
Woman by any accounts. She wore a cream white silk dress
to her graduation in 1892. She was said to be very fond of
company and to possess many friends. Whether it was hyper-
bole created after her death is impossible to say, but some
claimed she was known as the "belle of Putnam county."
Beyond that little is known about what type of person Pearl
Bryan was, what her dreams might have been, or what she
might have feared.

Her second cousin and one of her closest friends was Will
Wood, who was not quite two years younger than her and

was at one point enrolled at DePauw University. Some accounts describe Will as Pearl's boyfriend; and after the murder there were a few parties that claimed he was, in fact, the father of her child. However, there no clear evidence suggesting that. Still, due to the lack of paternity tests, we'll never know for certain. It is clear that Will Wood was the link between Pearl and Scott Jackson.

Jackson's personal history is better known than Pearl's, but it is hard to say how much of it has been pulled through the lens of his later crime. Scott Jackson's mother had been married twice. The first marriage had produced a daughter, while the second produced a son, Scott, born in Maine. His father, sometime referred to as "Commodore" Jackson, was the captain of a merchant vessel that traveled the Atlantic. It was said that once Jackson reached the age of fourteen, he began to make journeys with his father and learn "the ways of the world." The implication being that the life of a sailor is not known for social purity. After Scott's father died, he and his mother moved to New Jersey for a short time, where Jackson was said to enjoy society in general and was believed to frequent saloons and brothels. It was also said he became a member of the Entre Nous, an exclusive social club in New Jersey that some believed engaged in debauchery.

Jackson then gained employment with the Pennsylvania Railroad and was quickly involved in a scam conducted by his boss, who would be charged with embezzling about $32,000 from the company. After two trials, Jackson arranged a deal that he would testify about everything he knew concerning the scam and would receive immunity from any prosecution.

His half-sister had by this point married a professor at DePauw University and his mother was living in Greencastle, too. Scott traveled there and moved in with her. His mother received some sort of steady income, perhaps a pension from one or both of her previous husbands, and this allowed the Jacksons to live comfortably. Their house happened to be next door to that of the Methodist reverend Wood and his young son, Will. Scott and Will soon became good friends.

After meeting and working with a dentist in Greencastle, Jackson decided he wanted to go to dental school and so enrolled in a school in Indianapolis. There he became acquainted with another student, Alonzo Walling. After a year in Indianapolis, however, Jackson decided to withdraw from that school and enroll at the dental school at the University of Cincinnati instead. Later rumors stated he did this because he was no longer welcome at the school in Indianapolis because of his habits and personal conduct. He was, it was claimed, drinking and visiting brothels the entire time he was enrolled. None of the rumors was ever confirmed, and no clear explanation was ever given as to why he switched schools.

While Jackson was looking for a room to rent in Cincinnati, he ran into Alonzo Walling, who had also switched schools at the same time. This chance meeting would change both of their lives. As Walling would later describe it, "Well, I was standing on the doorstep of our boarding-house, at 222 West Ninth Street, the second day of our school term here in October, when Scott came along Ninth Street and recognized me. On the strength of our being acquainted in Indianapolis we roomed together at 222 Ninth Street and took our meals out." This was the house where Jackson would be stopped by the police and arrested for the murder of Pearl Bryan the following February.

Between dental school in Indianapolis and his move to Cincinnati, Scott Jackson spent time in Greencastle. He frequented the local dentist's office, as did his young friend Will Wood. The first time Pearl Bryan met Scott Jackson might have been there, when Pearl was coming to have some dental work done. Will naturally introduced the two. Later, Wood and Jackson called upon the Bryan household, Will being a regular guest because of his familial connection. At social gatherings Pearl Bryan and Scott Jackson found themselves in each other's company. Pearl was generally regarded as a beautiful girl. Scott, who was five years older than Pearl, might have been attracted to the wealth of her family; he might have fallen for her reportedly innocent charm. Pearl might have been taken with Jackson's striking blue eyes and his worldliness. Most everyone agreed, even if later they believed him to be a monster, that he could be very charming.

Will Wood, who was probably in the best position to comment on it, later said, "Pearl was stuck on Jackson from the first time they met, Jackson would come and get my horse and buggy and drive over to Pearl's house, when they would often go out driving together. Pearl was pretty and ambitious, but I never thought she would do wrong. Now I can see she was perfectly infatuated with Jackson from the start; so much that I am firmly convinced, she was completely in his power, and he took advantage of his influence over her."

Will's words, though delivered with a certain coached feeling, are vaguely revealing. Perhaps the most striking word choice is when he called Pearl "ambitious." After it was learned that Pearl was the victim, the general attitude appears to have been that she was innocent and, as Will says, "completely in his power," but the idea of her being ambitious twists the perspective, if only slightly. She might have been ambitious, but in the sense of seeking Jackson's love or perhaps his hand in marriage. We cannot assume that Wood meant that she was an ambitious person who sought fame and fortune. We do not know if Pearl dreamed that Scott Jackson might take her away from the routine life she had always known in Greencastle. We cannot determine if

Jackson's worldliness excited Pearl's hope for a life that was different than her dutiful mother's.

Pearl is often described as a "country girl." These sorts of labels are often relative and do little to accurately describe the person in question. The supposition is that this was a polite way to explain that she was unsophisticated, part of the presentation that she was innocent and pure and thus susceptible to Scott Jackson's devilish charm. Within the delicate framework of painting the portrait of a murder victim, the idea that Pearl was a country girl helps to keep her in a positive light. Because of this, we may never know if Pearl longed to be a New Woman, like the kind described in so many novels and plays. We don't even know if she was a reader or what she might have read.

Perhaps her father received the *Indianapolis Journal* and perhaps, being an ambitious and educated young woman, Pearl glanced through it on January 1, 1895, months before she would meet Scott Jackson. She might have seen the article titled "On the New Woman" that explained that the New Woman had the "lawlessness of Eve," the "moral standard of Lacedaemonia," and the "domestic failings of Greece." Lacedaemonia is the name for the region controlled by ancient Sparta. Women in Spartan society had unprecedented domestic freedoms and received similar education as men; they could legally own and inherit property. They were alleged to have been promiscuous and controlled their husbands. The author's meaning was clear: the New Woman was a threat to society. The article in particular addresses the problems the New Woman posed to religion.

Any number of similar articles in regional papers and magazines that appeared at the time would have made it clear to Pearl that if she wished to be more than an innocent "country girl," she would be better off doing it somewhere else, perhaps outside Indiana altogether. The possibility exists that she might have seen such an opportunity in Scott Jackson, who came from the more progressive and sophisticated East Coast, who had belonged to exclusive social clubs of young, open-minded individuals, and who seemed to have such a bright future. Needless to say, this is mere speculation. Pearl, as far as anyone knows, didn't leave behind a diary that might have shown us who she really was. Yet, she was certainly something more than an innocent murder victim. She was more than a headless body lying in the brush on Colonel Locke's farm. She was more than the blood that soaked the ground and splattered the leaves, more than the macabre souvenirs and ghost stories.

Born decades before Pearl, Mary Abigail Dodge would die in the same year that young Pearl was murdered. Mary might, at one point, have been called a country girl, growing up in Hamilton, Massachusetts. She was educated and came from a respectable and well-liked farming family. While people would say only that Pearl was sweet and charming, Mary was often called "headstrong." She became a teacher before giving it up to write poetry and essays. She was a governess for her publisher for a time and took on the pen name Gail Hamilton, a standard literary device for cultural critics. Her writings first came out in antislavery publications. From watching her own mother toil endlessly for her family, Mary grew to despise housework and defied the idea of confinement in a "woman's sphere." She wrote critically of men and spoke out about women's rights. She would write twenty books on women, religion, travel, and rural life, not to mention biographies, a novel, and children's works. She sued her publisher for not paying her as they would a male writer, and although she lost the suit, she established a precedent of women fighting for equal pay. She criticized the treatment of women writers, raising issues that many believed helped to ensure better circumstances for female writers.

Dodge's biographers don't often call her pretty, innocent, or a country girl; they do not paint her as blindly falling through life, unable to control her own destiny, hoping instead that she might find herself in the arms of a virtuous man. There is nothing about the story of Pearl's life up to and including her first encounters with Scott Jackson that indicate that she might not have had a future like Mary Dodge, had things gone differently. She was young and was in love with a charming man.

Pearl and Scott met in the spring and became lovers sometime in the summer. Scott Jackson never indicated that he felt anything particular for Pearl. She might have been simply a conquest or he might have toyed with the idea of a future with her at some point. However most accounts of the story indicate that Scott ended the relationship by the end of the summer, before he went off to Cincinnati. It is also generally agreed that Pearl was unhappy with the termination of the relationship, which might also help explain her depression that fall and into the winter. It is not clear when Pearl began to show signs that she was pregnant, but most likely in October through December 1895. Letters passed between Wood and Jackson. Based on Jackson's reaction it must have been apparent that he had no intentions of marrying Pearl or supporting the child in any way; instead, he wanted to rid himself of the problem.

It is not known what Pearl thought of this, but the implications are that she went along with Jackson's plans. Perhaps he persuaded her it was too early to start a family, that it would be better once he was a practicing dentist. For her own reasons, which we will never know, she was willing to end the pregnancy, or at least, she was at times. As is often the case in these circumstances, there is every reason to believe that Pearl struggled with the decision. However, she made no efforts to keep the child, either. One can only imagine the turmoil Pearl faced regularly as she dealt with the father of her child who didn't want her or the child, the multiple failed attempts to abort the pregnancy, and the fact that with each passing day her condition would be more and more obvious.

The reports on Scott Jackson seem to indicate that if Pearl did have any dreams or designs, he wouldn't have thought much of them. It must be kept in mind that the moment Pearl was discovered to be the victim, Scott Jackson was cast as the monster of the story. This does not mean that he was not. Regardless of the truth, he never stood a chance of a presumption of innocence. He was a "libertine" and "boasted of his conquests." There were certainly letters that passed between Pearl and Jackson, but none appears to have survived. Louis Poock, in his book on the case, states that Pearl learned of her condition after Scott's fall term at the dental college had ended. "No doubt she was pleading with him in her letters to save her from her shame in a honorable way," he presumes.

While this might be nice to believe, Will Wood never indicated this, nor did Scott Jackson—the only two people who were in a place to know. However, each had reason to cover up any chance that Pearl might have not wanted an abortion. Poock also says that Jackson returned to Greencastle during the holiday break, having previously sent a prescription for drugs that Pearl should use. According to Poock, Pearl ignored the prescription, much to Jackson's consternation.

Poock goes on, "Now that it was no question but that he had deceived her and proposed to continuing to deceive her, she realized, as she never had before, that all his love for her was but a pretense for wicked designs. All her pleadings with him proved to be in vain, and while he may have held out some hope to her of amending, he never proposed in his heart to carry out his promises to her."

It is very tempting to believe this fiction, but we must admit that Poock, as far as anyone can tell, had no way of knowing any of this. There is nothing that demonstrates that Pearl pleaded with Scott to "do the honorable thing." There is no correspondence that shows a struggle between the two over what to do about the pregnancy. There is most assuredly nothing that tells us the inner workings of Scott Jackson's mind, however much we might wish for such a thing. What we can say for certain is that Pearl and Scott knew she was pregnant and both, it would seem, agreed the best course of action was to secure an abortion.

ELEVEN

ARRESTED

Scott Jackson, giving off every indication of nervousness, sat in the mayor's office and did his best to answer the questions being fired at him. His pale blue eyes scanned the room.

"Do you know William Wood?" Chief Deitsch asked dryly.

"I do," Jackson answered

"What is his business?"

"I don't know. He used to be connected with the school at Greencastle. Saw him last about January 6."

Chief Deitsch then read the dispatch from Detective Crim ordering Jackson's arrest.

"What have you to say about that?" the chief asked.

Jackson looked at the man. "The charge is entirely false. I don't know anything about that."

"That's what everybody says who is arrested, but the identification of the clothes and other facts point to you as the man who took Pearl Bryan or her body to Ft. Thomas. Where were you last Friday evening?" the chief asked

Jackson paused briefly, "I must have been in my room."

"What time did you go to your room?"

"I think I had supper about 7 o'clock and went home about 7:30."

"What did you do?"

"I studied in my room," Jackson said.

It was Wednesday night, 5 February 1896, five days almost to the hour since the murder.

"Was your roommate there?" the chief asked, looking intently at Jackson.

"I think he was," Jackson responded.

Jackson was then asked about what he did last Thursday night; the investigators were probably trying to establish a timeline between when Pearl arrived in Cincinnati and her murder. He said he was home and his roommate was out. Saturday evening, the evening after the body was discovered, he said he went out with a friend and went to the theater. He was asked who ate with him Friday evening; in other words, who could account for his actions. He ate alone. They asked him what he had done that day, Wednesday. He said he had left his rooms in the morning, saw a young lady and took her to dinner. He was with her all afternoon. They had gone to the Emory Hotel.

Speaking of the moment when Jackson was arrested, the chief asked, "Why did you pass the house and look up at it?"

Jackson seemed confused, "Well, I don't know. I am turned around now."

He sat on a long sofa in the mayor's office, surrounded by men who, for the most part, seemed to already have determined him guilty, though it seems they might have been uncertain what he was guilty of. The *Enquirer* plainly called him Pearl's "slayer," though the chief of police seemed to be uncertain just how Pearl died and where.

All day the police had been at work tracking down the coming and goings of Scott Jackson before they were able to apprehend him. They asked him if he remembered leaving a valise at a saloon on Saturday night. He said that he did remember it and that he came back for it later on. When pressed, he said there was nothing in the valise, that it was empty. When asked why he took an empty valise out with him, left it in a saloon, retrieved it, and then, according to him, gave it to a fellow student whose first name he could not recall, he was uncertain.

Until this point in the interview Jackson's answers were of the sort that could be seen as innocent. He spent time alone, ate out, and studied in his room for much of the time in question. There was nothing particularly unusual about that. He did not have a list of witnesses who could confirm his presence on that crucial Friday evening, besides possibly his roommate; but innocent people don't feel compelled to provide witnesses to their every move. However, the conversation about the valise became a stumbling block. Jackson admits that he bought the valise in Indianapolis, and that he had it with him, but claims it was empty and gives no clear reason why he would be carrying it, why he might leave it in a saloon, and why he might give it to an acquaintance.

The interview ended and Jackson was taken away. A reporter stopped him on his way out.

"Why don't you tell Colonel Deitsch the truth about this?" the reporter demanded.

Jackson looked at the man. "I did tell the truth, all but about the valise. I got that back."

This is the ink drop in the water of Jackson's first interview. He lied about the handbag. Scott Jackson had something to hide, but the investigators, despite their preconceived notions, did not know what that might be. This became the heart of the investigation. How much was known and by whom? Who was involved and in what way?

As a later, unidentified writer would ask, "Was it cruel fate which led pure, beautiful, innocent and attractive Pearl Bryan into the toils [snare] of such a fiend in human shape?"

After the interview, at about 11 o'clock that night, Jackson was taken to the city jail and put in a cell. At the same time Will Wood had been located and arrested in South Bend, Indiana, and was on his way to Cincinnati. When Jackson was registered in the jail, he was briefly searched and three women's handkerchiefs were found on his person. He said that he had found them on a streetcar. Reports would later indicate that Jackson had appeared cool under pressure, "a bundle of steel." His slip-up about the valise, he later explained, was because he was confused under the circumstances.

THE DESCRIPTIONS OF JACKSON at his arrest are limited. They focus mainly on his pale-blue eyes, on his shifts between apparent nervousness and then his moments of cool collection. They mention his blond hair and whiskers, and one comments on his stiff hat. The illustrations of him show his face and perhaps part of a collar. His dress was not much remarked on. But the implication was that he looked much like H. H. Holmes and Theo Durrant, like a banker or someone in middle management, a doctor, druggist, or dentist. He gave the appearance of what one might call a gentleman, not a "rough." He was not the product of a neglected childhood, not the result of an upbringing marked by petty crime and violence. His face was not marred; his clothes were not dirty. Taken out of the jail cell, he might have been someone you would like to see courting your daughter, as perhaps the Bryans did.

Of course the term "gentleman" had become of such a relative nature that a *Popular Science* article of the time could read, "Until the present century drunkenness was almost universal, and the gentleman who did not drink himself under the table was thought at best to be a poor sort of man." Here the word "gentleman" obviously bears no positive connotations; it is seemingly synonymous with "man."

In England, going back centuries, a gentleman indicated a particular man of noble birth, a landowner without an occupation. The word went through a series of shifts; at times people insisted that a gentleman could only be so by birthright, and then that birth alone could not make one a gentleman. As the nineteenth century progressed, certain occupations could establish someone as a gentleman, though which occupations was debated. English writers spent countless words arguing whether being an author or poet could make one a true gentleman. There was also the argument that a man could only be a gentleman if he obtained a liberal education from certain exclusive schools.

In America, where no one held titles, the question became one of presentation. A man was a gentleman if he acted and dressed as a gentleman should. Several publications and books addressed just what a man needed to do to be considered a gentleman by fashionable society. Yet it was not just the hats, gloves, walking sticks, and suits. It considered a man's manners, his gentleness, his kindness, his strength of character, his proper attitudes and behavior according to the norms of the society he lived in. There were rules to how a gentleman should handle himself in a fistfight or in times of war. In many ways, the American gentleman was marked by a certain self-assurance, clothed in humility.

The author Henry Lunettes, writing in 1860, described meeting a son and father from Kentucky on a steamboat. During a storm in which everyone was driven into the cabin, Lunettes and the father were engaged in quiet conversation, while the son and a group of young men were nearby engaged in a loud, boisterous talk that is a universal exchange among young men. As they grew louder, the father became perturbed.

"Fredrick," he said firmly, "make a little less noise, if you please."

The son stood up quickly and bowed respectfully, "Gentlemen, I beg your pardon! I really was not aware of being so rude."

Lunettes was deeply impressed with the son's response and so included it in his book, *The American Gentleman's Guide to Politeness and Fashion*, as an example of gentlemanly conduct.

By the end of the nineteenth century, however, the idea of the gentleman was beginning to lose its distinction, and as the *Popular Science* article shows, it began to mean simply any man at all. Still, this didn't mean that society in 1896 didn't have a general idea of what a "good" man should be and that he could be identified by his dress and manners. Scott Jackson had this, as did Theo Durrant and H. H. Holmes, and this is what made them the monsters of popular imagination. A dead prostitute, a lynched black man, a killer tramp, or a street rough usually only produced a few headlines. A charming, well-dressed, but brutal killer—this was beyond belief and the public had an insatiable desire to learn more.

JACKSON WAS NOT LONG IN HIS CELL before he was taken out again and brought to a separate room to be searched. He undressed and quickly the detectives searching him noticed two large scratches on his right arm. The right sleeve of his shirt also had bloodstains that showed signs of trying to be washed out.

"Where did that blood come from?" one of the officers asked.

"I was bothered with bugs the other night," Jackson explained. "And I scratched myself."

Neither of the officers believed the explanation.

Jackson was taken back to his cell and it was noted that he seemed nervous and out of sorts. At around half past midnight he called the guard. The guard approached and asked what he wanted.

"I want you to get a chair and sit in front of my cell all night," Jackson replied.

"Are you afraid of getting lynched?" the guard asked.

"Never mind that," Jackson said. "I prefer to be well guarded whether I am in danger or not."

The turnkey tried to stay near Jackson's cell as much as possible, but he was not able to sit in front of the cell as the prisoner had asked. For his part Jackson, despite the earlier reports of appearing to be cool under pressure, showed every sign of distress. He tried to make himself more comfortable by removing his jacket, hat, vest, and necktie. He laid on the bed in his cell and put his hands behind his head. But he did not sleep. He laid there, staring at the ceiling, and speaking in short sentences, being sure to divulge as little information as possible. He admitted only that he was from Indiana, but beyond that he remained evasive. He did not sleep at all that night.

Jackson had no intention of trying to get out of jail, unlike the prisoner in Sandusky, Ohio, who had almost escaped a few weeks earlier. The prisoner cleverly fashioned a handmade key from tin, lead, and copper shavings he had collected from his mealtime cups. He might very well have been successful, if another inmate had not reported him to the guards. Scott Jackson probably didn't have the skills to conduct such an escape, but he also had every reason to stay safely guarded in jail. The papers would all carry his name and likeness the next morning, and he must have known that in short order he would be the most reviled man in the city and that eventually his name might share the stage with the other monsters of the day—unless he could prove himself innocent.

PEARL HAD APPARENTLY SAID she was going to visit her friend, Miss Fisher, the daughter of Mr. Lou Fisher of Indianapolis, when she left Greencastle on January 28. A few telegrams confirmed that Pearl was not in Indianapolis and that she had never gone there. When Will Wood and Jackson's family were contacted, they expressed their doubts to the reporters that their sons were in any way involved in the terrible crime.

A report from Cincinnati appeared in the *Louisville Courier-Journal* the day after Jackson's arrest. "His account of his whereabouts last Friday was not by any means conclusively satisfactory, nor was it conclusively convicting," they relayed. More incriminating was the report concerning his confusion about the valise; the article added, "The theory is that the head of the murdered girl was probably in the valise, and he traveled about with it to destroy it without being discovered." There did not appear to be much possibility of Scott Jackson's innocence, and considering the circumstantial evidence already pointing to him, it seems understandable that the papers and the public might easily accept his guilt. The investigators were beginning to think they definitely had their man as well.

The conditions of Jackson's cell are not given, but the general opinion was that Cincinnati's jail was cleaner and better maintained than many others. Something that is ubiquitous now, a flushing toilet, was most likely not present. As might be expected, prisons varied greatly around the country, and the penitentiary system was relatively new in many places. Jackson, because he had not been charged or tried, was in a small-scale lockup. There is no mention that he shared a cell with anyone, but it is possible that an occasional homeless person or drunk joined him. Beginning in the 1870s, prison reform had led to what was now called the "correctional system." One of the key tenets of this new system was that a criminal could face a range of sentencings, from five, ten, or fifteen years to life, depending on the crime and circumstances; in addition, prisoners who behaved well within the system could be released early. Scott Jackson must have known that if he were found guilty, he would likely be sentenced to life in prison or death; but there were certain key pieces of information that could affect his fate. The most important was whether Pearl Bryan was dead or alive when her head was removed. If she had died before, then the question was whether her death was murder or an accident.

The thoughts must have been a small portion of the turmoil that raged inside Scott Jackson's head as he lay in his cell. He must have also been wondering if they had found his friend—not Will Wood—but his roommate, Alonzo Walling.

Born in 1872, Pearl Bryan was the youngest daughter of a well-respected farmer from Greencastle, Indiana. This is her only known photograph. (*Northern Kentucky Views*)

Scott Jackson was a dental student when he met Pearl Bryan. He had been kicked out of a school in Indianapolis before enrolling in the Ohio College of Dental Surgery in Cincinnati. (*Cincinnati Enquirer*)

Fellow dental student Alonzo Walling ended up sharing rooms with Scott Jackson after a chance encounter. Like Jackson, Walling had transferred from Indianapolis to the dental school in Cincinnati. (*Cincinnati Enquirer*)

A view from an old postcard of John Locke's field where the decapitated body of a young woman had been found by a worker on February 1, 1896. (*Northern Kentucky Views*)

Louis D. Poock owned a shoe store in Cincinnati. Intrigued by the shoes found on the body, Poock was instrumental in breaking the case by using his expertise to identify the shoes and ultimately the body. (*Northern Kentucky Views*)

Police Chief Philip Deitsch from a photo taken in 1885. Deitsch assigned two of his best detectives on the case. (*Cincinnati Police Historical Society*)

Detective Cal Crim believed the unidentified body had not been dumped where it was found, but murdered at the spot with the head being taken away to prevent the body from being identified. (*Northern Kentucky Views*)

Pearl Bryan's cousin William Wood sketched at the time of the Jackson and Walling trials. He introduced Pearl Bryan and Scott Jackson and testified against Jackson during his trial. (*Northern Kentucky Views*)

The 6th Infantry Regiment at Fort Thomas around the time of the Spanish-American War, two years after the Pearl Bryan case. Bryan's body was found not far from the fort, which led to suspicions that a soldier had been involved in the crime. (*Kenton County Public Library, Covington, Kentucky*)

Fifth Street, Cincinnati, Ohio, c. 1900. At the time of Pearl Bryan's murder, in 1896, Cincinnati was the most populous city in Ohio and the ninth largest in the United States. (*Library of Congress*)

The Ohio College of Dental Surgery where both Scott Jackson and Alonzo Walling attended. (*University of Cincinnati*)

Atlantic Garden on Vine Street between Sixth and Seventh streets featured saloons, pool halls, gambling houses, and other entertainment. Frequented by prostitutes, the body found on John Locke's farm was initially thought to be a woman who had been last seen here. (*Public Library of Cincinnati*)

An illustration of prostitutes in Cincinnati. Scott Jackson was said to have frequented bordellos, leading to speculation that Pearl Bryan was simply another "conquest" of Jackson's. (*University of Cincinnati Library*)

Sheet music for "Forgive me, I'll come home," published in Cincinnati in 1895. Popular songs such as this one reinforced conservative female role models. Like many other young women of the late nineteenth and early twentieth centuries, Pearl Bryan was exposed to both old and new ideas about the role of women in American society. (*New York Public Library*)

The Drew, Selby, & Co. shoe factory in Portsmouth, Ohio. Louis Poock discovered that the unusual shoes worn by the body had been sold in Greencastle, Indiana. (*Portsmouth [Ohio] Historical Society*)

The Bryan family home in Greencastle, Indiana. It was here where Pearl's family learned of the tragedy and confirmed that the body was indeed that of their daughter. (*Northern Kentucky Views*)

The all-male jury that convicted Scott Jackson of capital murder. (*Northern Kentucky Views*)

Scott Jackson, left, and Alonzo Walling, right, on the platform beneath the gallows a few minutes before their execution. They were hanged on March 20, 1897. (*Cincinnati Enquirer*)

The pock-marked gravestone of Pearl Bryan in the Forest Hill Cemetery, Greencastle, Indiana. Visitors have chipped pieces from the stone over the years as well as left coins heads-side-up on top.
(*Jennifer Wiggins/GraveyardGirl.net*)

Cal Crim later in life. After leaving the Cincinnati Police, Crim established an independent detective agency. His most well-known case was investigating the "Black Sox" scandal following the 1919 World Series.
(*Crim Detective Agency*)

TWELVE

THE ROOMMATE

A T AROUND TWO O'CLOCK IN THE MORNING OF FEBRUARY 5, it is said, Scott Jackson approached close enough to the bars of his cell to speak to one of his guards.

"Hasn't Walling been arrested yet?" he asked.

Authorities knew he had a roommate named Alonzo Walling, but up until that point they had no particular reason to think he was involved in the murder.

"Why should he be arrested?" the officer asked.

Jackson said nothing else, but it was enough. Walling had actually spoken to the police earlier, but had been let go. The details at this point aren't entirely clear, but it appears that an *Enquirer* reporter, upon hearing Jackson's words, took it upon himself to impersonate a police officer and "arrest" Walling at his rooms on Ninth Street. Upon bringing him to the police station, the police must have agreed with the reporter's reasoning, because they booked Walling.

Alonzo Walling's past is particularly difficult to uncover. The general story, which seems to be passed over with hardly a care, is that he was raised on a farm in Mt. Carmel, Indiana. It is said his father died when he was young. From there nothing much is known except that he found himself in dental school in Indianapolis, where he met Scott Jackson. Why he would feel the need to leave Indianapolis and go to Cincinnati has never been clearly explained. His coincidental encounter with Scott Jackson on Ninth Street, in Cincinnati, is the moment he emerged from obscurity.

While Jackson and Walling maintained that they were only acquaintances before they began the fall semester in 1895, over the course of the coming months they quickly became bosom companions. They ate many of their meals together. They became friends with the barber, Albion (the man who claimed to have seen Jackson first with the valise). The three of them often went out drinking, and while the papers never clearly state it, probably kept company with prostitutes. They seemed to be familiar with the Tenderloin district and establishments on George Street in particular. Scott Jackson was the older of the two by about seven years, and it is easy to imagine Jackson as the teacher in decadence and Walling as the student, although neither gave this impression.

It was later on February 5 when Walling was taken to Chief Deitsch's office and interrogated for the first time.

"Well, now Walling," the chief said. "Your friend Jackson has been up here talking, and he told me an awful lot of bad stuff about you."

"Well what did he say?" Walling asked.

"He said that you killed the girl."

"Well, I didn't. The only time I saw Miss Bryan was when he told me to meet her at Fourth and Race streets and tell her that he was busy with a class and could not see her, but would meet her later."

He contended that this was the last time he saw Pearl. He explained that later on, after he heard the news of the body at Fort Thomas, he told Jackson that something appeared wrong with him. Jackson told him that he was tired and that he would be fine if it weren't for "those damned shoes." Walling noticed women's clothes in their rooms, which he thought Jackson had shoved up the chimney. He did notice that Jackson had two valises with him and seemed to leave one and take the other out and then switch at other times. Friday night, the night of the murder, Walling said he stayed in his room, but Jackson went out about 11 o'clock and came home around 1 o'clock in the morning.

The house where Jackson and Walling lived was of newer construction, three stories, and situated in the shadow of City Hall and within walking distance of most of the entertainment in Cincinnati. Two widows occupied the bottom floor, while the rest of the rooms were given to male lodgers, many of them students. Each resident had a night key and so could come and go as he pleased. This was a common set up. Rooms were rented and used primarily for sleeping and little else. There was usually no kitchen and a common bathroom, though rooms might contain a wash basin. Bachelors were not expected to have much need of luxury.

Jackson and Walling's accommodations were palatial compared with many in the city. In one neighborhood, the West End, which surrounded the Tenderloin district, 60,000 people were crowded in a few dozen blocks. Tenements were precariously built and seemed to lean against each other. Barefoot children in dirty rags played in the alleyways, and parents struggled to keep them safe or simply gave up. Disease was common and the physicians assigned to these poor districts were constantly overwhelmed. The city recognized these areas as problems, but finding decent housing for the poor was a massive task. There were attempts to build model communities in the suburbs and arrange for the poor to be sent there, but this proved highly impractical since those in poverty could not afford the lifestyle presented by these communities. Decades later city planners would hit upon the idea of housing projects, though this was still far in the future in 1896.

During the winter months the police complained that their jails were filled with homeless people with nowhere else to go. So it is reasonable to assume that while Scott Jackson and Alonzo Walling, two men accused of beheading a young woman, sat in jail, they shared the space with people guilty only of being poor.

At some point on that same day, Jackson and Walling were dealt another blow. A saloon keeper named Wallingford came to the police with his black porter Allen Johnson and said that he and Johnson saw Jackson, Walling, and a young woman at his saloon on the night of the murder. Johnson gave a description of the woman and the police believed it matched Pearl Bryan. Wallingford added that Jackson had said to him in passing that he wished he had a woman's head to dissect; this statement was given without any pretext and seemed amazingly bizarre. He also said that Jackson borrowed two dollars from him to get a cab.

The next day, February 6, Will Wood arrived from South Bend and was interviewed in the mayor's office. In short order Will explained that he was twenty years old and second cousins with Pearl. He said that his family visited hers every few days.

"Were you intimate with the girl?"

"No, sir."

"Did you know that she had been betrayed?" (in other words, that she was impregnated out of wedlock).

"Yes, sir."

"How did you find that out?" the interviewer asked.

"Jackson told me," Wood said.

The investigators could hardly have been surprised. This seemed to fit with the narrative that had been trickling into them for some time. Wood told them that Jackson said he had betrayed her in September, which tallies with the estimate of the postmortem. There were several telegrams and letters sent back and forth between Jackson and Wood. At one point, Wood said, Pearl was set to go to Indianapolis and have an operation done there, but Wood advised her to wait for word from Jackson. Wood's motives here are unclear; when asked about his interest in the case, he said that he wanted to "shield" her. Unfortunately he did not specify what he was trying to shield her from, whether shame, a painful operation, or Jackson. However, his actions seem to clearly rely on Jackson in his explanation. He waits on Jackson's word and does as Jackson commands. Here again is Jackson, pulling the strings.

There is no question that things looked bad for Jackson, Walling, and Wood. They place the blame on each other, making them all seem the more guilty. Louis Poock in his book *Headless, Yet Identified* explains that Jackson would never have had a problem betraying a girl as he did Pearl, except for the fact that she resided in Greencastle where his mother and sister lived, and that would bring ruin to their good names in that community. So he thought to make the problem disappear. If Jackson was the mastermind and the killer, then one might wonder why he stayed in Cincinnati after the news about the shoes had appeared. One could argue that in 1896 it was much easier to disappear. Scott Jackson could have gone West, like so many others. He might have changed his name and would never be heard from again. Walling might have done the same, if he was more involved than he claimed. So could have Will Wood. But none of them proved hard to find. Perhaps as Jackson walked past his boardinghouse he was thinking of making a run for it, but by then it was too late.

The Pearl Bryan case was an anomaly because on the surface it seemed to offer only dead ends and nothing in the way of solid leads, yet the victim was identified and suspects were found. As Jackson was supposed to have said succinctly, "if not for those damned shoes." Detectives in the late nineteenth century were primarily used to find stolen goods. The fact that Plummer, Crim, and McDermott were the ones to track down the suspects was a departure from the way of normal policing in the previous several decades. Often it was the coroner who identified the suspect, often based on public hearsay more than anything else. Murder cases at the time were solved either quickly or not at all.

Establishing the rate of unsolved murder cases at the time is nearly impossible. First there is the issue of determining whether a death was a murder, which as could be seen in the Keller case was not always clear. Then there are the large number of disappearances, which might be innocent misunderstandings or actual homicides. However, homicides were increasing, specifically in the urbanized regions of the country. An estimate for pre-1900 cities puts the chance of homicide at 1 in 100,000, much higher than the 0.3 per 100,000 in the rural North. However, the rural South had a surprisingly high range of 0.4 to 1.8 per 100,000.

Over the next several days, items were discovered across Cincinnati that seemed to belong to Bryan or Jackson. Jackson's coat was found on February 7 in a sewer at Richmond and John streets. On the 9th Pearl's hat was found in Newport. There was a rumor that Pearl had some jewels on her that were pawned. Someone claimed to have found her hairpin, but it would seem this was only assumed because one was found on the floor of Wallingford's saloon on the morning the body was discovered, and Pearl was supposed to have been there the night before. It was given to the police so that they could show it to the Bryans for identification.

From this point on, the case became a sensation. Papers throughout Indiana, Ohio, and Kentucky were covering the case heavily, and papers across the country related in lengthy columns the story of the innocent country girl seduced to her doom by a demon in human form. The papers needed to only write the name "Pearl Bryan" and it conjured up the lurid details of the headless body found near Cincinnati and the two dental students arrested for her grisly death. The *New York Times*, the *Rock Island Argus* in Illinois, the *Topeka State Journal* of Kansas, and the *Record-Journal* of Sacramento, California, all covered the story. Readers learned of poor Pearl in the pages of the *Seattle Post-Examiner* and the *Pioneer Express* from the new state of North Dakota. Many of the reports were reprinted articles from Cincinnati papers with slight editorial changes, which was common practice.

Readers in Wheeling, West Virginia, read on February 6 about Jackson's arrest and his unease in his interview in the mayor's office, his lie concerning the valise, and the rumor that he carried the head around with him all day on Saturday. After reading such articles, it is not surprising that the city, the region, and the country were sure Jackson and Walling were guilty.

The *Evening Star* in Washington, D.C., printed an interesting article on February 6, which claimed that Jackson had confessed, or at least that was what the headline said. "Scott Jackson, accused of the murder of Pearl Bryan of Greencastle, Ind., near Fort Thomas, Ky., last Friday night, has confessed his guilt, and he implicates Alonzo M. Walling" might have surprised Jackson had he read it. Walling, too, would have been surprised, as it continued: "Walling has also confessed to a personal knowledge of the murder of the girl last Friday Night. Walling tries to lay the whole blame on Jackson. Jackson, on the contrary, while he admits his own guilt, takes pains to implicate Walling." The statements were accurate to note that the pair placed the blame on each other, but that Jackson or Walling had confessed to any knowledge of the murder or having taken part in it at all was false information. The article states that Jackson said that Pearl had undergone an abortion which had gone bad, and she died. Jackson never said where this happened, nor how Pearl's body ended up decapitated in Fort Thomas. Also, curiously, the *Evening Star* mentioned Scott Jackson telling a guard or police officer that he was "afflicted with fainting spells" and that when he was a boy he would rise in a delirium from these spells, dress himself, and wander around for hours without knowing what he was doing. The paper suggested this might be the beginning of some sort of defense.

The papers employed artists to make quick sketches, since printing photographs in newspapers was still a rarity. In short order, the likenesses of Alonzo Walling, Scott Jackson, and Will Wood were being circulated around the nation. A sketch of Pearl Bryan, done from a photograph, was included as well.

Walling appears the most confident in many of these drawings. His hair rises from his head and then descends away from his part in tight, thick waves; all of it appearing slicked to a shine. His heavy dark eyebrows and mustache make him look almost exotic, but his thick, fine tie and the cut of his jacket mark him as someone of a higher class. His neck is elongated and his shoulders pushed back as if he were challenging the viewer to something. Jackson, on the other hand, appears completely at ease. His receding hairline makes him look older than his twenty-seven years. He has a thin mustache that curls to a point at each end. His expression is one of mild interest, as if he were in the audience at the theater. Will Wood, if anything, seems even younger than his age. His lips appear too big and his ears too large. His hair is parted in the middle and he appears the picture of a country boy. Yet he is handsome, at least to judge by the sketch, and it is not hard to imagine that he might have been the favorite of a few young women in Greencastle.

Pearl's likeness appears to have been primarily drawn from a photograph of her during her senior year of high school. The artists, it would seem, were more comfortable with drawing from life. Where the men are drawn with minimal lines, Pearl is overdrawn. Some of the sketches show her, for some reason, with dark circles under her eyes. One artist, seemingly without ever seeing a photograph of her, showed her with a weak chin and wide, high eyebrows, almost exactly like a woman from an advertisement. The actual photograph of Pearl shows an attractive girl, but with more of a low brow and a strong jaw. Later publications, like the sensational *Headless Horror*, used illustrations that made no attempt to show the players accurately.

THIRTEEN

METHODS

THE CINCINNATI POLICE DEPARTMENT USED SOMETHING they called the "Bertillon system," which was nothing like the real Bertillon System, used to identify repeat criminals. The method used by the Cincinnati Police appears to have been to identify the accused's personality, using measurements of the head to determine the type of person the suspect was. The person responsible for conducting these examinations was Sergeant Kiffmeyer. What qualifications were needed to gain this position is not clear.

Kiffmeyer's official reports don't survive, but the summary of his findings was related to reporters. He took careful measurements of Scott Jackson's head, while the prisoner presumably sat patiently. His assessment of Jackson: "Every man's head tells its own story. Jackson is another H. H. Holmes. He has a head such as Napoleon would have. Jackson's skull is abnormal, and unusually long in proportion to its breadth. It is abnormally developed on the right side in front and on the left side in the rear of the head."

Kiffmeyer examined Alonzo Walling and concluded, "Walling's head is that of a commonplace criminal, he is just the opposite of Scott Jackson. . . . Walling is utterly void of any ability or cunning to plot and plan and to conceal. Jackson knew fully and realized what lay before him in the murder of Pearl Bryan. Walling had not realized the enormity of the crime, and is supremely indifferent to the consequences and to the crime committed. No appeal, not even the fear of punishment, will have any impression on Walling."

It is impossible to say if the public and authorities took Kiffmeyer's results as inarguable truths or if his findings happened to coincide perfectly with their own opinions, but his summation of the two suspects' characters appears to have been the general assumption by almost everyone involved with the case, with the exception of Jackson and Walling and perhaps their defense attorneys. Will Wood eventually agreed with the assessments.

Yet how Kiffmeyer came to these results and why it was called the "Bertillon system" is something of a mystery. It is clearly not the Bertillon system, considering that that system was never meant to reveal a person's character. Kiffmeyer's technique bears the closest resemblance to phrenology, a pseudo-science that claimed that studying various areas on the scalp could determine a person's personality and propensities. Phrenology was typically used in a positive light, and parents would have their children examined to better determine what sort of profession to guide them to. Phrenology was well known at the time, so it is unlikely that anyone could have simply confused the two.

Phrenology had come to the United States mainly through Johan Spurzheim in the 1820s and 1830s. The method itself was quite complicated and required the practitioner to feel and measure the subject's head to find specific locations, known as "organs." The size, shape, rise, indent, and so on of these areas would then tell the phrenologist whether the person was strong or weak in a particular organ. Since each organ coincided with a different trait or characteristic, the examination could reveal just what sort of person the subject was. Whether they were kind, patient, brave? Yet in only a few decades the scientific community abandoned phrenology. In 1887, the chair of the London Anthropological Society, Frances Galton, read a paper to the society to suggest that a new, scientific phrenology be established to determine if a link could be made between the shape of the skull, the shape of the brain, and any characteristics of the subject. The group discussed the paper and determined it was an idea for further consideration, then passed on to other business.

By 1896, most of the scientific establishment in the country had abandoned phrenology, but not everyone. Some phrenologists were also mesmerists—another popular treatment at the time—while other charlatans who claimed to be phrenologists traveled around giving examinations. The term phrenology might have fallen out of favor but the concept still held weight with people. In 1896, the *Enquirer* ran a lengthy story about the disdainful way young women were acting. One example was of a young lady who was caught up in phrenology and used phrenological exams when first spending time with a young man. The article implied that this was merely an excuse for her to run her hands through his hair, just as her interest in palmistry was an excuse to touch his hand.

A new science, though, was being developed at the time that bore a marked importance on the Pearl Bryan case: criminology. Employing scientific techniques to help solve crimes was an innovative concept, and like many new ideas its growth was complicated and not altogether uniform. The use of fingerprints to identify a person was known to some, but was not universally accepted, and it required police to allocate funds for fingerprint analysis, personnel, and equipment that departments often could not afford. Evidence was often sent to local professionals instead to analyze and was not handled by the police. While scientists did not have the experience or training to apply their specialties to actually solving crime, they were able to create a revolutionary approach that sometimes assisted those who could. At the end of the nineteenth century, enterprising scientists had developed a specialized microscope that allowed them to compare markings on bullets and determine whether they had been fired from the same gun. A jury could then be shown that a particular gun was used in a crime and no other. In the Pearl Bryan case, rudimentary forensic analysis aimed to link Scott Jackson to the crime scene. His pants, which were found stuffed in Walling's school locker, were sent to a local chemist to have the mud analyzed to see if it matched the mud in Locke's field.

At the end of the nineteenth century, science was entering American public life in a way never seen before. It was in the chemistry of various cleaning products and in the vaccinations for diseases like measles. It fueled the machines of progress and saved lives. In some ways science was unbridled in its growth and expansion, allowing for many forms of pseudo-science to spread among the public as well. If a product, treatment, or cure was presented in the guise of a scientific break-through, some people would accept it regardless of the source.

A January 1895 article in the *Louisville Courier-Journal* entitled "In the World of Science" related the following items: aluminum pencils that could write on glass; machine-spun platinum threads that they were invisible to the naked eye; a telephone line proposed between England and Holland; a German discovery that cream made with steril-

ized equipment lasted longer than cream made with unster-
ilized equipment; and a report that electricity could be used
to keep meat fresh.

As with so many things, science was dominated by men.
Women were beginning to study sciences in Europe in larger numbers—Marie Curie began her brilliant career in 1893
that would eventually lead to a Nobel Prize with her husband, Pierre—but American schools were, for the most part,
not as progressive. There was one luminary, a woman who
came from simple origins and helped explore the universe.
She is not often remembered now, but in the mid- and late
nineteenth century Maria Mitchell caused a stir in the world
of science.

Mitchell was born to Quaker parents on Nantucket Island
in 1818. The Quakers believed in equal education for both
boys and girls, and in addition to her regular schooling,
Mitchell's father taught her the navigational sciences used by
the whalers of the island. She quickly learned math and
astronomy and was able to predict the solar eclipse of 1831
while still a schoolgirl. Her father had a telescope and they
began making observations and publishing their findings.
The Mitchells were among the first to observe the return of
Halley's Comet in 1835. Soon their small "lookout" came to
be one of the most respected observatories in the region. In
1847, Maria discovered a previously unknown comet, which
resulted in her winning a medal from the king of Denmark.
The comet came to be known as "Miss Mitchell's Comet,"
although officially it is the less quaint "1847 T1."

Though Maria Mitchell's story was interesting and surely
inspiring for young girls across the country, her work was
overwhelmed in the flood of new scientific discoveries at the
end of the nineteenth century. One area that seemed to interest people the most was not the motions of the stars, but the
secrets of the mind. Just as Kiffmeyer sought to divine

Jackson and Walling's true personalities through measurements of their heads, many people wanted a way to determine why one man might become a loving husband and another a cold-blooded killer, and if there might be a way for science to identify one from another.

Whereas Maria Mitchell's interests were focused on charting the stars, there was another scientist of the age that seemed to have a hand in every area of study. Francis Galton's *Fingerprints* (1892), as we have already seen, was immensely important in the development of criminology. Galton, born in 1822, was a polymath who would be known as a travel writer and explorer, a scientist and thinker, who seemed to dabble in anything that grabbed the interest of his brilliant mind. He wrote on meteorology and mapping English weather. He was a statistician at heart and seemed to love to compile data and draw conclusions from what he found. He shared much with his half-cousin Charles Darwin. Galton wanted to better understand the science of humanity, and one area that intrigued him was heredity. Drawing from what his cousin had discovered and published, Galton began to look into the idea that certain psychological traits were passed through bloodlines.

"On more than one occasion," he once wrote, "I have maintained that intellectual ability is transmitted by inheritance." Through this line of thinking he came to argue that many traits were passed from parent to child, including some that were undesirable. He thought that the human race could be perfected if these traits were removed from subsequent generations. He called his idea "eugenics," which would become an influential and controversial idea for many years to come. Using Galton's theory, if Scott Jackson and Alonzo Walling were natural-born killers, a trait inherited from a murderous ancestor, then executing them would be an act of eugenics.

There was no way to know if Jackson or Walling had ancestors who were violent or killers, or at least no one bothered to find out. Still, psychologists of the time were uncertain on the source of the criminal or the killer mind, despite Galton's data and arguments. Some, like Galton, considered criminal activity as an expression of the individual's inherited traits, while others thought that criminal behavior was the result of certain societal conditions. In essence they were grappling with the nature versus nurture argument, a phrase that Galton helped to make popular. In a publication from 1896, "Social Problems," Charles H. Cooley attempted to address the argument: "A man's nature is like a seed, and his circumstances like the soil and climate in which the seed germinates and grows." In other words, nature and nurture worked together to form the man.

The stories beginning to circulate regarding Scott Jackson's past seemed to indicate that if he had not been born to do wrong, then he surely grew into it. While he lived in Indianapolis, people that knew him said he was "inclined to be wild and reckless, and his popularity with a questionable class of people led Lotshar [his landlord] to frequently remonstrate with him." In fact, the man Jackson was staying with in Indianapolis knew his family from Greencastle. One would think Jackson might have been on his best behavior because his actions could get back to Greencastle (what some regarded as his motive for killing Pearl Bryan). However, this didn't seem to be the case, according to Mr. Lotshar.

One of Jackson's dental school teachers in Indianapolis had this to say about him: "I remember him as one of my brightest pupils. His only fault that I knew of was that he would drink. He was rather wild in other ways, so I've heard. I know that he got into trouble with some women, and was arrested, but for the sake of his family the affair was suppressed in the newspapers. During a revival meeting at

Tomlinson Hall, led by the evangelist, Chapman, he was a member of the choir and was one of the leaders of the meeting."

The arrest his professor refers to was apparently for associating with prostitutes. There is good reason to believe this was the reason Jackson left dental school in Indianapolis and went to Cincinnati. Alonzo Walling, however, was not well remembered in Indianapolis, though he attended dental school there at the same time as Jackson. The students of the school who remembered both of them felt they were too cowardly to commit murder, but that it must have been an illegal operation that resulted in the girl's death, and then they attempted to conceal the act.

FOURTEEN

BLAME

On Thursday, February 6, 1896, a woman named Clara Bates called the police to say that a pair of rubber overshoes that appeared to have blood on them had been left at her house by a man she knew only as "Doc." She said that a girl in her house often met with a barber named Fred who had a friend he called "Doc." When presented with the suspects, she could not identify Scott Jackson, but said Alonzo Walling was the man she knew as "Doc." Walling conceded this and said that the rubbers were his. Two stains found on the inside of one of the shoes were believed to be blood.

While in his cell, Walling told the guard that the investigators should look in his locker at the dental school, as they would probably find something interesting. They immediately went and found a pair of pants wrapped in newspaper. The pants were black, but appeared to be covered in mud and blood from the knee down. When questioned, Jackson identified them as his pants, but said he had not worn them in some time. He said he believed Walling had worn them when he killed Pearl.

Jackson's initial story, which the *Enquirer* assured its readers was a tissue of lies, was that it was Will Wood who got Pearl pregnant and that he had approached Jackson for assistance. Jackson believed that his roommate, Alonzo Walling, was capable of performing the abortion; so he arranged to have Pearl come to the city. She did, staying at the Indiana House under the name Mabel Stanley. There Scott called on her and arranged a meeting between her and Walling on Wednesday. This, Jackson said, was the last he saw of the girl. When he read about the body in the newspapers, he reasoned that it was probably Pearl. Then Walling told him they needed to get rid of Pearl's clothing, to which Jackson agreed and helped.

"Who got Pearl into trouble?" a reporter asked him.

"It was Billy Wood," Jackson answered.

"How do you account for the blood stains in the valise?"

"I guess Walling carried the head in that."

Jackson's story obviously had a few problems. The idea that Will Wood was the father of Pearl's child is possible, but seems improbable. Pearl's family indicated that Jackson was courting Pearl and there is no evidence that they thought there might be anything between Pearl and Will other than a friendship of cousins. Still, there is a very slim chance that Pearl and Will hid their affair and Scott Jackson was the only one who knew the extent of it.

Even more problematic is Jackson's vague timeline of events after Pearl arrived in Cincinnati. He called on her and, according to him, spoke to her for only fifteen minutes and then never saw her again. She supposedly met with Walling on Wednesday, which is when the presumed botched abortion occurred. Yet, her body was not found until Saturday morning. Jackson does not say that Walling was missing during this time or that there might have been any indications that things did not go as planned with Pearl. It seems practically impossible that Jackson would arrange for an abortion and then not inquire as to the outcome. Yet, in his version of events, he does concede that he realized almost immediately that the body in Fort Thomas was the girl from Greencastle. He then, seemingly without question, assisted Walling in covering up Pearl's death.

A reporter was able to interview Walling about some of his activity the week before Pearl died.

"Jackson seems to be trying to put the crime on you," the reporter said.

"Yes, that's just like him," Walling replied. "Why don't he tell about borrowing the valise from Mrs. McNevin, the landlady?"

"Why don't you tell me?"

"Well, I will. He borrowed a valise from Mrs. McNevin last Wednesday week and told me to meet him at Wallingford's saloon at George and Plum streets. When I went there Jackson was in the back room with a girl. He came out in the bar and got the valise and a piece of twine and told me to follow him when he went out with the girl. I was frightened and went right home to bed."

"Why were you frightened?" the reporter asked.

"Why, he told me before that the girl would have to be fixed," Walling explained.

"Didn't you understand by that, that an operation was to be performed."

"No; I understood just what he meant, and that was to murder the girl."

Walling's story is not much more credible than Jackson's. Of course, both stories are scant on details and represent short interactions and not formal interrogations. Jackson and Walling don't agree on any detail except that curiously both indicate Pearl died on Wednesday night and not Friday, as the investigators seemed to believe. Walling's comments about the borrowed valise are interesting in that they make one wonder if Walling mentions the valise because he knows the reporters and investigators are focusing on the valise Jackson was supposed to have carried the head in, or if it was a truly important detail he wanted to share.

Walling added, as he said consistently in all his stories, that on Tuesday Jackson had met him and expressly said, "If it was not for those Goddamn shoes they would not have any clew."

The basics of Jackson's and Walling's stories were actually very similar except that Jackson states that he left Pearl to meet with Walling on Wednesday, and Walling states he left Jackson in the company of Pearl Wednesday night with clear intentions to kill her. In fact, there is even reason to believe the prisoners might have had contact with each other right after the moment they were arrested. They might have concocted the stories together, in order to confuse the investigators. There's no way to know.

Other reports make it clear that the two suspects didn't see each other after their arrests until ten o'clock on the night of Thursday, February 6. At this time they were both brought before Mayor Caldwell and Chief Deitsch in the chief's office. The suspects and the two powerful civic leaders sat in comfortable chairs facing each other. Only the four men were allowed in the room and they spoke for two hours. Then the saloonkeeper Wallingford and his porter, Allen Johnson, were asked in and the two men identified Jackson as having been at the saloon Friday. Wallingford said he was in the company of a man and two women. Another saloon keeper was brought in, but all he was able to do was identify Jackson as a dental student for whom he had cashed a few checks. The prisoners were sent back to their cells and the chief admitted nothing much was gained by the meeting. Jackson said Walling was the killer, while Walling laid the blame on Jackson.

No one from Campbell County, Kentucky, appears to have been part of the interviews with Jackson, Walling, or Wood, even though the body was found there. Sheriff Plummer, of Campbell County, arrested Will Wood and brought him to Cincinnati, but it seems he did not express a wish to take custody of the prisoner himself. Cincinnati, being the larger city and with more facilities at its disposal, was the logical choice to take the lead in the investigation, especially since the suspects were living in that city. But the question remained where, exactly, had the crime been committed and who, then, had jurisdiction. This was one of the challenges facing the investigators. They knew that both Jackson and Walling were probably lying, but they didn't know what was being left out and what was being fabricated.

Pearl had come to the city at the urging of Jackson—that seemed clear—and she had been seen off by her cousin Will Wood. She had spent a few days in the city and then her headless body had been found that Saturday morning. There were reports that she had been seen with Jackson and Walling at saloons, but no one mentions her demeanor or her attitude toward the two men. The investigators must have entertained two possibilities: one was that Pearl was killed, possibly by accident, then her head was removed and her body left in Locke's field, or that she was brought to Locke field's alive and killed there. Cal Crim had said he believed she had been killed in the field because of the amount of blood and the splatter on the leaves that seemed to indicate her heart was pumping. In contrast, Coroner Tingley had said he thought she had died somewhere else and then was decapitated in the field.

To help clarify matters, another postmortem was conducted, with the specific purpose of determining whether
Pearl was alive or dead when her head was removed. The
examiners noted that they could not locate a drop of blood in
her body; she had completely bled out, indicating that her
heart was still pumping when she began to bleed. They
reviewed the reports from Tingley and others at the scene
and concluded that every bit of blood she had had bled out
into that field.

Dr. Charles S. Phythian gave his conclusions to a few
reporters: "The cut on the left hand shows that she fought
with her murderer. The cut goes clear to the bone and proves
that she did not receive it by making the weak attempt at
defense that a person in a semi-comatose condition would
have made."

He also added that no puncture mark was found. This
was a reference to a story that had been circulating that Pearl
had been killed with an injection of prussic acid. According
to an article in the *Enquirer*, Walling had confided in a
reporter for the paper that no abortion had actually been
attempted. Instead, Pearl had been injected with the acid
specifically to kill her. There is no clarification on who
administered the acid or when. The paper even carried a
detailed, life-sized illustration of the syringe and needle that
according to this theory was most likely used to kill Pearl.
However, this is the only time an injection of acid is mentioned and neither of the postmortems appears to be able to
back up this story.

That same day Crim and McDermott filed the necessary
paperwork to formally charge Jackson and Walling with
murder. They also cited Wood for procuring an abortion.
With Jackson and Walling blaming each other while slightly
implicating themselves as accomplices, if only to help cover
up the crime, it would seem they might both be thinking they

could testify against the other and then escape the noose. The investigators involved seemed to have other plans. With the results from the postmortems, the circumstantial evidence, and the bloody clothes and valise, they were probably beginning to see that they had the makings of two solid cases against both dental students and wouldn't need one to testify against the other.

While the officials in Kentucky might not have been overly concerned with the prosecution of the murder at that moment, the people of Campbell County were beginning to believe Jackson and Walling should face justice in their county and not Cincinnati. Colonel John Locke, when he visited one of the police stations to get word on the suspects, warned an officer that they should do whatever they could to keep the two prisoners on that side of the Ohio River because the people of Campbell County were ready to lynch them on sight.

This exchange between Locke and the officer was overheard by a reporter and promptly printed the next day. Except for the private meeting with Mayor Caldwell, the police chief, Jackson, and Walling, reporters were present at almost every interview or examination of the prisoners. They traveled with investigators to follow up on clues and at least one impersonated a police officer and "arrested" a major suspect. Never at any point later on did investigators reveal a detail that they kept from the press. In the Pearl Bryan case, the press did not just report on the investigation; they were actively engaged in it. The authorities appeared to be keeping nothing from the press, and they maintained this attitude through the rest of the investigation, inquest, and trials.

Later on, the Cincinnati authorities would come under criticism for allowing such transparency, so it would seem this might not have been the approach taken by all or most police in this type of case; but they never changed their approach to the press. In a society that seemed overly concerned with decorum and appropriate behavior, it is amazing to see reporters present for some of the most intimate and emotional moments in the story. When Plummer, Crim, and McDermott brought Pearl's things to be identified by her family, reporters were there to capture the scene. Because so many details were made public, however, it became impossible to determine if a witness's information was authentic or if he or she just read the papers and, for example, saw the drawings of Jackson and Walling and so could identify them.

In the end, from our vantage point it is hard to fault the authorities for being so open. First, it gives later generations insight into this case and, second, had details not been published in the papers, key features of the case might never have been revealed, much less preserved for posterity.

FIFTEEN

THE VALISE

O N THE MORNING OF FRIDAY, FEBRUARY 7, 1896, WILL
Wood, Scott Jackson, and Alonzo Walling appeared
in police court. They all looked ragged and worn,
their faces dirty with a few days' growth of unkempt beard.
Their clothes were disheveled, and their general demeanor
was one of exhaustion. Walling, however, seemed to keep
cool, looking straight at the judge as the charge of murder
was officially laid against him. Jackson's cold, blue eyes dart-
ed around, as if trying to see everything at once. Wood was
allowed to be released on bond, but his father refused to pay
it.

Crowds gathered in the halls to get a glimpse of the prisoners, and the general question on everyone's mind seemed
to be: where was the poor girl's head? Chief Deitsch had
come into his office that morning and found several letters
telling him where the head could be found, but he took none

of them seriously, depositing them into the trash. At this point, it seemed most people were convinced that the head had been in the infamous valise that Jackson carried with him and then had left empty in Kugel's saloon.

Kugel brought the valise to the police station at city hall and explained that it had been left, taken away, and left again by a young man with a blond mustache who he believed was Scott Jackson. The satchel, which was made of brown leather, was brought to the chief, who examined it. It was empty but heavily stained with what appeared to be blood. He asked that Jackson be brought up. Chief Deitsch ordered Jackson to pick up the satchel and open it. He asked Jackson what he saw.

"Nothing that I can see, except that it is stained," Jackson said.

"What is it stained with?"

"It looks like blood," Jackson responded.

"Looks like blood? Don't you know it is blood?" the chief replied with indignation.

Jackson paused and ran his hand through his hair.

"I think it is blood," the prisoner said, "but I have not examined it carefully."

The chief advised him to examine it carefully.

"Yes, that is blood," Jackson admitted.

"Isn't that the valise in which you carried the head?"

"I guess it is, but I did not carry it."

"Well, who did?"

"Walling."

The chief knew he would get nowhere, as Jackson had fallen back on his same refrain. Kugel was brought in and identified Jackson as the man who had left the valise. Then Jackson was taken back to his cell, but not before he added that he believed the head had been thrown into the river but he was not sure.

Around this time the investigators also intercepted a letter sent from Jackson to Will Wood, written just two days earlier. It read as follows:

2-5-96
Hello, Bill—
    Write a letter home signed by Bert's name telling the folks that he is somewhere and going to Chicago or some other place—has a position etc—and that they will advise later about it —Say tired of living at home or anything you want. You know about the way he writes. Send it to someone you can trust— How [about] Will Smith at La Fayette—tell the folks that he has not been at I[ndianapolis] but at La Fayette and traveling about the country get letter off without one seconds delay—and burn this at once. Stick by your old chum Bill—And I will help you out the same way—some time. Am glad you are having a good time
—D
Be careful what you write me.

When presented with the letter, Jackson admitted that it was about Pearl. Explaining that "Bert" was a sort of code name for her, he insisted that Walling had told him to write the letter. Walling read the letter and said only that Jackson had told him he was going to write such a letter in order to get away with the murder. Walling also included another detail. He claimed that on Christmas day, Jackson had told him he was going to kill Pearl.

Walling explained that Jackson said that "he and Billy Wood had gotten Pearl into trouble and that he must get rid of her. He suggested two ways in which it might be done. One of the plans he suggested was to take her to a room and kill her there and leave her. Then he spoke up quickly and said: 'No, I have a sudden thought as something often tells me when I am on the wrong idea. It would not do to leave her there, so I will instead cut her to pieces and drop the pieces in different vaults around town.'"

Mrs. McNevin, Jackson and Walling's landlady, came to give a statement, but she could not shed any light on the mystery as she wasn't sure of her tenants' comings and goings. She did say that for the past week Jackson and Walling had acted cool toward each other. They seemed to be keeping their distance, and when Mrs. McNevin asked Walling about it, he said that Jackson liked to be on his own when he had money and this had led to a falling out between them. Walling had come in one night and sat in the dining room and mentioned the creaking of a rocking chair coming from the floor above them. He told Mrs. McNevin that that was Jackson and that Walling wouldn't go to their rooms until after he was sure Jackson was asleep. Walling, in fact, ended up spending that night at a hotel.

Ora Greene, a clerk at the Indiana House, came to police headquarters and stated that a girl he recognized as Pearl Bryan from the illustrations, but who gave her name as Mabel Stanley, had registered at his hotel Monday night, January 27, and stayed again on Tuesday night, and then he had never seen her again. He recognized Jackson and Walling as men who had called on the young woman Monday night and Tuesday. Greene's statement was not regarded as particularly noteworthy, but it does beg a question that the investigators never seemed to address. If Pearl left the Indiana House Wednesday morning and her body was found Saturday morning, where was she between those times?

There are glimpses of her possibly with Walling and Jackson at saloons, but there is no clear answer to where she might have been staying. She could have taken rooms some-

where else, but no one ever came forward with this information. Coinciding with this hole in Pearl's timeline is the fact
that both Jackson's and Walling's stories concluded with last
seeing Pearl on Wednesday, the day she left the Indiana
House. The postmortems had indicated that Pearl had been
alive when she went to Locke's field, so she would have needed a place to sleep and food to eat for those three days. Mrs.
McNevin never saw any evidence of a woman staying with
the men or she would have presumably brought it up to the
police. There is the chance that the postmortems and
Detective Crim had been mistaken and that Pearl was
already dead when she was brought to the field. For those
three days her body might have been hidden away, yet this
doesn't explain the blood spatter in Locke's field—unless
Crim and others were mistaken and those were not spots of
blood on the leaves of the bushes.

Jackson, for his part, believed he could account for Pearl
on those three days. He said that he believed Walling rented
a room somewhere and brought Pearl there Wednesday
night to perform the abortion. He had her undress and then
administered chloroform to render her unconscious. Jackson
stated that he knew Walling had chloroform, but that he
must have given her too much. Walling then spent the next
day trying to revive Pearl, but to no avail. He finally concluded that she was dead. He had to wait until the cover of night
on Friday to take her body, possibly in a wagon borrowed
from the college, to Fort Thomas. The explanation for her
clothing being in disarray was that he had been unable to
dress her completely, but brought the clothing she was wearing to the dump site. Jackson guessed that Walling was
frightened and so began to remove her head to conceal identification. This was when Pearl came to and Walling realized
that she was not dead after all, yet he had already cut her
throat. This is when she received the cuts on her hands as she

tried to defend herself. Jackson stated that this was all guesswork on his part.

Chief Deitsch told reporters that he believed finding the
head was no longer of much importance to the case, as the
body was clearly that of Pearl Bryan. He said that he was sure
Jackson had killed the girl, though he knew Walling was
somehow involved. It did not make sense for Walling to be
the killer, since he had not known or been intimate with the
victim. Deitsch believed that the evidence they had was
enough to convict Jackson as the murderer and Walling as an
accomplice, and he had no doubt about the outcome of the
trials. He believed the head had been thrown into the Ohio
River and that for all he knew, it might be in the Gulf of
Mexico by now.

Still, the resting place of Pearl's head remained of interest
to the public, not to mention her family. Rumors that the
head was buried in a sandbar resulted in a horde of men and
boys with shovels who in some cases dug as deep as six feet
but were not able to find it. The stories about Jackson being
seen with the valise grew and grew. At the most extreme he
carried the head with him for several days and was seen talking to it. In these accounts we see Jackson slowly take on the
appearance of a psychopath. His cold, blue eyes dart around,
taking in everything, his madness barely concealed behind
the mask of a gentleman. He lied with ease, he played the
part of innocence, but now his evil nature was revealed and
he could not hide from the truth—or so the narrative seemed
to go.

On the night of February 7, Jackson requested a visit from
Secretary George F. Tibbits of the YMCA. The jail came
alive with the speculation that Jackson might confess. Tibbits
came and asked Jackson what he wanted.

"I want you to pray with me," Jackson said and began to
cry.

They prayed together and Jackson said aloud, "God, have mercy on me!" Jackson prayed for his dear mother, who must be heartbroken at the news of her son charged with murder.

Tibbits saw his chance. "Now, Jackson, tell all about this horrible deed, and relieve your mind."

"I have nothing to tell," Jackson said quietly and then he took his right hand out and placed it on the Bible that Tibbits held. "I swear to God I did not murder that girl."

"Who did?" the secretary asked.

"It was Walling," Jackson said and repeated his theory that the abortion had been attempted on Thursday night, as Jackson said he couldn't account for Walling's whereabouts. It is worth noting that Walling, himself, couldn't account for his whereabouts on Thursday night, either. His landlady did not believe he stayed in his room that night, and the clerk at Helder's Hotel said he checked in at three o'clock in the morning on Friday and left by 8 o'clock the next day. Jackson stated that he wasn't with Walling, and Mrs. McNevin seemed to support this assertion.

The fact that Jackson swore on a Bible proclaiming his innocence was no idle gesture, given the strong Christian current that flowed through society in the late nineteenth century. No one, it was reasoned, except a dead-hearted killer would swear on a Bible in jest. As Frances Willard and the Women's Christian Temperance Union exemplified, the reform movements, often called "crusades," were spearheaded by Christians, socialists, union leaders, and progressives; sometimes the same person could be considered to be all of these. In fact, there was a specific group known as "Christian socialists," of which Frances Willard considered herself a member. Christian socialism was an international movement, though the approach varied from country to country. It was believed that the Christian socialist movement came mainly from German immigrants, though American Christian socialism did not share much with the movement in Germany, specifically its anti-Semitic leanings.

American Christian socialism was not an effort to convert socialists to Christianity or to convert Christians to socialism, but to combine the two in an open relationship. Jewish socialists were lecturers at Christian socialist rallies. Christian ministers spoke in support of socialist candidates without proclaiming themselves socialists. These Christian socialists were aware of the contradiction in their philosophy. Many others believed no one could be called a socialist unless they were an atheist and adhered to Marxian ideals. The American Christian socialists, in contrast, felt that socialism should be expanded to include the Christian religion, an equal marriage between Christianity's virtues and socialism's ideals. However, this did not represent the opinion of most Christians or Americans, who viewed socialists with suspicion.

The majority of Americans in 1896 were Christians. According to the 1890 census, of the number of registered ministers, Methodists and Baptists were the most numerous. Religious ceremonies marked the key moments in most people's lives, whether they lived in the city or country: baptism, marriage, and, finally, burial.

SIXTEEN

FUNERAL

ON FRIDAY, FEBRUARY 7, SIX DAYS AFTER HER BODY HAD been found, Pearl Bryan was dressed in her cream white silk graduation dress. Satin slippers were carefully slid on to her feet. A pillow was placed where her head should have been. She was laid in a white-cloth-covered casket trimmed with cord and tassel. The handles on the coffin were burnished silver. On the center of the lid was a silver plate inscribed with "Pearl" in gothic letters. Her body had been removed from Newport and taken to John P. Epply's funeral home in Cincinnati. Pearl's brother and sister, Fred Bryan and Mary Stanley, had come to claim the remains and have them sent back to Greencastle, but they desperately hoped that Pearl's head might be found so that she could be buried whole.

A little while later, Detectives Crim and McDermott brought Jackson and Walling into the parlor where Pearl lay in her casket. Her brother and sister sat nearby in grief.

Fred Bryan had already been to see Scott Jackson in his cell. They knew each other from when Jackson had been courting Pearl. A detective had brought Fred down to confront Jackson. Jackson looked at Fred briefly and then turned his eyes to the detective. Fred spoke, his eyes never leaving Jackson's face. "If they let him out of here I'll fix him." Nothing more was said. Fred continued to stare at Jackson, while Jackson looked away. A drunk in an adjacent cell broke the silent tension and began to sing a song called "A Mother Was Bidding Good-By to Her Boy." Jackson sat down and put his head in his hands. Fred Bryan left without another word.

When Jackson and Walling were brought in to the funeral parlor, Fred remained silent, but Mary Stanley however saw it as her only opportunity to right things, as best she could. The men stood around, unease and tension in the air. Mary turned first to Jackson, whom she had known the previous summer as someone who was growing close to her beloved sister, but who was now accused of killing and mutilating her. She must have thought that a decent man still remained somewhere within him.

"Mr. Jackson," she said in a quiet voice. "I come to you and ask where is my sister's head. For the sake of my poor mother and for my sister and for my brother I beg of you to tell me where my sister's head is. It is my last chance and I want to send it home with the body. Won't you please tell me, I beg you?"

Jackson looked at her with his clear blue eyes unblinking; anyone involved in the case might have given the world to know what thoughts raced behind them.

"Mrs. Stanley," he said flatly. "I do not know."

His demeanor indicated that he would say no more of the matter.

Mrs. Stanley, surely feeling a heavy heart and bitter disappointment, turned to Walling and pleaded with him to tell her where she could find her sister's head.

If anything, Walling was cooler than Jackson. Without a hint of emotion he replied, "I do not know where it is."

After Walling and Jackson were brought back to their cells, Chief Deitsch was heard to comment, "I've been in many trying situations, but I never saw anything to equal that. How they could refuse to tell that poor woman where the head was I cannot understand."

Of course, if Walling and Jackson knew where to find the head, giving out that information would only prove their guilt. If the head had been destroyed then there would be nothing to give Mary Stanley anyway. If the head had been thrown in the river, then it was most likely lost and nothing would be gained by telling Pearl's family. If Jackson or Walling didn't know the whereabouts of the head, then they were only speaking the truth. It should not have come as a surprise to the chief that neither of them would tell Mrs. Stanley what she wanted.

The two most likely resting places for the head could not have been more different. Since the two suspects admitted to throwing Pearl's clothes into the river, then it is entirely possibly that her head was dumped into the icy waters of the Ohio as well. The river, one of the main waterways of the nation, flows at a steady pace and depth and so the head, after several days, could have been almost anywhere. A search would have been fruitless; the river was too long and wide to make the use of nets or hooks feasible. In addition, wildlife would have most likely consumed it. The other possibility is that her head was thrown into a furnace and quickly turned to ash. Coal-burning furnaces were commonplace, and the dental school had a large one. Either Walling or Jackson could have easily thrown the head in, burying it under red-hot coals.

~

THE INVESTIGATORS, after conducting the postmortems and examining the scene a week before, had come to a general conclusion: Pearl was alive when she went into Locke's field and her cause of death had been decapitation. Decapitation, as a method of death, can be relatively quick and painless, as far as anyone has been able to determine, if it is done properly. That is to say, if the head is severed in one swift motion, there is no reason to believe the person suffers. The guillotine, for instance, was invented to cause the least amount of suffering of the person being executed. Though different societies felt differently about decapitation, many employed it as a method of executing various kinds of criminals. It was often reserved as capital punishment for royalty and nobles, to distinguish them from common persons, who were hanged. Swords and axes were the most common weapons employed, and a good headsman could decapitate with swift precision. There are various accounts in which the accused required two or three blows—even stories of upward of ten blows, but these are rare or doubtful.

Beheading as a method of murder was, however, rare. This is specifically due to the time it takes to remove a head and the fact that the victim might still be conscious and able to fight back. In 1875 in New Hampshire, Joseph Lapage, a French-Canadian woodcutter, was accused, tried, and hanged for raping, murdering, and mutilating a seventeen-year-old schoolgirl. He had removed her head and wrapped it in a cloth, but it is probable she died from her earlier injuries, and a heel print that helped convict him was pressed into her cheek. In the summer of 1895, while Scott Jackson and Pearl Bryan's love was supposedly blossoming, an African American man named Henry Taylor killed his wife and infant child and left their other children locked inside the house when he left. Locals heard the screaming children, broke down the door, and found the wife and baby dead, both beheaded, and an ax lying nearby covered in blood. The evidence at the scene indicated that both victims were beheaded while alive. Bloodhounds were soon put on the trail of Taylor. There was never any word if he was captured.

In the Henry Taylor case, he had tied his wife down and then removed her head with an ax with presumably one or two blows. It would seem that a person being attacked with a knife by a killer intent on beheading him or her, who was not bound or otherwise held down, would have multiple wounds all over the body as he or she fought with every ounce of strength against the assailant. A person who was unconscious or even dead at the time of the beheading would have no wounds on the body as the killer would have plenty of time to remove the head. Pearl, however, had those distinct, deep cuts on her hand. The investigators and eventually the prosecutors felt that the only way for this to be the case was if there were two killers. One man (they cast Walling in this role) held Pearl down, while another, Jackson, removed her head. The cuts on Pearl's left hand happened when she briefly was able to slip out a hand in a vain attempt to protect herself, but Walling held her fast.

The idea that Pearl was in a delirious state was dismissed in the second postmortem, though there was not much explanation for this. She certainly had a large amount of cocaine in her stomach, and it is hard to say what state she might have been in, especially if she had also consumed alcohol or any other intoxicant. One man could have sat on her back and began to cut at her neck. Her hand might have reached back and been cut. If the beheading happened in the field then it would have been dark and wet and perhaps foggy. If the killer or killers did not have a light then it would have been hard to see just what was being cut.

With an ax or sword, a decapitation can be performed in a second. Using a knife requires more time and focus. From very early on in the investigation, people wondered what kind of knife had been used. Walling told a reporter that it wasn't a knife that cut off Pearl's head, but a razor, Jackson's razor that he kept in a red case. Police searched the suspect's rooms several times but could not locate the razor among Jackson's belongings. Finally, searching one of Walling's trunks, they found the razor in a small compartment. It was in a red case, thin and properly sharpened. There were small stains on the blade that may or may not have been blood, but nothing particularly incriminating. The blade was taken by the police.

Another possible weapon was a scalpel, what the papers called a "dissecting knife," which Jackson was said to own and carry with him often. One saloon keeper, a Mr. Stenger, said that Jackson often came to his bar and talked physical science with others gathered there and while doing so, would take out his knife and twirl it around. Stenger said he once saw Jackson trim his fingernails with the knife and accidentally cut his finger. Reporters asked Jackson if he had ever done any dissecting, but he claimed that he never had. Walling, however, according to Jackson, had extensive experience in dissecting. The police were in possession of Jackson's dissecting knife for a time, but then a week after Jackson's arrest, the knife went missing. There are no reports of it ever being recovered.

As studying anatomy was probably part of their professional training—the formal name of the school they attended was the Ohio College of Dental Surgery—Jackson and Walling would have been instructed that the head was properly severed from the neck with the subject lying face down. To make it as easy as possible, the student cut between the major muscles. The hardest part would have been separating the vertebrae, which needed to be cut with care. Skilled doctors could easily remove a head in a few minutes. A deranged killer with clear motivation could make short work of it, even with a knife—as brutally demonstrated by religious fanatics in our own time.

The sharper the knife, the easier it would have been. The cuts on Pearl's hand go to the bone and at the very least the cuts along the back of her neck are clean and even show that the knife was especially sharp. By a rough measurement of the cuts on her hand, it would seem the blade must have been of a decent length, not a short pocketknife. This makes Jackson's dissecting knife a good candidate. In the late nineteenth century, scalpels did not have a uniform shape. Most resembled the scalpels of today, with a long handle and a short, wide blade; but some had considerably longer blades. Some scalpels folded up, much like a straight razor, which would have been practical if Jackson had carried one around in his pocket. However, his knife was mysteriously lost and with it possible answers as to the murder weapon.

HAVING GIVEN UP on finding Pearl's head, her family sent her body back to Greencastle. It was buried there in Forest Hill Cemetery.

WHILE JACKSON AND WALLING waited for the coroner's inquest, scheduled for February 11, the volunteer soldier, George Jackson, captain of the Caldwell Guards, was presumably struggling with great personal risk. As an African American man he had to have known that getting himself involved in a murder case, particularly one involving only white people, was probably not a good idea. Yet there were other considerations, and we cannot know which weighed more heavily on him. On one hand there was the chance to help the authorities—to help Mayor Caldwell—hang these terrible men who had murdered an innocent country girl. And on the other hand, there was the reward money.

SEVENTEEN

GEORGE JACKSON'S STORY

I N CAMPBELL COUNTY, WHERE THE BODY WAS FOUND, Coroner Walter Tingley's inquest began as scheduled. A jury was quickly appointed, including a shoe dealer (who no doubt knew Louis Poock) and a steamboat captain. Sheriff Plummer took the stand and explained in brief how he came to identify the body found on Locke's farm as that of Pearl Bryan. When asked how she was killed, he stated, "The evidence we have leads us to believe that she died of having her throat cut."

Tingley then took the stand and was asked if he thought Pearl was killed where she was found.

"It did not seem so to me. There was not enough blood on the ground to lead me to that conclusion," the doctor said. He added that he believed the head had been removed by someone familiar with anatomy, specifically because it appeared the removal of the head was begun at the back of the neck.

Tingley stated that according to his observation on that Saturday morning, there was no more than a quart of blood on the ground and he did not see any blood on the bushes. Even though the amount of blood in a human body depends on the person, Pearl's body most definitely held more than a quart, more likely about ten pints at least.

There was brief discussion in which it was suggested that Pearl's head could have been removed in Cincinnati, and if her body were held in an upright position then some blood would have remained when the body was dumped near Fort Thomas. However, this scenario seems implausible. It is hard to imagine circumstances in which it would make sense to decapitate someone in Cincinnati then take their body to northern Kentucky, via a wagon or carriage one would presume, all the while carefully keeping the body upright.

Locke was then put on the stand and stated the condition and position of the body when he first saw it. He said he saw blood on the bushes, only about two feet high. He agreed with Tingley that the girl had not been killed in his field. He stated that the body was about a hundred yards from Alexandria Pike and that he heard no one cry out in the night. Also he stated that he canvassed his neighbors and no one heard any sort of cry that night, another indication that Pearl may not have been fully conscious in the field, although it is impossible to cry out if your throat is slashed.

Detective Cal Crim was then called to the stand. The bulk of his testimony was that he believed Pearl was killed in Locke's field. The questioning attorney then asked, "State from your examination to your best knowledge and belief who committed the crime?"

The jury paused in their various movements to better hear the answer.

"Scott Jackson and Alonzo Walling," Crim said with confidence.

Crim then stated his and McDermott's findings so far. The trip to Greencastle; what was learned from Pearl's family and other residents; Scott Jackson's relationship with Pearl and her pregnancy; her departure to Cincinnati for an illegal operation; and most important, that she was last seen in the company of Walling and Jackson on Friday night, the night of the murder, at Wallingford's saloon where they entered a hack they had stopped, and for which Scott Jackson had borrowed two dollars from Wallingford.

Crim could not definitely account for Pearl, Jackson, or Walling from about 7 P.M. to 3 A.M. the next morning, but the conclusion was obvious, even though this was based solely on the statements given by Wallingford and his porter, Johnson. These witnesses could very well have been telling the truth, but there was no supporting evidence to verify their stories. There isn't any obvious reason why they might be making the story up, but they could easily have been mistaken. They might not have had the correct times or even the night. The girl they thought was Pearl Bryan might have been someone else entirely, as it was often indicated that both Walling and Jackson were regularly seen in the company of various women. Also there is the curious detail that Jackson borrowed two dollars for a cab, which the trio then took off into the night. As we shall shortly see, this is problematic. The nature of this cab, who the driver was, and what company operated it became extremely important to the case. A large cash reward of $700 was eventually offered for information about the cab.

Wallingford, the saloon keeper, was called to the stand and testified that he knew Jackson and Walling well, but did not know Pearl Bryan at all. Most telling, though, was that Wallingford identified the dress on Pearl's body when found as the dress worn by the woman who was with Jackson and Walling on the night of January 31. This, perhaps more than

anything else, demonstrates that Pearl was still alive and in
Wallingford's saloon on that Friday night. Wallingford
would seem to have little reason to lie, but there are other
possible explanations. One is that Wallingford only thought
he recognized the dress. The other, admittedly far-fetched, is
that Jackson and Walling had another woman dressed in
Pearl's dress in some effort to give evidence that she was still
alive, though she was not. (These are offered only as speculation.) Allen Johnson, Wallingford's porter, substantiated his
employer's statements and added that the cab driver had been
white and that he did not recognize him.

Rogers, the clerk from Heder's Hotel, was then called to
testify; he was not asked about Walling staying there earlier
in the week, but rather was asked if Walling stayed there
Friday night or Saturday morning. Rogers said Walling
came in at about 3 o'clock on Saturday morning and refused
to register, and that he was very curious in his behavior and
appeared to be very nervous. The clerk did not say that he
saw any signs of blood about Walling.

The jury returned an indictment the next day: Pearl
Bryan had been killed by decapitation in Locke's field,
despite the testimonies of Coroner Tingley and Colonel
Locke.

About three days later, George Jackson first told his story
to the police and reporters. He explained that he was the captain of the Caldwell Guards, a semi-official regiment in
Cincinnati. On the night of January 31 he drilled with his
men, in the rain, then walked toward his home at George
and Elm. He was walking with a group of his fellow soldiers
when they were hailed by a white man, whom he identified
as Walling, who said, "Who wants to make $5?" The man
turned directly to George then and added, "All I want you to
do is to drive us over to Newport. I am a doctor and another

physician will be with me to take a very sick woman home."
George agreed.

The carriage was closed and with it being dark, George
did not see who exactly he was driving. He simply followed
the directions as they were called to him. He crossed the river
and came to Newport. At this point, he said, Walling climbed
out of the back of the carriage and sat next to George. George
could hear moans in the back and he made a quick attempt
to escape, but was stopped when Walling pulled a revolver
and threatened George with it. They eventually came to a
relatively secluded spot along the Alexandria Pike near Fort
Thomas. The two men dragged the woman out of the carriage and into the field. George became even more afraid. He
quickly hitched the horse by means of a weight and fled back
toward home. Regardless of the route he took, it was several
miles. "I did not stop running until I was back in Cincinnati,"
he said. He guessed that he arrived home around 3 or 4 in the
morning. He said that he thought he heard the men yelling
for him as he ran away.

Within short order, Mayor Caldwell told reporters that he
believed George Jackson's story. A few days later, Chief
Deitsch, who had just returned from a vacation in New
Orleans, told reporters that he had heard George's story and
believed him as well: "You may say that I believed in the colored man's story. I see no reason why it should not be
believed. I had a talk with the man last night and he
impressed me as being truthful. When I have examined the
written reports of his testimony I shall send for him, and I
will make a careful examination of his whole story. Unless
something develops then which has not yet come to light, I'll
believe Jackson's story of the fatal cab ride to be the truth."

It is interesting that in 1896, a time of racial discord, the
word of an African American man, particularly in the South,
should be so readily believed; George was captain of the

Caldwell Guards, which honored the mayor, and so possibly that afforded him additional credibility, but his story also fit nicely with the narrative being developed of the end of Pearl's life. It seems clear that, whether purposely manipulated or not, the case was becoming more defined as time went on. It became accepted that Pearl died Friday night of decapitation in Locke's field. Jackson was the knife wielder, and Walling was the one to hold her down. She was conscious at the time, even if not fully so. The abortion may or may not have been attempted, but was not of importance because Jackson had been planning on killing Pearl all along. George's story provided that crucial link between the trio being spotted in Cincinnati and then ending up at the murder scene.

George said he was afraid to come forward, even though he had read all the stories in the paper and believed his experience was directly connected to the murder in Fort Thomas, because the killers had taken his name and address and told him that they had friends that would "fix him" if he told anyone about the matter. Finally he considered telling his story and asked an officer if the police would do anything to the cabman that drove Jackson, Walling, and Pearl Bryan. The officer said they would do nothing and only be glad for the information, so George told his story. He was able to pick out Jackson and Walling from a crowd of forty men. However, this is interesting because nowhere in his story does he say he got a good look at Jackson, but only Walling, who threatened him with the revolver and supposedly uttered the memorable line, "You drive this cab or I'll drive you to hell!" George repeatedly stated that it was dark and so he could not make out what the woman was wearing or much else except the man that sat next to him.

There are a few problems, of course, though these don't necessarily discredit George Jackson's story. Almost coincidentally, Wallingford's saloon was robbed just when George came out with his story and Allen Johnson, the porter, went missing. This might be of no importance, but it was Johnson who said Pearl, Jackson, and Walling left in a cab driven by a white driver. Between that moment and Walling approaching George on the street, Jackson and Walling must have left the white man's cab, if this was the case, and then rented a carriage, which they then asked George to drive for $5. If they had money to rent a cab and pay George $5, it seems peculiar that Jackson would need to borrow that $2 from Wallingford for the cab. Also, there is no logical reason that they needed a driver for the rented carriage, especially since Walling spent part of the journey on the bench next to George, threatening him with a revolver. It also added George Jackson as an unnecessary witness.

When not at the coroner's inquest, Detectives Crim and McDermott met with Mayor Caldwell, Chief Deitsch, and Sheriff Plummer of Newport. These men agreed, before the inquest had reached its conclusion, that the murder had occurred in Kentucky and so Scott Jackson and Walling would need to be removed from Cincinnati and then taken to Newport. This would require Plummer to travel to Frankfort, Kentucky, to get the proper papers to transfer the prisoners across the river. This included the official indictment that was first filed on February 13, 1896.

A copy of the indictment from the grand jury in Campbell County is undated, but reads that Scott Jackson and Alonzo Walling "did willfully feloniously and with malice aforethought kill and murder Pearl Bryan by the said Scott Jackson with a knife or other sharp instrument cutting off the head of the said Pearl Bryan so that the said Pearl Bryan did then and there die. The said Alonzo Walling being then and there present aiding and assisting the said Scott Jackson in the killing and murdering of said Pearl Bryan by holding the person of the said Pearl Bryan whilst the cutting as afore-said was done by Scott Jackson."

Plummer and the others knew that Jackson and Walling's attorneys would demand all the necessary paperwork to pass the prisoners from Cincinnati to Campbell County. The charges of murder in Ohio would need to be dismissed and then Plummer would need to immediately arrest Jackson and Walling based on the warrants Plummer obtained in both Frankfort and Campbell County. They needed to address the chances that Jackson and Walling might be lynched if they went to Newport, something that their defense attorneys would probably use to keep them from being taken across the river. It was understood that the process would take time and that it would need to be handled with care.

After George Jackson's story appeared in the papers, the case was basically solved as far as the public was concerned. "Clinched," read the headline in the *Cincinnati Enquirer* when they interviewed George Jackson. However there were letters to various editors that asked the public to keep an open mind, to look at the case with fresh eyes, remain skeptical, and remember that these men should be treated as "innocent until proven guilty." It was possible that George Jackson's story was completely fabricated. The fact that he could pick Walling and Jackson out of a lineup is not remarkable since their likenesses had been widely published, and anyone read-ing the newspapers for the past few weeks would have been able to do the same. He would know that they were last seen at Wallingford's saloon since the papers had printed that multiple times, and he would know that they needed to end up at John Locke's field in Fort Thomas off of the Alexandria Pike. There is also the fact that Scott Jackson and Walling did not need a driver under the circumstances George Jackson described, nor did they need to involve another witness. The revolver that Walling supposedly threatened George with was never found.

The carriage as George described it was believed to have come from Mullen's Livery and Stable, which rented out carriages regularly. The particular carriage in question was shown to George, who said it was the same one he drove that night. He asked someone to look at the right-hand lantern and there they found a small dent. "I made that dent when I tried to get out at the distillery," George explained. Everyone gathered at Mullen's, including Sheriff Plummer, Crim, McDermott, a few officials, curiosity seekers, and reporters, agreed that George Jackson gave off an air of believability and honesty.

However, to the credit of the investigators, George's story was not accepted as fact without challenge. On February 16, close to one o'clock in the morning, a grand procession of carriages left Cincinnati and headed toward Fort Thomas. At the head of the bizarre parade was George Jackson, driving a carriage which contained Sheriff Plummer, Night Chief Louis Renkert, and a reporter from the *Cincinnati Enquirer*. Behind them were carriages with other reporters, Chief Deitsch, Detectives Crim and McDermott, and other police officials.

Everyone agreed to let George lead and not to offer any assistance or suggestions in which direction to take. George, for his part, was confident he could find his way. As they crossed the river, the watchman on the Cincinnati side said he remembered no such carriage on the night in question, but the watchman on the Newport side said he thought he remembered the carriage and had charged a toll. George said that he didn't remember Walling paying a toll, but it was possible Scott Jackson paid the toll through the carriage window. The procession went on into Kentucky. They meandered around the streets of Newport and finally left in the

direction of Fort Thomas, and into the countryside. This is
when trouble seemed to arrive.

George came to a house and said, "Don't seem to me that
I remember this house." He then turned the carriage around.
"I'm afraid we ain't on the right track." Sheriff Plummer,
who knew these roads probably better than anyone else in the
group, said nothing, but he became concerned because he
knew that the only way to Locke's field was to keep going the
way they were heading and that they now were heading in an
entirely wrong direction. George then turned onto a road
which Plummer knew ended at a barn and went no farther.
The road was terribly treacherous, and the procession went
through creeks and muddy bogs. One carriage overturned
and the entire party inside fell into the mud. The journey
seemed fruitless and it must have taken every ounce of
Sheriff Plummer's patience to not speak up. However, his
concerns proved unfounded.

When the road came to the point where Plummer thought
it ended at a barn, it carried on and up a hill and led right out
onto the Alexandria Pike. "This beats me," Plummer was
heard to remark. George then came to the spot where he said
the men took the woman into the field while she moaned.
Then, as George had previously said, he hitched the horse
and ran off back home.

That George knew the location of the crime scene is not
remarkable; it had been general knowledge for almost two
weeks. What made his journey impressive was that he took
such an obscure route to get there. It was impressive, but also
confusing. Presumably Jackson and Walling had planned out
this route, suggesting that Locke's field had been the chosen
killing field and dumping ground, and that Jackson and
Walling had decided they needed to take a treacherous route,
at night, to get there. Not just that, but that they would need
to hire a stranger at the last minute to drive them through

this roundabout way, which held the very real danger that their carriage might be overturned. Also, this route was not devoid of habitations—the procession passed several houses along the way and some were very close to the track.

It would seem obvious that the investigators would want to question the residents of these homes to see if they noticed a carriage travel by on the night of January 31. However it doesn't seem anyone had the presence of mind to do this. Instead, they all seemed to agree that George had passed his "test" with flying colors and so his story was undoubtedly true. And perhaps it was; there is much that seems to ring of truth, although parts bring up only more questions. Everyone involved in the investigation found George Jackson believable, and yet his story so perfectly convicts Scott Jackson and Alonzo Walling, it can't help but call the investigator's motives into question. George, who claimed to have no knowledge of Campbell County, knew a back route to Alexandria Pike that even Sheriff Plummer wasn't aware of. That such a route was taken seems bizarre and remains unexplained. Yet it might have been simply dumb luck.

EIGHTEEN

COMPLICATIONS

O N FEBRUARY 10, 1896, A TWENTY-TWO-YEAR-OLD WOMAN known variously as May or Lulu Hollingsworth was held by the Indianapolis police. It was believed that she had important information regarding the death of Pearl Bryan. The police had brought Miss Hollingsworth in after a letter was sent to a woman in Greencastle stating that information might be obtained from her about the case. When questioned, May admitted to knowing Scott Jackson, Will Wood, and Pearl Bryan. She first said that she believed Pearl had committed suicide and her body had been taken to the field and decapitated afterward. She said that she had happened to meet Pearl Bryan in Greencastle at the train station, where Pearl told her of her situation. They discussed the use of drugs to produce a miscarriage, and May had recommended one particular drug which, if used incorrectly, could easily result in death. May said that she had been in a previous situation similar to Pearl's and that the recipe she gave her had worked for her. It consisted of whiskey and a deadly poison which needed to be mixed very carefully. May Hollingsworth said that her only reason for talking about it now was that she firmly believed that Pearl had died as a result of ingesting the drug and that Jackson and Walling were only trying to dispose of the body without any questions falling on them.

"I do know this," May told the police. "Pearl Bryan died by her own hand. Scott Jackson is not guilty of her death. Before this murder occurred there was an affair in which Pearl Bryan, Scott Jackson and I were involved. I will never tell what that was until they are condemned to hang. If they are condemned to die, then I will tell the whole story, but not until then." Later she would add to the story, saying that she knew it was actually a black man who cut off Pearl's head, and that Scott Jackson had actually sent her a letter which explained that Pearl had died in his room after taking some concoction to induce an abortion.

May Hollingsworth said she saw Will Wood after her meeting with Pearl, but that they had not spoken of her trip to Cincinnati or of Scott Jackson. The police also learned that she had destroyed a letter just before she was brought in to the station. She would not comment on the nature of the letter, but many of those present thought that it might have been from Scott Jackson and contained some important details about the case that were now lost.

May Hollingsworth caused something of a stir for a few days until Indianapolis authorities came to see Jackson, Walling, and Wood. Each man in turn was told of Miss Hollingsworth and each man admitted that he had never heard of the woman before in his life. Wood said he never met her and had never heard her name. Walling claimed to never have heard of her from Jackson and that he didn't believe there was anything to her story. Jackson, after hearing her story, said, "She must be crazy." With that May and her stories faded from the public's attention. The affair that she said involved her, Pearl Bryan, and Jackson was never told, and most agreed it had never existed in the first place.

OVER TWO WEEKS AFTER the murder, scores of men and women came to the prison daily to try and gain admission and speak with Jackson and Walling. Many young women were turned away, and the elderly were sent away as well. Jackson and Walling bore their visitors with patience, though by the end of each day they looked exhausted and ready for some privacy. However, it was noted that Jackson always seemed pleased by a visit from a good-looking lady. Walling, when not tired, was seen to be pleased to be visited by anyone. He had been told by his lawyers to not speak of the case to anyone and, perhaps surprisingly, the majority of the visitors talked about everything except the case.

Reporters, in contrast, wanted to talk of nothing else when they visited the prisoners. After George Jackson came out with his story of the night of the murder, Scott Jackson and Walling were quickly told the details. Not surprisingly, they dismissed the story. Jackson, when he was first told of George's story, responded, "I don't know a damned thing about any driver."

"Didn't you hire a colored man to drive you and Walling at George and Elm?" an *Enquirer* reporter asked him.

"No, I didn't," Jackson was lying on his bunk with his hands behind his head.

"The jig is up and you might as well tell," the reporter pressed.

"For God's sake, what am I to tell?"

"Don't you know that you hired this man and that you sat in the back of the rig while Walling sat with the driver?"

"I don't know a thing about it," Jackson replied. "These cab stories are making me tired."

With that he covered his face with a blanket and turned away.

Walling was even less talkative. "See here, I've said all I'm going to say. I've put the whole story on paper and I'm sick of repeating it."

Will Wood was also told of George Jackson's story, but seemed little interested.

"Is that so? You say they found the driver?" he responded.

"Yes."

"I'm glad of it."

"Didn't you know something about this?" the reporter asked.

"How could I?" Wood asked.

"Didn't you learn of it afterward?"

"No, I didn't. Say, have you got a cigarette?"

The reporter handed over a cigarette.

"I've told all I know, so help me God," Wood said, "Good night."

Will Wood remained important to the case as a key witness. He was essential to the prosecution, since his story clearly linked Scott Jackson to the betrayal of Pearl Bryan, to the attempts at an abortion, and finally to Pearl's trip to Cincinnati. However, the fact that he had burned Jackson's letter undermined his testimony since it was partly his word against Jackson's. Furthermore, he could do little to implicate Walling. One can only guess at his mental state, viewed by Pearl's family as the source of her downfall and death, never far from suspicion, and admitting to trying to help Jackson abort Pearl's pregnancy. However, not far from Cincinnati another tragedy was about to happen, and though not connected to Pearl Bryan's case, it shared headlines in the area and the offender would become close to Jackson and

Walling, eventually forming a supernatural pact between them.

On the morning of February 15, the people of Augusta, Kentucky, learned that a well-to-do farmer's house was on fire a few miles outside of town. The farmer, named Robert Laughlin, had run from his burning home, covered in blood, stating that his wife and young niece had been killed by unknown assailants. He had barely escaped with his life, he said, after they slashed at his throat. These masked attackers then set fire to the house. Laughlin had two cuts under his chin, one a long gash that spread from ear to ear. His wife was an invalid, and the niece was just thirteen years old. Laughlin could not say whether they were killed before he was attacked or after, just that he had fled the scene when chased by multiple masked men.

Right from the outset, investigators questioned Laughlin's story. Again and again they had him go over the details, and his stories began to conflict in serious ways. In one statement he said he did not think of getting his revolver from his trousers, which were at the foot of the bed, but then later he said he did get his gun, but the murderer grabbed the gun from him and he simply ran away. He said he ran the quarter of a mile to his neighbor's house in his bare feet. The detectives took note of the road between the two houses and saw it was particularly rough; Laughlin's feet showed no bruises or scrapes when examined. The detectives thought he must have worn his shoes, which undermined the idea of him racing out of his house to save his life. The gash under his chin turned out to be not very deep and it seemed unlikely that all the blood on his shirt was from this cut, suggesting that some of it might have been from the victims. Because of these details, Laughlin was kept under careful watch by the authorities.

The next day, Laughlin broke down. He admitted that he had raped his young niece, apparently in the presence of his invalid wife. Then, perhaps to cover his guilt and shame, he had killed them both, and then burned the house. Almost immediately rumors of a possible lynching were heard. Laughlin asked to be taken to Maysville, Kentucky, as the jail there was newer and supposedly more secure.

Authorities needed to be cunning in their movement of Laughlin, usually sneaking him through towns and villages by night. They finally brought him to Maysville, where he was guarded due to newspaper reports of lynch mobs forming. He officially confessed his multiple crimes and said he was ready to be hanged for his crimes but he wanted it to be done legally. As time went on, Laughlin's reason seemed to break down and those who spoke to him were sure he would be raving mad before his trial. His lawyers attempted to put forth an insanity plea, but it did not work. He was found guilty and sentenced to death. He would later be moved to the Covington jail, where he would come in contact with Walling and Jackson, the latter of whom some said he resembled. It seems that the three men might have shared some sort of macabre friendship, for a pact was said to be made between them that Laughlin would return to the other two in spirit form after his execution.

On January 9, 1897, Robert Laughlin was hanged in Augusta, Kentucky, before a crowd so eager to see him die that they broke down the barricades keeping them back from the scaffold. He was collected and calm while facing his fate, and the hanging was clean; he died almost instantly. Due to his free and complete confession, there was no doubt of his terrible crimes. Jackson and Walling were said to have written him letters of farewell.

NINETEEN

MISTAKES

OVER THE FOLLOWING DAYS, SHERIFF JULE PLUMMER AND the authorities in Campbell County continued to try to move Jackson and Walling to northern Kentucky, while the prisoners' lawyers fought against the move. The major concern, as in the Laughlin case, was that any attempt to move them would be met with a lynch mob. The city, as a whole, had not forgotten the two men. Visitors still came to the prison to see them. The papers still reported on any developments, no matter how mundane or sensational, in the case. Séances were conducted and mediums consulted, purportedly producing spirits that spoke of Pearl Bryan. Possible locations of the missing head came from a seemingly endless supply of helpful citizens, sure that they knew where it could be found. A cellar in Chicago turned up nothing. Sewers were searched in vain, as were outhouses. A spot near Ninth and Elm streets in Cincinnati proved empty. Scott Jackson curiously made a claim that the head "would not be found tonight," which led to a flurry of speculation, though nothing of substance. He later said he could not tell where the head could be found for a million dollars.

At the request of the sheriff, Will Wood wrote down, from memory, letters he said he had received from Scott Jackson. George Jackson's story had not been contested, except for the denials of the prisoners; however, he added that two white men had been on the corner with him when Walling approached him. A search was conducted for these men, but they were never found. By February 20, George Jackson had not yet received the reward for providing the key information on the cab ride to Fort Thomas. In fact, while the mayor and other authorities continued to express their opinion that George Jackson was telling the truth, the papers published letters claiming that he was lying, that he was not of sound mind, and that he was actually involved in the murder. George responded angrily in a letter of his own and offered his own reward if anyone could prove any of the accusations against him.

Howard Scott, an African American man who was apparently part of the Caldwell Guards, came forward to the police and said that on the night of January 31 he was with George until one o'clock in the morning, so Jackson could not have driven the two accused murderers to Fort Thomas. The police were unable to confirm the story and George Jackson claimed it was actually the night before, not the 31st, that he had spent with Howard Scott, so it was not looked into any further. George told the police a few days later that there was a black man with him when he was hired by Walling; the police searched for this man too but were unable to locate him.

Despite the support of papers like the *Enquirer*, George Jackson was not the only one under criticism. In March, the

Kentucky Post ran an interview with J. L. Graman of the Graman Detective Bureau unambiguously titled, "Mistakes of the Police in Handling the Pearl Bryan Case." Graman admitted that he had not worked on the case at all, and that in fact he had been asked to take part in the investigation but declined.

"Do you believe Jackson and Walling killed Pearl Bryan?" the *Post* reporter asked.

"I have my opinion, but it might do someone an injustice," Graman replied. "The circumstances of the case look very dark for the guilt of the accused men, but the necessity of proof rests with the authorities."

When asked if he thought Jackson and Walling would be found guilty, he stated that it was his opinion that an unprejudiced court would convict them based on the evidence made public. He did retain hope that the police had not been "so foolish as to publish to the world their evidence."

Graman's criticisms, which he claims not to have wanted to express, quickly came to light in the interview. He said that too many individuals were involved in the case from the beginning. No one person was in charge, according to Graman. The police did not use ciphered telegrams when communicating with one another. The detectives should have worked more in secret and should not have shared so much information with the papers. Jackson shouldn't have been interviewed in the mayor's office, but at police headquarters, and the press should not have been allowed in for the interview. Jackson and Walling should not have been arrested right away, but shadowed in the hopes that they would provide additional clues. The chief of detectives was not directly involved in the case, and Graman thought he should have been taking the lead. Crim and McDermott were called in the case, but Graman felt they did not have enough experience to conduct the investigation properly, as seasoned detectives would have.

The *Kentucky Post*, which seemed to be more critical of the investigation than other papers, stopped Sheriff Plummer and asked him to answer some criticisms against him, including questions of expenses used in the investigation.

"I have never said that the Greencastle trip cost me $237. As a point of news and a matter of fact, I am $400 in the hole personally on this case and I don't see where or how I am to be reimbursed, or to whom I shall render my expense account. That's a matter for my county and state to settle. Why, I spent over $50 in telegrams and I didn't abbreviate them so as to save 4 or 5 cents. I sent them so they would be understood."

The *Post* also questioned Mayor Caldwell.

"You should not ask me whether Jackson and Walling are guilty," he explained to the reporter. "I doubt the propriety of asking an official to express an opinion about accused men. There is no question in anybody's mind about Jackson and Walling's guilt, but it is for the court and jury to determine. I really don't think I ought to talk. . . . You must remember that not all the evidence of the police had been printed."

He defended himself against Graman's criticism and then abruptly ended the interview. The reporter closed the article stating, "During the interview the Mayor made several statements which he insisted should not be published. His manner indicated that the subject was not a pleasant one."

While Graman was fairly vague about his opinion on the guilt of Jackson and Walling, Sheriff Plummer didn't comment on it at all; Mayor Caldwell, however, barely tried to cover his opinion. "There is no question in anybody's mind about Jackson and Walling's guilt," he said, and there could be no doubt in anyone's mind what he meant. It was an inappropriate statement and perhaps in another time would have led to the trials being moved to another jurisdiction. However, his words seemed to simply add to the flood of sentiment against Jackson and Walling. The *Kentucky Post*, while being critical of the authorities at times, never directly challenged the idea that Jackson and Walling were guilty. All of the region's papers did publish reports that questioned the strength of the case against the two men, but the papers didn't give these tales much credence or column space. If the papers and the mayor of Cincinnati were any indication, there seemed to be small chance that Jackson and Walling would get impartial trials.

This sort of corruption of the justice system was not unusual for the time. In fact, it is easy to see that true impartiality is practically impossible. However, in the late nineteenth century, the justice system and the government at large were rife with corruption. It was something the public was aware of and part of what the reformers of the time wanted to change. Cincinnati, while officially run by Mayor Caldwell, was unofficially under the control of George B. "Boss" Cox, who slowly came to power in the 1880s.

Cox was the son of English immigrants. His father died when he was young, so to help support his family he worked a string of odd jobs. In his twenties he bought a saloon and became a popular figure in his neighborhood, and at twenty-four ran for and won a seat on the city council. This started a thirty-year career in politics, in which he slowly gained control of the votes of the city. Although he held great power, there is no mention of him being involved in Pearl Bryan's case; he left it in the hands of the police.

The month of March would prove to be a decisive time for Jackson and Walling. The main concern the two most likely had, although they did not outwardly show it, would be that they would not get a fair trial in Newport. On March 11, the *Enquirer* printed a short passage that appeared to be responding to the general opinion that Jackson and Walling might not get a fair trial in Newport and that they might be

lynched. A Newport lawyer felt the need to respond directly
to the public. "I am thoroughly familiar with the feeling
among my fellow townsmen about the case," he claimed. "I
can say, without any doubt, that the prisoners will be accord-
ed a fair trial in every respect." While the unnamed lawyer
may have believed every word he said, some people must
have obviously thought differently. While these might have
been the lawyers and supporters of Jackson and Walling, it
should have also included those who believed in the necessity of a fair trial to the credibility of the justice system.

On March 16, a court ruling finally settled the battle to
move the two prisoners. They were ordered to Newport as
soon as possible. Neither of them showed any reaction to the
decision, most likely because they expected it, but also, one
can imagine, because they had become exhausted by the
ordeal. Jackson might not have heard that a group of boys
had hung him in effigy in Newport a few weeks before. Nor
was either prisoner much bothered by the strange visit of
Nathoo, the "high caste Brahmin priest" who was engaged in
locating Pearl's head through the use of his mystical mental
abilities. The Brahmin priest met with each man, talking for
several minutes while they smoked cigarettes, and left each
with the warmest regards and offers to see them again soon.
The Hindu seer wouldn't divulge details of his meetings
with the two men, only to say that if Walling was involved in
the murder, it was not in malice, and that his beliefs would
not lead him to convict the men as he could not have a hand
in anything that might lead to the death of beast or man.

TWENTY

SUPPORTERS

THE TRANSFER OF THE PRISONERS FROM OHIO TO Kentucky proved to be a mad dash through both cities. On March 17, the prisoners were taken out of their cells, with Walling handcuffed to Detective Crim while Jackson was cuffed to McDermott. Reporters who had gathered and had been waiting for hours were politely asked to leave; they complied. No one knew quite when and where the prisoners were going. Some were certain they wouldn't be moved for several more days. They were hustled into a waiting carriage and taken quickly to Cincinnati's central police station, where they were put in a temporary cell for two hours. Then in quick succession a carriage arrived and the prisoners were brought out and took their seats. The carriage then took off on its race to Newport. The trip took only eight minutes. Neither prisoner seemed particularly happy to be on the other side of the river. Reports indicate that there was a crowd waiting for them when they arrived, so the prisoners were rushed inside, though no violence broke out. It was about 4 o'clock in the afternoon.

The crowd dispersed after only an hour and the scene grew quiet. As the *Louisville Courier-Journal* described it, "The metropolis of Campbell County was never more quiet than it is tonight. The forlorn looking shack called by grace of legal phraseology a jail never looked more lonesome. One solitary sentinel stands guard in danger of being overcome by nothing violent then somnolence superinduced by extreme solitude." The fears of lynching and mob violence turned out to be unwarranted. Apparently enough time had passed and the people of Newport were collectively calmer than expected.

An *Enquirer* reporter managed to get into the Newport jail and speak to the prisoners. Jackson was in a particularly biting mood.

"All right. I'm used to being placed on exhibition," he said. "How do you want to see me? Coat-collar turned up, hat pulled down over my eyes and hands in my pockets? Want to hear me say, 'Can you tell me and so forth.' That's the way they generally demand of me to exhibit myself."

The reporter assured him he only wanted to see how he was doing. He asked him if he was nervous to come to Kentucky.

"Well I wasn't stuck on the idea," Jackson admitted.

"Why not?"

"I had read and heard so much of lynch-law in Kentucky and of mob violence before the guilt of the accused was positively established, that I felt some anxiety. Then I understood that a great deal of prejudice existed against us in this particular case, and well, you can understand."

Walling, on the other hand, said he felt no fear whatsoever.

"I understand the gentleman on the first flat [meaning Jackson] is scared to death," he joked. "At a fair trial, I will

be acquitted. I had not motive in committing the murder and
never knew Pearl Bryan."

Later Jackson gave a more direct response to the difference between Ohio and Kentucky. "This is quite different
from the Hamilton County Jail, where everything was at
least nice and clean. If I could only exercise a little it would
not be so bad. I am really losing the use of my legs, and I cannot see what harm there would be in allowing me to walk in
the corridor with one of the guards."

Reading the *Enquirer* through February and March 1896,
it seemed that each day presented more proof of Jackson's
and Walling's guilt. It didn't help that the paper continually
referred to them as the "murderers." "Two men saw Jackson
in Kentucky." "Damaging: The Latest Evidence..." "A
Missing Girl: Has she been spirited away by Jackson and
Walling?" A questionable story appeared on March 13 with
the headline "At Last," which said that a woman, who would
not give her name, claimed Pearl Bryan had spent the
Thursday night before her death at the Indiana House. There
is no mention if this information could be verified or why it
did not match the statement given by the clerk of the Indiana
House. In other words, it seemed the *Enquirer* had already
convicted Jackson and Walling. However, other papers were
not much better. The *Kentucky Post* and *Courier-Journal* all
sounded as if their guilt was a foregone conclusion.

There were supporters of Jackson and Walling, though
they preferred to remain anonymous. These unknown apol-
ogists wrote scores of letters to the prisoners according to the
jail guards, though none of them survive and only one
appears to have been printed. It was a letter to Walling that
began, "Dear Alonzo—I now venture to write you this
evening: cannot say what kind of note it will make, for I cannot do anything but cry since I first read of this terrible crime
you are supposed to be implicated in. I could never believe

you guilty, if you was to hang tomorrow. Therefore I am willing to get you anything you want while you are in prison." The letter was signed "C.M.M.L." and spoke of an "Aunt Hat and Uncle Jim," but if Walling knew who the letter was from, he never told the papers.

Jackson and Walling, besides everything else, were now celebrities. Jackson had a scheme to sell pictures of himself to his many visitors, but he did not go through with it. No one seemed to know how many of these visitors were curiosity-seekers, supporters, or something else. No one tried to harm either prisoner, though they were often suspicious of gifts. When offered a cigarette, it was noted, Jackson and Walling usually waited for the other person to light their own cigarette first. There are plenty of references to young women who seemed to be fascinated with the alleged killers.

On one day Jackson, who liked to keep track of the total numbers of visitors he received each day, counted almost five hundred different persons who came to see him. The guards began to notice that a large number of the visitors were young women and that many of them were sympathetic to the prisoners, which led to Jackson and Walling acting "brazen." In the language of the day this speaks to a more flirtatious manner than what the word might imply today. The field of psychology would one day call these possible cases of "hybristophilia," or a person who derives pleasure from having a sexual partner who has committed a terrible crime, specifically rape or murder. The guards were keen to keep an eye on these women and there was no indication that their interactions with the prisoners went beyond looks, words, or letters.

The most important supporters for the prisoners were their attorneys. Though Jackson and Walling had been represented by a number of different lawyers throughout their various legal battles, they would each eventually be defended by a separate attorney. Walling's counsel was Col. George Washington, Jr., while Jackson was represented by Leonard J. Crawford. Rumors began early that the two lawyers were at odds with each other, much like the defendants; but these tales were exaggerations. They were actually working together, spending many hours poring over the details of the case. Washington's experience was mainly with constitutional and equity law, but he had been a defense attorney in several criminal cases, including murder, and even one feud involving the death of a dozen people. He was able to secure acquittals in many cases and had a good record. Crawford was one of the most respected attorneys in northern Kentucky and had a wide range of experience as well. He was active in Republican politics and held a number of party leadership roles, but never an elected office.

By March 19, the legal process was set to begin. At the first hearing, much to the disappointment of the spectators who had come out, Jackson and Walling were not present. The attorneys presented themselves and received orders from Judge Charles J. Helm, but not much else was done. The defense team indicated to reporters gathered there that they had evidence which would help to provide alibis for their respective clients, though they did not elaborate. On March 23, the prisoners were both present in court to enter pleas of not guilty, and it was also officially decided that they would have separate trials, which Colonel Washington had requested from the beginning. For this session tickets were sold, a relatively common occurrence for any trials of great interest. About 300 people were present, including, it was noted, almost every attorney from the three neighboring cities.

Before the prisoners were brought in, most people were trying to get a look at Louis Poock, the shoe man who famously played such a key role in the investigation. His story had been told in the papers many times over, and the fact that such a seemingly mild-mannered man should figure so prominently in the "crime of the century" made him a person of great interest. Poock, as was his gentleman's nature, didn't mention anything of his rising fame when he wrote his book on the case. However, there is no doubt from his writings that he believed in the guilt of Jackson and Walling from early on.

Besides female admirers and their defense attorneys, the only person who seemed to think Jackson and Walling would not be found guilty was, surprisingly, Joseph W. Pugh, the chief of police in Covington, Kentucky. "In the shape which the case now is," he told a reporter, "there is neither credible testimony nor reliable witnesses to present to the jury. There are several points which are of vital importance and which have been absolutely neglected." He doubted the motive proposed for the crime, that Pearl should be killed rather than having an abortion that could have been easily obtained. He wondered why she would have been drugged, when his understanding was that abortions were usually done without the use of drugs. He questioned George Jackson's story of driving the carriage to Fort Thomas and taking Pearl to Kentucky by such a bizarre route to a place that was relatively heavily populated and close by a main road and electric car line. He pointed out that two of the key prosecution witnesses, both African Americans, were George Jackson, who he claimed was "crazy to get in the papers" and of questionable character, and Allen Johnson, the porter from Wallingford's saloon, who had finally been arrested for robbing his former employer. Because of all these points he felt it was impossible that Jackson and Walling would be found guilty, though he seemed to personally think one or both of them were probably guilty.

At the March 23 hearing, Jackson's trial was set for April 7, while Walling's remained to be determined at a later date.

Crawford tried to get Jackson's case moved back, as he had only been attached to the case for the past week and a half, but Judge Helm did not allow it and kept the date firm. Jackson, for his part, expressed his opinion that he wanted the trial to be over as soon as possible. With that Jackson and Walling were removed, the crowd was ushered out, and the courtroom stood empty within a few minutes. In short order, Jackson and Walling were back in their cells. Life, for them, resembled closely what it had on the other side of the river. They read and slept and paced about their cells. They received visitors, but typically refused to speak of the trial or their present troubles. Jackson felt compelled to point out, however, that his cell in Cincinnati had been two paces larger than the one in Newport, though it was not said as a complaint, simply an example of the monotony of his existence.

IT IS OPEN TO THE READER to determine whether or not Jackson or Walling had a chance at a fair trial in Newport. Being tried in an area where the population was already sure of your guilt was not uncommon at the time. As previously noted, humanity seems to always have had a fascination with murder and mayhem. But it was the late nineteenth century, with the abundance of papers, the free access of the press, and the speed of information thanks to telegraphs and telephones, when these stories seemed to grab and hold the attention of so many people at the same time. There was a report, around the time Jackson and Walling came to Newport, of a woman who had become so obsessed with the case and afraid that she would be decapitated, that she needed to be confined to an asylum.

Murder stories were front-page news everywhere. Cheap pamphlets, often filled with more rumor and exaggeration than fact, were sold with lurid illustrations to the hungry public. The kidnapping of four-year-old Charley Ross in

Philadelphia; the murder of John Whipple by his wife's lover in 1827 in Albany; the murder of Mansfield Walworth by his son in 1873; H. H. Holmes, Theo Durrant, Lizzie Borden, and many others were all the centers of public frenzy at one time or another. Some continued to be known for decades, while others faded quickly from memory. It appears that men were more likely to be found guilty than women, though no conclusive studies have proved this. The plea of insanity was often used but only occasionally successful. It is impossible to say how good the odds were that a defendant would get a fair trial, especially since a "fair trial" is a relative statement. Judges and attorneys certainly did the best they could do in most situations, though some were more conscientious than others.

There was a report that someone—the police or the prosecution—set men in unseen locations near Jackson's and Walling's cells and, using listening devices, tried to obtain any information that might help convict the men while they conversed with visitors and other prisoners. One reporter was offended by the idea. "The procurement of evidence by means of spies set upon a prisoner is subject to one very great objection. The task of a spy is one that is repugnant to the feelings of most men of high character." He pointed out that the word of a man eavesdropping on unknown prisoners was not likely to be held high in the mind of a jury since this spy would be of a character that might be inclined to lie or exaggerate what he heard.

Still, it should not come as a surprise that juries could be biased and quick to convict. Many terrible crimes went unsolved at the time, thus a suspect and enough circumstantial evidence was more than enough to feel that justice had been done. St. Clair County, Illinois, for example, struggled for decades with a heinous unsolved murder. In 1874 an unknown killer or killers came to the Steltzenrider farm and killed all five people in the house. The butchering was done with an ax and a corn knife. The owner had his head bashed in and his throat slit open. His elderly father was killed in the same way. The wife had her throat slit in bed and lying by her was a year-old baby killed with the knife. A three-year-old child lay at the foot of the bed, brutally killed as well.

The most likely suspect was Frederick Beltz, Steltzenrider's brother-in-law. Yet he was able to leave town, and even when he turned up in Texas, there was never enough evidence to arrest him. Other suspects included George and Charles Killian, members of a gang thought to possibly be involved in the killings. Charles Killian was shot, years later, and on his deathbed asked to speak to the sheriff about the case, but died before he could divulge any information. The motive was apparently $800 that Steltzenrider had told his brother-in-law that he had and was going to put in the bank. Various grand juries looked at the case and a few arrests were made, but there were never any trials. The house where the murders occurred stood abandoned for some time; its fate is unknown. The murder remained unsolved until time washed it from living memory. A case like that has the potential to undermine the public's trust in authorities. It could end the career of an otherwise successful sheriff, chief of police, or mayor. There was more than just justice at stake in the capture and conviction of a suspect.

TWENTY-ONE

SCOTT JACKSON'S TRIAL

THE WEATHER PREDICTION FOR APRIL 7, 1896, WAS "generally fair." Perhaps the most curious thing to happen nationally on that date was that Mrs. C. A. Curtis would be elected mayor of the town of Cimmaron, Kansas, prompting the papers to report that the community was now "in control of the women." The other news of the day was largely concerned with baseball, boxing, and horse racing, as well as the presidential campaign in which the candidate William McKinley, from Ohio, was viewed as the frontrunner going into the November election. There was also the trial of Scott Jackson for the murder of Pearl Bryan. The Newport courtroom was filled, ready for Jackson's trial to begin. Louis Poock, as would be his custom, was present, and many eyes were drawn to him. There were a few women in the courtroom, and a rumor spread that one of them was May Hollingsworth, the woman from Indianapolis who claimed to have talked to Pearl and had letters from Scott Jackson. It was said that she was there to threaten Walling if he thought of testifying against Jackson, but it turned out to be a complete fabrication—the woman was actually a friend of detectives Crim and McDermott.

There was a general press when Jackson was brought in from an anteroom, but no one made a move except for one curious incident. Noticed by only a few people, a comely and seemingly respectable woman sitting along Jackson's path put her leg out and kicked him twice, hard upon the leg. The judge and the sheriff, who was acting bailiff, did not see the action and no one made any sign that they had seen it. It might not have been recorded if a reporter had not been close by and witnessed it. Jackson gave the woman a surprised look, then composed himself and went on. That was the only violence he ever suffered from the public.

With hushed tension in the air, the judge brought the court to order; however, the spectators would be disappointed. The first thing Jackson's attorney Leonard Crawford requested was a continuance, and Judge Charles Helm granted him two weeks. Even with this extension, Crawford would have less than a month and a half to prepare his case in defending Jackson. The judge clearly indicated that this should be more than enough time. Crawford, for his part, seemed doubtful. He pointed out that he did not have the time to determine the credibility of the various witnesses, to speak to people in the various neighborhoods associated with the case. Judge Helm, who was thin and in his thirties, surprisingly young for his position, would hear none of it. "The prisoner merely needs to tell where he has been and this he knows of his own knowledge. You have only to gather supporting evidence." In other words, the judge was saying that Crawford, as the defense, did not need to challenge any of the evidence presented by the prosecution.

The highlight of the day was perhaps not the legal arguments, but the state of the people outside the courtroom. They all seemed bent on Jackson's and Walling's deaths as soon as was possible. One large man yelled, "He'll hang, and he ought to, damn him!" A woman with an infant nearby replied, "Yes, and Walling ought to follow him in five minutes."

JACKSON'S TRIAL WAS NOW SET for April 22. In the following two weeks, the world seemed to carry on much as it had. There were unsubstantiated reports that hundreds of Americans were wasting away in Spanish jails in Cuba while the Spanish continued to oppress the Cuban people. There were suicides and murders, but nothing to compare to Pearl Bryan's story. The presidential race was gaining momentum, and would be one of the most defining in American history. Grover Cleveland was essentially ruined by the Panic of 1893 and declined the nomination of part of the fractured Democratic Party. William Jennings Bryan would gain the Democratic nomination, while McKinley, governor of Ohio, would accept the Republican nomination. This election is often cited as the beginning of the Progressive movement, although McKinley was not a progressive candidate and mainly represented the wealthy and generally higher-skilled workers, while William Jennings Bryan was seen as the populist.

Women of Cincinnati met to learn cultural subjects, such as the importance of French Romantic painting and the history of English churches, while the papers printed illustrations of the new and latest spring headwear—straw hats with plaited tulle around the brim. In early April, H. H. Holmes wrote a confession of his crimes. He admitted to twenty murders in all, nine more than he was convicted of. The confession was written in Philadelphia in the "shadow of the gallows" and declared him to be a "professional murderer." In all, he would write three confessions and claim to have killed hundreds.

APRIL 22 WAS A PLEASANTLY COOL and breezy spring day, a break from the recent warm spell the Ohio Valley had experienced. The Newport courtroom was once again crowded. All eyes were on Jackson, who sat in apparent calm. Once things were settled and Judge Helm had entered, the first witness was called. This was Jack Hawling, whom the *Enquirer* now called John Hulling. His testimony indicated that he had discovered the body and made particular note of the arrangement of her dress and that her corset lay about five feet from her body. Coroner Tingley next took the stand and stated plainly that he believed the head was cut off while the victim was still alive. He had noted blood on the leaves of the bushes, and he thought the victim was killed in the field. His statements fully contradicted what he had stated at the inquest, when he specifically had said that he did not see blood on the bushes and that there was not enough blood at the scene to have been the site of the murder. It would seem that this might be a perfect opportunity for Crawford to confront Tingley with his contradictions, but he did not. He hinted that the coroner had previously believed something different than what his current testimony reflected, but there was no direct accusation. Crawford let the chance pass by him.

The jury which now had the burden to condemn or set free Scott Jackson was, as by law, all men. Their ages ranged from thirty-three to eighty-eight, and they were all from Newport or nearby towns. Among them were a newspaper agent, carpenter, clothing cutter, teamster, and three grocers. Eleven of the twelve jurors admitted that they had, in fact, formed an opinion already on the innocence or guilt of the defendant, but they assured the court they would remain impartial. Though never clearly stated, it is not hard to imagine what their opinions were.

The second day of the trial started with Sheriff Plummer bringing a headless dummy wearing Pearl's blood-stained clothes into the courtroom, apparently to be used as evidence. The courtroom erupted with disgust and horror; some of the women present were heard to let out exclamations of shock. Crawford, who apparently had no knowledge of this display, jumped up immediately and objected to the presence of the dummy. Judge Helm agreed and had the dummy removed, but it had already had an effect. It was as if the body had been brought into the room in all its ghastly detail, and there was no longer any doubt that the majority of people in the room blamed Jackson for everything.

Mary Stanley, Pearl's sister, was then called as a witness. Sitting in deep mourning, she spoke with a tremor in her voice. She handled the dress and other clothes and identified them as her sister's. Her sorrowful words moved everyone present; one of the jury members was seen to wipe tears from his eyes. She turned and identified Scott Jackson as the man who had courted her sister. Her face was blank and Jackson did not look back. Dr. Carothers was called and repeated his earlier statements that Pearl had come to the city for an illegal operation and that she was alive when her head was removed. He added that he did not believe there was a scientific way to determine if Pearl had been killed where she was found or somewhere else, only that he believed she died from the arteries in her neck being severed.

The following day was mainly concerned with the chief question of the trial: Was Pearl Bryan's head cut off while she was still alive? Several physicians weighed in for the prosecution and the defense. Due to the specific nature of the indictment and the decision at the coroner's inquest, it seemed that

Crawford merely needed to present a plausible scenario in which Pearl's head was removed after she was dead. His main argument was that Pearl might have been killed with an overdose of chloroform, which would cause the heart to stop beating and so blood would stop flowing. Then the head could be cut off and her blood would seep out in Locke's field. This might also explain the large blood clots found at the scene. The prosecution, given chiefly by the well-regarded Mr. Lockhart, presented evidence that the head must have been cut off while the victim was still alive because of the condition of the skin around the wound. Crawford argued against this, stating that it was well known that animal skin would draw back in the same way even when the head was removed after death. The witness, Dr. J. O. Jenkins, simply said that animal skin and human skin were different due to the presence of undeveloped muscle under animal skin which allowed them to shake off flies. The prosecution continued to present experts who declared the head was removed while the victim was still alive. Crawford tried to refute their reasoning, but was unprepared for the task.

By the fourth day of the trial, the papers had all but declared victory for the prosecution. "Apparently the only hope of his [Scott Jackson's] attorneys is to prove error in the present trial, and secure a rehearing under more favorable circumstances." Allen Johnson, the porter from Wallingford's, stuck to his story that he had seen Jackson and Walling leave that Friday night with a woman in clothes like the ones on the body. He could add no more to the story, but the courtroom seemed to place much stock on his testimony even though it didn't prove that it was Pearl whom he saw with Jackson and Walling, and did nothing to place the murder at their hands.

Pearl's mother was put on the stand and Crawford, understandably, refused to cross-examine her.

Louis D. Poock was called next, and he detailed his involvement in the case and how he helped to determine the identity of the victim. He was also asked what he knew about what Jackson had told Mayor Caldwell in their first interview, Jackson's inconsistencies, and his lack of a clear alibi. Crawford objected since this was second-person hearsay, but Judge Helm overruled, and Poock told the jury what he had heard.

Next came Dr. Crane, a chemist, who testified that Pearl had two grains of cocaine (about 120 milligrams) in her stomach at the time of his examination. He said that it was most likely taken orally, and he calculated that she had consumed enough that would cause death. He stated that he knew of at least two cases where cocaine had been used to try to cause an abortion, but both were unsuccessful. There is no record whether Crawford pursued Dr. Crane's admission that Pearl may have died of an overdose.

Dr. Dickore came next and stated that the soil sample taken from Jackson's pants and the earth removed from Locke's field were a match. On cross-examination, however, it was discovered that Dickore did not conduct a chemical analysis of the samples, but only viewed them both through a microscope and declared that they appeared similar.

Will Wood then took the stand and told the story of his contact with Jackson and Pearl and his involvement in the case. Wood had admitted to receiving scores of letters from Jackson, but that per Jackson's instructions, he had burned them all. Later, when Jackson accused him of being the father of Pearl's child, he said that he wished he had not burned those letters, but that he had kept the originals. He was asked to reconstruct the letters from memory, and he complied.

At some point the charge against Wood of attempting to procure an abortion must have been dropped or in some other way changed to complicity in Pearl Bryan's murder. After he had languished in jail for over three months, Wood's case was brought up in police court and dismissed for a lack of evidence before the trial began. Those involved in the case claimed there was no agreement that Wood agreed to testify against Jackson and Walling in exchange for the charges against him being dropped. On cross-examination, Crawford confronted Wood with evidence that he had actually boasted of being intimate with Pearl and that he had told someone that he had gotten a girl in trouble. Wood steadily denied these accusations.

In the following days the prosecution largely spent their time presenting Scott Jackson as a depraved character. Will Wood was allowed to read the letters that he had written from memory that were supposed to be from Jackson. Why Crawford didn't object to this, especially since there seems to have been no precedent to allow letters written from memory as evidence, is baffling. Wood could have fabricated every word in those letters and yet they were allowed to be read in court as if they were Jackson's words.

Detective Cal Crim took the stand and was asked to describe what Jackson and Walling had said when they were arrested. Crawford objected on the grounds that according to Kentucky law, Walling and Jackson could not give evidence in court against each other, and that this would be second-hand information. He was overruled. Crim went on to relate more statements made by Jackson and Walling, and Crawford objected yet again. This time Judge Helm ruled that only statements made by Walling that Jackson agreed were true should be considered by the jury. This startling instruction presented a problem for the jury because they had already heard a large amount of testimony about what Walling had said which Jackson disagreed with. Crim then related the story that late on the night of January 31, Walling said Jackson entered their rooms with a valise, which he then spoke to, saying, "You're a beaut." Judge Helm ruled that this testimony should be thrown out, since Jackson claimed he had never said this.

The following days were consumed by George Jackson's testimony and cross-examination. His statement was much the same as what he originally told the police. Crawford eventually produced several witnesses, mainly members of the Caldwell Guards, who contradicted George Jackson's story. The state rested, confident they had proven Scott Jackson's guilt.

Scott Jackson took the stand in his own defense. While he occupied the witness box for over six hours, he repeated what he had claimed for some time. He admitted to an improper relationship with Pearl Bryan, but stated that he had left her with Walling and that he could only surmise that Walling had been her killer. In a surprise move, the state declined to cross-examine Jackson, though the papers seemed to indicate that his testimony was less than believable.

The defense presented witnesses who refuted much of what the prosecution had presented. Jackson's sister gave testimony trying to improve the impression of his character. There were suggestions that a third person needed to be involved in the case; a saloon keeper testified that he had seen Jackson and Walling and a third man discussing something of great importance before the time of the murder. Experts testified that the head could have been removed after death and in a different location, meaning Pearl could have died from other causes. George Jackson's character and truthfulness were attacked ruthlessly. Then Scott Jackson's defense made what might have been a fatal mistake.

They were to present a surprise witness, William Trusty, a cab driver found by a detective named Seward. This was to be the first of several witnesses put forward by Seward that would state that Pearl Bryan had died elsewhere before her body was found in Locke's field. Trusty said he witnessed a dead woman being brought out from a doctor's rooms. He then drove a cab to Fort Thomas where the doctor and a companion took the body into a field. Trusty then returned to Newport in the cab. None of those involved was Jackson or Walling.

The only problem was that Seward was a fraud, and all of his witnesses were paid to give false testimony. The plot had been uncovered before Trusty had even taken the stand, but the police and prosecutors, who had been tipped off by one of Seward's fake witnesses, allowed him to tell his tale anyway, and then promptly charged him with perjury. Crawford was openly confused and then embarrassed; he stated that he had no involvement with Seward (which was not his real name) and had only been presented with the witnesses by him. Crawford assured the court that he knew nothing of the plot, nor did his client. Yet it must have undermined their position with the jury. It was never clear who had hired Seward or if he had expected payment after bringing in the false witnesses. Regardless, it probably cost the defense their case.

To add to the troubles, a few of the witnesses who testified against George Jackson now made claims that they had lied as well, though this was only reported in the papers and they did not retract their testimony in court.

On May 15, 1896, it finally came time for the closing arguments. For the prosecution, Robert W. Nelson, a distinguished lawyer who hadn't had much of a role up to this point, gave what was agreed to be a stirring and convincing argument. Crawford spoke for the defense and there were reports that he moved some of the jury to tears in his effort to show that the prosecution against Jackson was unfair and inhumane.

The jury retired and deliberated for almost two hours. At noon they reached a verdict.

In the meantime Jackson smoked a cigar and commented that the biggest joke of the trial was the testimony of George Jackson, "That fellow is one of the most accomplished liars I have ever been in contact with."

The sheriff announced that the jury was ready with the verdict. Before the verdict was read, Judge Helm asked that no one react with approval or disapproval. The verdict was handed to the judge then to the court clerk, who read it aloud:

"We, the jury, find the defendant, Scott Jackson, guilty of murder and fix the punishment at death."

A single man, disregarding Judge Helm's warning, applauded. Scott Jackson dropped his cigar and the color drained from his face, he bent to pick up the cigar, but his eyes stared straight ahead at some unknown spot. The jurymen were thanked for their service, and the courtroom buzzed with excitement. Jackson was taken out of the courtroom in handcuffs, his head fell down, and he spoke no words but only shuffled back to his cell.

"Must Die" read the headline in Louisville, Kentucky, continuing, "The Public Generally Satisfied With the Verdict." The *Maysville Evening Bulletin* said plainly on the front page, "Jackson Is Guilty." The *Roanoke Daily Times'* front page read, "Murder In The First Degree." The front page of the *Arizona Republican* said, "He Was Found Guilty." The *Anaconda Standard* out of Montana reported the verdict as well, and related the same story printed all over the country: Jackson was guilty and sentenced to death. The defense had requested a new trial but was unlikely to get it.

Back in his cell, Alonzo Walling was satisfied with the verdict as he believed it helped his chances. Jackson was surprised and despondent about the results, as he believed his defense had been strong enough to get an acquittal.

TWENTY-TWO

STORIES

AFTER JACKSON'S TRIAL, THERE WAS A MASS ESCAPE FROM the Newport jail. Jackson and Walling could have made a run for it as well, but they declined the offer. Instead they remained in the safety of their cells, no doubt thinking of the fate they might meet if the people of the city learned the two prisoners were loose. In fact, a rumor had already spread that they had escaped, and a mob had gathered outside the jail waiting for any sign of them. Eventually order was restored and the mob dispersed.

Alonzo Walling, the perpetual afterthought, began his trial on May 26. Before the trial, Walling's defense, headed by Colonel George Washington, engaged a professional runner who held the world's record for the twenty-five-, fifty-, and hundred-mile runs. The runner was paid to run from the location where the body was found along the route George Jackson testified he had fled on the night of January 31, after leaving Jackson, Walling, the girl, and the carriage behind. The runner could not match George Jackson's claimed time. Not only that, but the runner was required to cross streams and climb fences, and at one point he ran through a back-yard, scared some girls, and caused their father to chase after him with a shotgun. At the end of it all he was covered in mud and behind Jackson's time by a large margin.

The jury proved to be hard to sit as every man in the area seemed to have already formed an opinion on Walling's guilt after Jackson's trial. Yet a jury was finally formed. At the same time Judge Helm denied Crawford's request for a new trial for Scott Jackson. Walling's trial progressed in much the same way as Jackson's, since many of the same witnesses were called and the same stories were repeated. George Jackson delivered his testimony as he had in Jackson's trial and the defense presented evidence, including the running test, to prove that his story was unfounded. Walling took the stand in his defense and blamed everything on Scott Jackson, pointing out that he had not even been around Jackson for the days surrounding Pearl's murder. This time the prosecution did move to cross-examine the defendant and challenged his every statement, but he did not waver from his story.

Closing arguments were heard, just as eloquent and convincing as in the Jackson trial; but it seemed the outcome was predetermined. The jury barely deliberated; the report from the jurors was that a ballot was immediately taken and the decision was unanimous on the first vote. "We, the jury, find the defendant, Alonzo Walling, guilty of murder and fix the penalty at death." For his part, Walling seemed unfazed. He took the news, like much else in the case, with greater composure than Jackson. While his attorney presented a motion for a new trial, Walling was led out of the courtroom. All requests for retrials were rejected.

Jackson and Walling were both transferred to a jail in Covington, where they made the acquaintance of Robert Laughlin, the condemned man who had raped his niece, then killed her and his wife, and set fire to his house. Dates were set for the executions, but they were frequently moved. Most of the news that summer concerned the presidential race. The public also seemed particularly preoccupied with staying cool and the papers reported regularly on the number of deaths from heat stroke. Short articles concerning the Bryan case appeared, like one in July that related the fact that the transcripts for the Jackson trial alone weighed fifty pounds.

After the trials were over, Louis Poock was forced to sell his business. Many claimed this was because he had become so preoccupied with the case that he neglected running his store or failed to keep it open while he traveled around hunting down the identity of the victim and then later spending days sitting through the trials. He had many creditors, and several shoe dealers from the area came to the sale, which began on July 28. For all his work and diligence in the case, and the importance of his role in identifying Pearl Bryan, he received no reward; there is no indication that he was compensated for any of his expenditures. His name and face became known, but with fame does not always come fortune, and so he was left to sell his stock and business in the hopes of paying off his creditors.

Then, unexpectedly, Sheriff Plummer came and stopped the sale due to a suit filed in the Campbell County Court. Poock must have been mystified. As it turned out, the suit had been filed by still more creditors from the East, for what seemed to be the fact that they wanted to organize their own sale of Poock's stock. To confuse matters more, there was another suit filed by Poock's attorney, apparently against his client, possibly for back pay. The attorney happened to be Colonel George Washington, who had unsuccessfully represented Walling. The sale was able to continue due to a lack of official documentation. When the documents were finally filed, most of the stock was sold and Poock was able to pay off most of his debts.

Kentucky governor William O'Connell Bradley regularly received letters begging that Jackson and Walling be pardoned. The letters appeared to be from strangers or were anonymous, and so one can only guess at their intent. Into the fall, Jackson and Walling made appeals for clemency but they all failed. Yet, there were some people, for unknown reasons, who felt sympathy or attraction to the two condemned men. Sheriff Plummer received threatening letters stating that he had perjured himself and had planted evidence. Women still came to see the two men and often left them bouquets to show their affection.

REPUBLICAN WILLIAM MCKINLEY was elected president and the dream of "free silver" died, but the populists and progressives were not deterred. Jackson and Walling were not asked their opinions on the matter. The holidays passed, followed by the anniversary of Pearl Bryan's death.

The date for the hanging was set for March 20, 1897. There, in the shadow of the gallows, Scott Jackson and Alonzo Walling gave their final confessions, written separately but matching in detail, telling what they said was the true story of the death of Pearl Bryan.

PEARL BRYAN CAME TO Cincinnati for an abortion, which Scott Jackson told Walling about and asked for his help. Walling asked the advice of May Smith, a girl of Louisville, who recommended he go to a Dr. Wagner of Bellevue, which is next to Newport. Jackson and Walling sent her to Dr. Wagner on the Wednesday she left the Indiana House. They repeatedly checked on her, between classes and other engagements. When they were both there on Friday, Dr. Wagner said her condition had worsened and sent Jackson to a druggist to get ergot (a fungus commonly found on rye that is also a hallucinogen and poison), which was supposed to help induce an abortion. Both men also said the doctor made an injection in Pearl's heart.

This confirmed an observation that came out in the trials that was overlooked. The embalmer said that he found what he believed was an injection site under Pearl's left breast, which would indicate an injection in the heart. Dr. Wagner examined Pearl closely and pronounced that she had died during this process.

The doctor then got his own carriage and they took the body out a back door. They drove to an area that neither man said he recognized, which would prove to be Colonel Locke's field. Jackson said he held onto the body while Dr. Wagner removed the head with a scalpel. The doctor took the head and Jackson and Walling were charged with getting rid of the girl's clothing, which they threw into the Ohio River.

Dr. Wagner was, in fact, a physician in Bellevue, but after the murder of Pearl Bryan he was committed to the Lexington Insane Asylum. There was no known connection between Jackson or Walling and Dr. Wagner, thus it is unclear where they got his name, if the confessions were fabricated. These stories also explain the injection site on Pearl's chest and answer the holes in George Jackson's story, which would have to be a complete fabrication.

The confessions were sent to Governor Bradley, who stayed in his office late into the night with his advisors, discussing the subject. He was clear about a few points to the reporters who waited by his door. First, if these statements proved to hold any truth then the condemned men had previously lied in their testimony and so then, he could not trust the word of liars. Also, he said that he would look at the case by Kentucky law and no other. Specifically he was referring to the fact that in Ohio infanticide was only manslaughter, while Kentucky treated it as murder. So Jackson and Walling had admitted to helping to kill the child that Pearl carried and so were still guilty of murder.

Dr. Wagner was interviewed at the asylum and claimed he had never met Jackson or Walling or heard of Pearl Bryan until after the tragedy. The superintendent of the asylum was also interviewed and stated that Dr. Wagner was completely recovered from his mental troubles and that his hallucinations had nothing to do with the Bryan case. In his ravings, his caretakers said, he never mentioned the case or abortion or decapitation. His doctor was concerned this new attention might cause Wagner to have a relapse into his previous illness.

The confessions were coolly received by officials and the public. The problems with the confessions are fairly apparent. The prisoners were allowed to talk to one another, so they could have easily worked out the story together. Furthermore there is the question of why they didn't confess this information until what was essentially the last minute. Also, there was no real way to prove the story, especially since Dr. Wagner professed complete ignorance and had a friend back up his alibi for the night of the murder.

On the other hand, now that people had the time to process all the information from the trials, they began to form the story of Jackson, Walling, and Pearl Bryan. This is exemplified in Louis D. Poock's book, *Headless, Yet Identified*. Scott Jackson had been from one end of the country to the other filling his time with crime and debauchery. He came to Greencastle and in short order brought shame upon the innocent Pearl Bryan. From very early on, before he ever called her to Cincinnati, he had planned to kill her. He included his roommate, Alonzo Walling, in the plan because he knew

Walling would do whatever he said and was, like him, lacking in any moral character.

Jackson lured Pearl to Cincinnati, using Will Wood as his unsuspecting agent. She might have come with the intention of getting an abortion, but it was just as likely that Jackson had promised her that he would do right by her, as she may have secretly hoped. Jackson and Walling had been planning the murder for some time. People said they saw them walking along the roads of Fort Thomas for no obvious reason. Clearly they were looking for a good site to dump a body. Poock included in his speculation that Walling, for his part, might have tried to dissuade his partner, but Jackson would hear none of it.

Pearl came to Cincinnati and stayed at the Indiana House. Both Jackson and Walling called on her over the next two days, and it was believed that on Thursday she was "strolling about the streets" and went into a hairdresser's and a piano store. She ran into a boy she knew from Greencastle. She was then seen in the afternoon in Kentucky, taking a walk near the river. That night she and Jackson went to a medium, who claimed Pearl confided in her, and the medium told her to go to her mother and confess everything and all would be right. The next day, her last day according to the story, she was seen arguing with Walling in Cincinnati. Then she was seen waiting in the Grand Central depot, apparently intending to board a train. Walling came and took her back, refusing to give her her clothes or money so that she could return home to Greencastle. From there she was taken eventually to Wallingford's saloon with Jackson and Walling, where they got a cab. Then, for some reason, they rented a carriage and hired George Jackson as the driver. In Locke's field, Jackson attacked Pearl and slit her throat. Then Walling held her down as Jackson removed her head. Jackson carried the head with him for several days in a valise, until he disposed of it by throwing it in the river or by burning it. Walling helped get rid of Pearl's clothes, and they stayed in the city, confident that they had gotten away with a gruesome murder. Poock determines all of this from a few witnesses and perhaps a little imagination. Yet, this was basically the story that everyone in the nation agreed upon.

There are problems with this story as well. The claims that Pearl was spotted in various places around the area over the course of that week are questionable as they rely on people who did not know Pearl, but recognized her only from a published drawing or photograph sometimes weeks after the fact. In a case with this much attention, there must have been many supposed sightings, and it is not clear why the prosecution believed these particular accounts. Much of Poock's story was assumed, such as the head being in the valise or that Pearl wanted to leave but was not allowed.

The end result was that the truth, if it was to be found, had been buried under lies and half-truths, stories that never completely added up. George Jackson, the unsuspecting driver, would seem to have the most damaging story for Jackson and Walling since it puts them in Locke's field on the night of the murder with an unnamed girl, who could only be Pearl Bryan. Yet, there was no one that could corroborate his story; several people testified against it (a few later recanted), and there is the fact that it seemed unlikely that George Jackson could have made it back to Cincinnati so much faster than a world-record-holding long-distance runner.

Probably the most damaging testimony for Jackson and Walling came from Jackson and Walling themselves. They blamed each other from the start and implicated each other in Pearl's death, while at the same time suggesting they weren't involved. The public, the police, and eventually the juries seemed to think this was an admission of guilt on both their parts and instead of believing one over the other, the juries found both guilty. Since both men admitted to certain things, like meeting with Pearl when she was at the Indiana House and then disposing of her clothing in the river, it seems almost certain that they were involved in her death, but the details of what happened from the Wednesday when Pearl left the Indiana House to the Saturday morning when her body was found remain out of reach.

She might have been killed by the cocaine in her stomach, or the mysterious injection under her left breast, or even a blow to the head, which would never be known since the head was never found. She might have been killed by an abortion gone wrong. She might have died in Cincinnati, in the carriage ride to Fort Thomas, or in Locke's field under those bushes. The testimonies on how much blood was in Locke's field are contradictory and the presence of blood spatter is uncertain, especially since most of the evidence was taken away by souvenir hunters. Detective Crim did save a few leaves, but there is no record of these being tested or examined to determine if there was blood present. At the end of it all, the case is filled with many "might bes" and "possi-blys," but no satisfactory end to the mystery. Each person must look at the evidence and make their own conclusion.

TWENTY-THREE

PENALTIES

Mr. Frank Vonderheide, a cordage dealer, made two twenty-five-foot-long sturdy ropes. They were made of silver finish flax sewing twine with four strands of 110 threads each. As asked for by Sheriff Plummer, the rope intended for Jackson had four red threads woven in each strand and Walling's rope had four black strands. They were declared to be fine examples of the rope-maker's craft, though they were made only to be used one time. The scaffold, erected in a fenced-in yard behind the Newport jail, was finished on March 18, 1897, and tested the next day by Sheriff Plummer. Plain black suits were ordered for the prisoners to wear. Sheriff Plummer received the official death warrant.

On the night of the 19th, the prisoners were moved from Covington to Newport; as usual, a crowd gathered to observe them. The date of the double executions was set for the next day at noon. It was a Saturday morning that dawned clear and bright, and light flooded through the windows of the little Newport jail as the condemned men raised themselves for the last time. Scott Jackson and Alonzo Walling were surprisingly calm, Walling even joking with someone outside his window. They watched the crowd gathering and donned their black suits. Jackson pulled a chair up and stood on it to get closer to his window, and in a clear voice he began to sing hymns to the crowd gathered below. "In the Sweet Bye and Bye" came out of his mouth like "a death chant," the *Enquirer* reported. Jackson then turned to the guard near him and stated that Walling was innocent.

Many people had been waiting for just such a statement from Jackson. Walling's defense and his remaining friends seized the opportunity. They knew that only Jackson could save Walling. Word came back from Colonel Washington, Walling's attorney, that if Jackson would agree to writing a statement or giving testimony that Walling was not present when Pearl was killed, the governor would save Walling. Jackson, however, would not admit this. "I can't say that. That's a trap. I can't say that Walling was not there without admitting that I was there." Sheriff Plummer was told that if Jackson made a full confession on the gallows, he might spare Walling's life; but beyond that the executions should go on as scheduled.

Their last meal was breakfast. They had been told they could order anything; Jackson asked for ham, eggs, buckwheat cakes, and coffee. Walling said he would simply have the same as Jackson. They sat down with each other and tried to eat, but barely touched their food or drank the coffee. They could hear the crowd outside, in the sunshine, and talked quietly of the happenings since coming back to Newport. They forced smiles and tried to appear calm and polite, but the veneer was thin and everyone in the room felt the weight of mortality upon them.

Just before noon they were taken out into the courtyard, where the gallows' shadow stretched out before them. The large crowd grew silent as they came out. There was no shouting or jeering. It had been over a year since the body had been found, on another Saturday much different than this one, but the crowd did not exude anger. As Pearl's visibly aged father, Alex Bryan, had told the press, he wanted justice, not vengeance. Perhaps this was the thought among the spectators; perhaps they were waiting to see if Jackson would confess all and save Walling.

THE COURT MIGHT have dismissed Wood's case, but not all parties were so forgiving. Pearl's family let it be known that they believed Will Wood was primarily responsible for the young girl's fate. Will had introduced Jackson and Pearl, he had helped her hide her shame, and he tried to abort the pregnancy by following Jackson's commands. Finally, he was the one that took her from her parents' home and sent her off to the villains who would take her life. Whatever ties existed between the Woods and the Bryans were destroyed.

Pearl's family's grief is evident even in the restrained mentions of it in the papers. Her family was hurt, yes, stricken with a pain that must have been unbearable at times. They had lost family members before, to disease, but this was different. The source of pain had names and faces. With this came a great feeling of anger, a wish, a desire, for vengeance. This emotional response resided mostly in the male members of the family, but it had been tempered by Pearl's father: "justice, not vengeance."

SCOTT JACKSON AND ALONZO WALLING ascended the wooden steps and stood before the crowd. A few photographs were taken, including those by Frank G. Sheppard, an *Enquirer* reporter, whose pictures were redrawn and printed in the paper the following day. From the distance it is hard to tell the two men apart, as they both wore the same dark suits; but Jackson is on the left and Walling on the right. The gallows extend behind them, toward a high wood plank fence in the background. Several men are standing on the platform and the crowd captured in the image appears to be all men, dressed in suits and hats. In contrast to the somber air in the courtyard, birds were said to be singing on the other side of the fence.

Detective Cal Crim stood in the crowd and later related his experience: "I could see them as they stood over the trap and before the black caps were drawn down over their faces. They were asked if they had anything to say, Walling first, and he said, 'I am not guilty.' Then the question was put to Jackson and I saw Walling turn to look at him with earnest expectancy in his face. With rare stolidity, Scott Jackson declared he had nothing to say. The trap was sprung and I turned away."

Crim was asked if he thought Walling was innocent. He replied that he believed Walling was "a simple country boy who fell under the blighting influence of an older and much more sinister man."

When the trap was opened, both men dropped with force. They were motionless for a moment but then both of them began to squirm and their bound hands began to clench the air. Their legs jerked, trying to find purchase that wasn't there. It was clear that the hangings had not been done properly, because they should have died instantly when they dropped. Instead they were being slowly strangled to death. It took both men several minutes to finally stop moving. A physician who had been standing by checked the men and declared them dead. For most people, justice was finally done. Pearl Bryan had been avenged and the monsters were slain.

The *New York Times* headline read the next day, "Jackson and Walling Die." Papers across the country and abroad spread the news. The details each article chose to print differed, but the outcome was the same, the murderers were now dead.

EPILOGUE

FIVE YEARS AFTER THE DISCOVERY OF THE BODY, COLONEL Locke estimated that hundreds of people still stopped at his house and asked to be shown where the body was found. A path had been worn from the Alexandria Pike to the low hill where Pearl Bryan's body had been discarded. There was even a register where some of the visitors had recorded their names and places of origin over the years. They came from California and Oklahoma, New York and Pennsylvania. There were even visitors from Europe, Australia, and one gentleman from South Africa who came specifically to America just to visit the crime scene. They wanted to see the spot where it all started, where young Jack Hewling stumbled through the fog and found the stuff of nightmares. Locke had tried for a short time to keep the curiosity seekers away, but it turned out to be impractical. Eventually he gave up and tried to entertain the visitors and continue to run his farm as best he could. Locke also tried to plant a rose garden on the spot—unknowingly he selected the Jackson Rose—but it made no difference as every last one was pulled from the ground as a memento. Despite the destruction, those who came were always somber and silent at the spot; some of them felt they knew what had happened there, but some probably wondered what really brought Pearl Bryan to this lonely bit of Kentucky farmland.

SCOTT JACKSON'S BODY was cremated, after the wishes of his family. His body was reduced to a few pounds of ashes and then placed in a plain earthen jar. His sister and her husband, Professor Edwin Post of DePauw University, took the jar. Its final resting place is unknown.

ALONZO WALLING'S BODY was taken to Greenwood Cemetery in Hamilton, Ohio, the current home of his family. There was a brief funeral with family members and a few members of the press, but the arrangements had been made secretly and the public was not aware, believing that Walling had been cremated like Jackson. He was buried in section L, without a marker, in a steel coffin that boasted heavy locks. The service and burial were constantly disrupted with the cawing of the large number of crows who had made their home in the cemetery. By the time it was done night had set in and the mourners left, leaving the disturbed earth to the darkness and the still rustling crows.

In April, the *Enquirer* ran an article headlined, "Verdicts: From an Excited Public, Often as Unfair as the Edicts of a Despot." The heart of the article was that Alonzo Walling was completely innocent of all charges and that Scott Jackson had implicated his roommate simply as a scapegoat, "the cowardly bloodhound clutched at his roommate as the drowning pirate of one of Gerstaeker's sea tales of the ship-

wrecked sailor at his side." The author stated firmly that the
tale of George Jackson was a complete fabrication, without
naming the witness directly. The chief argument is that brief
moment when it seemed Jackson might confess all and free
Walling, though it seemed clear Jackson never intended to do
such a thing. The author points out that Walling had consistently proclaimed his innocence, not mentioning that Jackson
did the same. In fact, this author had saved all his or her sympathy for Walling, while Jackson was "a dastard stained by
every infamy and every vice, a thief, a slanderer, a whining
hypocrite, a libertine, a pimp, a parasite, a liar devoid not
only of the sense of truth, but of its substitute, the sense of
probability." How many people shared this view is unknown,
but it was obvious that even though they were dead, Jackson
and Walling would live on.

It did not take long before the spirit of Scott Jackson tried
to communicate with the living. In Anderson, Indiana,
Jackson's spirit was said to manifest itself to a group of spiritualists. Disappointingly, he said nothing about the murder
mystery, but only asked for sympathy. Pearl Bryan's spirit
had previously come to spiritualists and claimed that Scott
Jackson and Alonzo Walling had not murdered her.

Baptist reverend Lee, who had spoken closely with both
Jackson and Walling, was immediately caught up in a scandal after the executions, as he was accused of offering to sell
confessions from the dead men to a newspaperman. The
Baptist Ministers' Association investigated the allegations
and was expected to censure Reverend Lee and speak out
against the newspaperman who had tempted and trapped the
minister.

By early April, the publishers Barclay & Co. of Cincinnati
were selling for twenty-five cents a copy an anonymously
authored pamphlet with the sensational title *The Mysterious
Murder of Pearl Bryan or: The Headless Horror*. Copies were

sold on street corners and at train depots. The small book contained full-page illustrations that didn't bear much relation to any trial testimony or known likenesses of the primary actors, but were exciting all the same. Certain details were taken directly from the newspaper coverage of the case, while other details seemed to have been invented for effect. For instance, despite the many times that experts commented on the fact that the weapon used against Pearl must have had a razor-sharp edge, the writer or writers of *The Headless Horror* say her head was removed with a "dull knife." These sorts of short books or pamphlets recounting sensational crimes were very common, and the publisher no doubt made a fine profit.

The years stretched on. America finally went to war with Spain—Fort Thomas's 6th Infantry Regiment charged valiantly up San Juan Hill—and a new century dawned. The names of Pearl Bryan, Scott Jackson, and Alonzo Walling were heard less and less. Slowly the nation forgot the case, though it remained an occasional topic in Cincinnati, Covington, and Newport, or in Greencastle. When Allen Johnson, the former porter at Wallingford's saloon, appeared in the papers regarding an investigation into a fraudulent charity, his connection to the case was briefly noted. Anytime the news mentioned anyone connected to the case, they would often add, "who, it will be remembered, figured prominently in the Pearl Bryan case." The claims of finding Pearl's head grew less common; none seemed plausible. At the end of the century, Chief Phillip Deitsch declared the Pearl Bryan case his most famous. Many crimes were compared to the case, and many killers and would-be killers were compared to Scott Jackson.

FIVE YEARS AFTER HIS daughter's death, Alexander Bryan passed away. Her mother, Susan, lived until 1913 when she passed on as well. Of her twelve children, only six survived her. Mary Stanley, Pearl's widowed sister who pleaded with Jackson and Walling for her sister's head, lived until 1939. There is no evidence that she ever remarried, but what she did for the forty-three years after her sister's murder is not known.

PEARL'S SECOND COUSIN, Will Wood, who introduced her to Jackson and sent her off to Cincinnati, faced a possible federal investigation into his involvement in the crime after Jackson and Walling were executed. The investigation was never carried out. In 1897 he joined the navy and was recorded to be aboard the battleship *Iowa* in 1898, serving as secretary to the lieutenant commander. The USS *Iowa* saw plenty of action in the Spanish-American War, firing the first shot in the Battle of Santiago de Cuba. In 1901, living in Lebanon, Indiana, Will Wood related a tale that for the past several years someone, or some group of people, appeared to be intent on taking his life. He had been attacked multiple times over the years, not counting his time in the navy, when he was almost stabbed in a theater in Chicago and shot at in a hotel room in Baltimore, though the bullet missed its target. He seemed sure that it was connected to the fact that the Bryan family still blamed him for Pearl's death. After this, Will Wood disappears from the record. There is a William F. Wood of the right age living in South Bend, Indiana, in 1910. He has a wife, Blanche, and two adopted children, Mary and Calvin, and a servant by the name of Pearl Brown, born in Indiana.

IN 1899, GEORGE JACKSON, the cabman whose testimony put Jackson and Walling in Locke's field on the night of January 31, came back to the spot where the headless body was found. He was now officially a soldier, in the 9th Infantry Regiment.

He happened to run into Colonel Locke, who asked him to have his picture taken so that he could add it to the mementos concerning the Bryan case on display at the farm. A year later, George, apparently having left the military, was back in Cincinnati and arrested on suspicion of stealing from his employer, a barber. George Jackson was not unknown to the wrong side of the law; while the Jackson-Walling trials had been taking place, he had been wanted on charges of perjury in Springfield, Ohio. He later spent some time in jail for the charges. Seemingly, the last mention of George Jackson is in 1902 when his wife, Fannie, was granted a divorce from him on the grounds of "willful absence."

Louis D. Poock would go on to write the short book, *Headless, Yet Identified*, which detailed his involvement in the case and the information he gained from the trials. He moved to Dayton, Ohio, not long after helping to solve the case and having to sell his business. Over the years he was consulted in various cases to try and identify bodies through their shoes, which became something of a hobby for him when he was not selling shoes. There is nothing to indicate he was ever able to solve another crime, however. Poock died in 1923 in his home in Dayton.

October 21, 1901, dawned bright, and Cincinnati's streets were busy with the usual traffic. Cal Crim, now sergeant of detectives for the Cincinnati Police Department, spotted a thin-faced man with a dark mustache and his collar pulled up. John Foley, otherwise known as Foley the Goat, was a convicted thief and practiced pickpocket. He had been released from prison the week before, and since then numerous cases of pocket theft had occurred and the police department was under general orders to pick up the Goat if they saw him. Crim was actually on his way to his first vacation in

five years, since the time of the Fort Thomas tragedy. He had
a small suitcase with him of things he would need for the
trip, to hunt rabbit near Aurora, Indiana. Yet when he saw
Foley, his instincts kicked in and he immediately approached
the man.

"Hello John," Crim said broadly. "The Colonel would like
to see you at headquarters. He wants to talk to you. Will you
ride or walk down?"

He grabbed Foley's arm, to which the Goat replied, "Say,
is it a pinch?"

Crim told him that it was. With that Foley pulled a
revolver from a coat pocket, put it to Crim's side, and pulled
the trigger. Crim turned, staggered, and fell to a sitting position. Foley shot at Crim again and then took off at a run. A
porter from a nearby hotel ran to Crim. The detective cried
out, "That man shot me. Catch him." Crim was helped up
with difficulty and a bullet fell from inside his clothes. It was
the second shot fired by Foley, which had been slowed by
Crim's hunting clothes and a stack of tickets, and so did not
pierce his skin. After that he was taken to the city hospital.
Foley was chased down by a mob and finally captured by two
policemen. He tried to shoot one, but the gun failed to discharge. The news of the assault quickly spread. Detective
Crim had become the most famous and popular detective on
the force. But his shooting was hardest felt in a small home in
Walnut Hills, to a grief-stricken wife and four children.

Crim's prospects did not seem good. On October 23, the
headline read "Physicians say He is Doomed." But by the
28th, the physicians said his condition was encouraging. In
November, Crim's condition had taken a turn for the worse,
and his attending doctors were giving him just hours to live.
Foley the Goat was in jail, awaiting his fate, his status as a
near-cop-killer made him popular with the other prisoners.
Yet Crim did not die. He steadily improved so much that,

despite a persistent cough, at Christmas he was able to present his attending nurses with gold watches.

Crim finally returned to the force after a year-long recovery. Through contributions from concerned citizens he moved into a new house in the nicer neighborhood of Hyde Park. His number of arrests was never officially recorded, but in his twenty-eight years on the force it must have been especially high. In 1913 he retired as chief of detectives and started the Cal Crim Detective Bureau, the first private detective firm in Ohio.

The firm investigated many cases, including murders and kidnappings, but perhaps Crim's most famous case was the 1919 Black Sox scandal. He was able to discover that the Chicago White Sox had purposely threw games in the World Series to the Cincinnati Reds. For his service, Cal Crim received a lifetime pass to any Major League Baseball game. In his later years he was driven around by a chauffeur in his Cadillac, still attending to responsibilities at what would become Cal Crim Security, Inc. He died in 1953, at the age of eighty-nine. The city he had always called home was then the eighteenth most populous in the U.S.; by 2014 it would be ranked sixty-fifth. Cincinnati is no longer the largest city in Ohio, having been eclipsed by Cleveland and Columbus.

IN INDIANA, THE NAME PEARL BRYAN is attached to numerous legends. She would take unwanted babies from female students at DePauw University. She is a headless ghost, who appears at the side of the road or is seen roaming Forest Hill Cemetery. No one is certain when or how it started, but visitors to Greencastle began to leave coins on her headstone, heads up. The idea being that it was figuratively giving her a head, in place of the one she lost, for the afterlife. Visitors too, not with the same sense of altruism, began to take chips from the gravestone as mementos. Of all the legends and ghost stories, this one is surely true, because the headstone meant to mark Pearl's grave is now nothing more than a blank, pock-marked block.

SOURCES

A FTER CONTACTING ARCHIVES, HISTORICAL SOCIETIES, museums, and various local government offices in Ohio, Kentucky, and Indiana, I learned that none of the police reports, trial transcripts, or evidence used in the case survived, except for a copy of the original indictment in the Kentucky State Archives, and a valise and pair of shackles rumored to be from the case, but without provenance. My main sources for information directly about the case were newspaper articles from the *Cincinnati Enquirer*, *Kentucky Post*, and *Louisville Courier-Journal*. Once the story gained national attention I pulled information from the *New York Times*, as well as the newspaper records of the Library of Congress.

Two other primary sources were Louis D. Poock's book, *Headless, Yet Identified*, specifically recounting his role in the investigation. This source provided much of the narrative of the methods used to identify the victim, specifically the parts that Poock relates in which he was present and part of the action. Also there is the sensational pamphlet *The Mysterious Murder of Pearl Bryan or the Headless Horror*, which I did not rely upon heavily since there were several errors and obvious fictions.

Much of the census data was pulled from Family Search, along with birth, marriage, and death records. For information outside the main narrative of the case I relied on books of the time: Charles Dickens' *American Notes for General Circulation*, Frances Willard's *Wheel Within a Wheel*, as well as books on homeopathic medicine from the end of the nineteenth century. H. Clay Trumbull's *Hints on Child-training* and Jacob Riis' *The Children of the Poor* provided helpful insight into the care and treatment of children in different classes during this period.

Much of my information regarding abortion and contraception of the time comes from Janet Brodie's book *Abortion and Contraception in Nineteenth-Century America*. Also I relied on journal articles found on JSTOR, some from the time period (such as those written by Francis Galton) and others more recent. All secondary sources are either from reputable journals on JSTOR or online information provided by accredited universities. Most of the details concerning Detective David Calvin Crim are from *Cincinnati Enquirer* articles and from a biographical article in *Cincinnati Magazine*.

I have separated out the sources used by chapter to make it clearer for those doing research on any of topics covered in this book. I have repeated sources used in several chapters. The sources are presented in the order they were used.

PROLOGUE

Primary Sources

Cincinnati Enquirer, Jan. 31, 1896, page 1, scanned image, accessed from www.proquest.com

"Fair." *Cincinnati Enquirer*, Feb. 2, 1896.

"For Woman's Eyes." *Cincinnati Enquirer*, Feb. 1, 1896.

"Frisco's." *Cincinnati Enquirer*, Oct. 24, 1895.

"Miss Cowen's Card Party." *Cincinnati Enquirer*, Feb. 1, 1896.

"The City's Health." *Cincinnati Enquirer*, Jan. 1, 1896.

"Black." *Cincinnati Enquirer.* Aug. 3, 1895.

"Special Dispatch to, T. E.: Never Thought of It." *Cincinnati Enquirer*, Jan. 15, 1894.

"Another Link." *Kentucky Post*, microfilm, Feb. 17, 1896.

Willard, Frances Elizabeth, "Address before the Second biennial Convention of the World's Women's Christian Temperance Union, and the Twentieth Annual Convention of National Women's Christian Temperance Union . . . , World's Columbian Exposition, Chicago, . . . 1893." LSE Selected Pamphlets, 1893.

Medical Century: An International Journal of Homeopathic Medicine and Surgery, Vol. 3, ed. Charles Edmund Fisher, MD, January–December 1895, Chicago (*information about Dr. Stella Hunt*).

American Homeopathist, Vol. 15, ed. Frank Kraft, MD, 1889, A.L. Chatterton & Co., New York (*information about Dr. Stella Hunt*).

Dickens, Charles, *American Notes for General Circulation*, 1842, Chapman and Hall, London.

Ouida, "The New Woman," *North American Review*, 158, no. 450, May 1894.

Willard, Frances Elizabeth, *Wheel Within a Wheel*, Women's Temperance Publishing Association, Chicago, 1895.

"United States Census, 1900," *FamilySearch*, accessed 18 July 2015, Helen D. Cowen in household of Nancy Frasier, Richland Township, St. Clairsville, Belmont, Ohio, United States, citing sheet 9A, family 208, NARA microfilm publication T623. Washington, D.C.: National Archives and Records Administration.

"Ohio, Births and Christenings, 1821-1962," *FamilySearch*, accessed June 20, 2015, Helen Denver Cowen, 5 Dec 1880; citing

St. Clairsville, Belmont, Ohio, vol. 2 p. 134; FHL microfilm 902,140.

Secondary Sources

"Population of the 100 Largest Urban Places: 1840," U.S. Bureau of the Census, Internet Release date: June 15, 1998; http://www.census.gov/population/www/documentation/twps0 027/tab07.txt. (This is Table 7, I also used Table 6, and Table 5 for 1830 and 1820 respectively. The paper on this data can be found here: http://www.census.gov/population/www/documentation/ twps0027/twps0027.html.)

"The Depression of 1893," http://projects.vassar.edu/1896/depression.html.

"Caldwell, John Alexander," accessed July 2015, http://bioguide. congress.gov/scripts/biodisplay.pl?index=C000034.

Buzwell, Greg, "Daughters of Decadence: The New Woman in the Victorian fin de siècle," Discovering Literature: Romantics and Victorians, accessed June 2015, http://www.bl.uk/romantics-and-victorians/articles/daughters-of-decadence-the-new-woman-in-the-victorian-fin-de-siecle.

Fisher, Jim, "Alphonse Bertillon: The Father of Criminal Identification," http://jimfisher.edinboro.edu/forensics/bertillon 1.html, accessed November 1, 2014.

Giffin, William Wayne, *African Americans and the Color Line in Ohio, 1915-1930*, Ohio State University, 2005. (This book contains information about the George Street Tenderloin District.)

Greve, Charles Theodore, *Centennial History of Cincinnati and Representative Citizens*, Biographical Publishing Company, Chicago, 1904.

The Encyclopedia of Northern Kentucky, ed. Paul A. Tenkotte and James C. Claypool, University Press of Kentucky, 2009.

Duke, Thomas S., *Celebrated Criminal Cases of America*, James H. Barry Company, San Francisco, 1910.

History of the Upper Ohio Valley with Family History and Biographical Sketches, Vol. 2, Brant & Fuller, Madison, Wisconsin, 1890. (This contains the history of the Frasiers in Belmont County from which Helen Denver Cowen was descended on her mother's side.)

Painter, Sue Ann, *Architecture in Cincinnati: An Illustrated History of Designing and Building an American City*, Ohio University Press, 2006, Athens.

Prout, Jerry, "Hope, Fear, and Confusion: Coxey's Arrival in Washington," *Washington History*, 25, Summer 2013.

Poole, W. Scott, *Monsters in America: Our Historical Obsession with the Hideous and Haunting*, Baylor University Press, Waco, Texas, 2011.

Schwantes, Carlos A., "Western Women and Coxey's Army in 1894," *Arizona and the West*, 26, no. 1 (Spring 1984).

Spence, Clark C., "Knights of the Tie and Rail—Tramps and Hoboes in the West," *Western Historical Quarterly*, 2, no. 1 (Jan. 1971)

Stradling, David, *Cincinnati: From River City to Highway Metropolis*, Arcadia Publishing, San Francisco.

Woody, Kaitlin, "H.H. Holmes (Herman Mudgett) Trial (1896): Selected Links and Bibliography," http://law2.umkc.edu/faculty/ projects/ftrials/holmes/holmeslinks.html.

CHAPTER I: ILL REPUTE

Primary Sources

"An Awful Find." *Cincinnati Enquirer*, Feb. 2, 1896.

"Murder is Done." *Cincinnati Enquirer*, Feb. 2, 1896.

"Local Brevities." *Cincinnati Enquirer*, June 4, 1885.

"Corner Tingley." *Cincinnati Enquirer*, April 22, 1896.

"Campbell County." *Cincinnati Enquirer*, November 7, 1894.

"The Inquest." *Cincinnati Enquirer*, Feb. 12, 1896.

"An Odd Mission." *Cincinnati Enquirer*, July 11, 1891.

Poock, L.D. (The Shoe Man), *"Headless, Yet Identified": A Story of the Solution of the Pearl Bryan or Fort Thomas Mystery Through the Shoes*, Hann & Adair, Printers, Columbus, Ohio, 1897.

"Sousa's Band Captures a Vast Audience at Music Hall—Brilliant Programme Admirably Rendered." *Cincinnati Enquirer*, April 6, 1895.

The Catalogue of the Phi Delta Theta, ed. Eugene Henry, Lewis Randolph, and Frank Dugan Swope, 6th edition, Phi Delta Theta, New York, 1894 (contains biographical information about Coroner Tingley).

Secondary Sources

Kuhnheim, Anthony W., *The Pearl Bryan Murder Story*, Campbell County Historical and Genealogical Society, Alexandria, KY, 1996.

The Mysterious Murder of Pearl Bryan or the Headless Horror, author unknown, Barclay and Company, 1896.

Brodie, Janet Farrell, *Contraception and Abortion in Nineteenth-Century America*, Cornell University Press, Ithaca, 1994.

Bryson, Bill, *Made in America: An Informal History of the English Language in the United States*, HarperCollins, New York, 1994.

Cohen, Anne B. *Poor Pearl, Poor Girl! The Murdered-Girl Stereotype in Ballad and Newspaper*, University of Texas Press, Austin, 1973.

The Encyclopedia of Northern Kentucky, ed. Paul A. Tenkotte and James C. Claypool, University Press of Kentucky, 2009.

"Walter Scott Tingley," http://www.findagrave.com/cgi-bin/fg.cgi?page=gr&GRid=48381431.

"In Praise of the Wrapper," http://walternelson.com/historia/2006/05/in_praise_of_the_wrapper.html.

Barnes, Jeffery G., *Fingerprint Sourcebook*, National Criminal Justice Reference Service, https://www.ncjrs.gov/pdffiles1/nij/225321.pdf, accessed June 12, 2015.

Shelton, Jacqueline, "Evil Becomes Her: Prostitution's Transition from Necessary to Social Evil in 19th Century America," dc.etsu.edu/cgi/viewcontent.cgi?article=2348&context=etd, East Tennessee State University, 2013.

Masson, Erin M., "The Women's Christian Temperance Union 1874-1898: Combating Domestic Violence." *Wm. & Mary J. Women & L.* 163 (1997) http://scholarshiplaw.wm.edu/wmjowl/vol3/issl/7.

"Frances Willard," http://www.wctu.org/frances_willard.html, accessed January 2015.

Reed, Addison, "Scott Joplin: Questions Remain," *Black Music Research Journal*, 10, no.1 (Spring 1990).

Reed, Addison, "Scott Joplin, Pioneer," *The Black Perspective in Music*, 3, no. 1 (Spring 1975).

Tenkotte, Paul, "Cincinnati's West End," History 515, Northern Kentucky University, Highland Heights. April, 2010. Lecture.

Warfield, Patrick, "March as Musical Drama and the Spectacle of John Philip Sousa," *Journal of American Musicological Society*, 64, no. 2 (Summer 2011).

Wilhelm, Robert, "The Mysteries of Pearl Bryan," http://www.nkyviews.com/campbell/text/pearl_wilhelm.html, accessed Feb. 2015.

CHAPTER 2: OUTRAGE

Primary Sources

"Mary Riggle." *Cincinnati Enquirer*, Feb. 2, 1896.

"In Newport." *Cincinnati Enquirer*, Feb. 3, 1896.

"Baffled." *Cincinnati Enquirer*, Feb. 3, 1896.

"More Mystery." *Cincinnati Enquirer*, Feb. 3, 1896.

"Accident." *Cincinnati Enquirer*, Feb. 1, 1896.

"Married in Covington." *Cincinnati Enquirer*, Feb. 2, 1896.

"Not a Clew Found." *Louisville Courier-Journal*, Feb. 3, 1896.

Bullitt, Joshua F. and John Feland, *The General Statutes of Kentucky*, Bradley and Gilbert Company, Louisville, 1887.

Hoffman, Frederick L., *Race Traits and Tendencies of the American Negro*, Macmillan, New York, 1896.

Poock, L.D. (The Shoe Man), *"Headless, Yet Identified": A Story of the Solution of the Pearl Bryan or Fort Thomas Mystery Through the Shoes*, Hann & Adair, Printers, Columbus, Ohio, 1897.

Secondary Sources

"Plessy v. Ferguson," Cornell University Law School, Legal Information Institute, accessed April 12, 2015, https://www.law.cornell.edu/supremecourt/text/163/537.

The Mysterious Murder of Pearl Bryan or the Headless Horror, author unknown, Barclay and Company, 1896.

Kuhnheim, Anthony W., *The Pearl Bryan Murder Story*, Campbell County Historical and Genealogical Society, Alexandria, KY, 1996.

Robertson, Stephen, "Signs, Marks, and Private Parts: Doctors, Legal Discourses, and Evidence of Rape in the United States, 1823-1930," *Journal of the History of Sexuality*, 8, no. 3, Jan. 1998.

O'Leary, James and Walter L. Moore, "Charles Gilbert Chaddock, His Life and Contributions," *Journal of the History of Medicine and Allied Sciences*, 3, July 1953.

Byrne, Lt. Charles, Adj. 6th U.S. Infantry, "The Sixth Regiment of Infantry," 1892, from *The Army of the United States Historical Sketches of Staff and Line with Portraits of Generals-in-Chief*, 1896, http://www.history.army.mil/books/R&H/R&H-6IN.htm.

Begley, Sarah, "'Redefining Rape': A Brief History of Rape in America," thedailybeast.com, 2013.

Wells-Barnett, Ida B., "The Red Record: Tabulated Statistics and Alleged Causes of Lynching in the United States," 1895, http://www.gutenberg.org/files/14977/14977-h/14977-h.htm.

Freedman, Estelle B., "Women's Long Battle to Define Rape," *Washington Post*, August 24, 2012.

Gullickson, Aaron, "Black-White Interracial Marriage Trends, 1850-2000," Sociology Department, Columbia University, Jan. 31, 2006, http://paa2006.princeton.edu/papers/60719.

Miller, Randall M., "Lynching in America: Context and a Few Comments," *Pennsylvania History: A Journal of Mid-Atlantic Studies*, 72, no. 3, Summer 2005, http://www.jstor.org/stable/2777 8679.

"Notable Kentucky African Americans Database," University of Kentucky Libraries, accessed May 13th, 2015, http://nkaa.uky.edu/subject.php?sub_id=153.

CHAPTER 3: BLOODHOUNDS

Primary Sources

"An Avenger." *Cincinnati Enquirer*, Feb. 2, 1896.

"At the Reservoir." *Cincinnati Enquirer*, Feb. 2, 1896.

"At the Reservoir." *Cincinnati Enquirer*, Feb. 3, 1896.

"Lizzie Borden." *Cincinnati Enquirer*, March 2, 1895.

"Filtration." *Cincinnati Enquirer*, Jan. 9, 1896.

"Numerous." *Cincinnati Enquirer*, Feb. 5, 1896.

"Special Dispatch to, T. E.: Whether." *Cincinnati Enquirer*, Feb. 1, 1896.

"Special Dispatch to, T. E.: Hard Blow." *Cincinnati Enquirer*, Feb. 5, 1896.

"Special Dispatch to, T. E.: Solution." *Cincinnati Enquirer*, Jan. 28, 1896.

"Special Dispatch to, T. E.: The Black Fiend." *Cincinnati Enquirer*, Jan. 13, 1896.

"Negro Lynched with Torture" *New York Times*, Oct. 31, 1895: http://query.nytimes.com/mem/archive-free/pdf?res= 940CE2DE 1139E033A25752C3A9669D94649ED7CF.

"Lizzie Halliday Dead." *New York Times*, June 29, 1918.

"Mrs. Halliday Seemed Sane." *New York Times*, June 2, 1894.

Barbour, John, *The Brus*, Book 6, accessed June 2, 2015, http://www.arts.gla.ac.uk/STELLA/STARN/poetry/BRUS/text 06.htm. One mention of the hound is as follows:

With him aucht hunder men and ma
A sleuth-hund had he thar alsua
Sa gud that wald chang for na thing,
And sum men sayis yeit that the king
As a strecour him noryst had
And sa mekill off him he maid
That hys awyn handis wald him feid.

Cais, John, De Canibus Britannicis/Of English Dogges, trans. Abraham Fleming, 1570, Project Gutenburg release date: Oct. 26, 2008, http://www.gutenberg.org/files/27050/27050-h/27050-h.htm.

Poock, L.D. (The Shoe Man), *"Headless, Yet Identified": A Story of the Solution of the Pearl Bryan or Fort Thomas Mystery Through the Shoes*, Hann & Adair, Printers, Columbus, Ohio, 1897.

Secondary Sources

Conway, John, "A Short History of Serial Killer Lizzie Brown Halliday," New York History Blog, http://newyorkhistoryblog. org /2014/08/11/a-short-history-of-serial-killer-lizzie-brown-halliday/. (This is not a traditional scholarly work, but the article cites newspapers within the text.)

The Mysterious Murder of Pearl Bryan or the Headless Horror, author unknown, Barclay and Company, 1896.

Kuhnheim, Anthony W., *The Pearl Bryan Murder Story*, Campbell County Historical and Genealogical Society, Alexandria, KY, 1996.

Masten, Scott E., "Public Utility Ownership in 19th-Century America: The "Aberrant" Case of Water," *Journal of Law, Economics, and Organization*, 27, no. 3, Jan. 22, 2010: http://www.kysq.org/docs/Masten.pdf.

Boyer, Mike, "Acclaimed City Water Works System Fueled Growth" (March 18, 2012), *Cincinnati Enquirer*, Reprinted online: http://cincinnatitriplesteam.org/documents/GCWW_Enquirer_Article_3-18-12_.pdf.

"The History of Drinking Water Treatment," EPA, (Feb. 2000), accessed June 14, 2015: http://www.epa.gov/ogwdw/consumer/pdf/hist.pdf.

"A Guide to Drinking Water Treatment and Sanitation for Backcountry & Travel Use," CDC, accessed June 30, 2015: http://www.cdc.gov/healthywater/drinking/travel/backcountry_water_treatment.html.

"The Trial of Lizzie Borden," accessed April 19, 2015: http://law2.umkc.edu/faculty/projects/ftrials/LizzieBorden/bordenaccount.html.

CHAPTER 4: TRAMPS

Primary Sources

"Not a Tramp." *Cincinnati Enquirer*, Sept. 8, 1895.

"At Brent Station." *Cincinnati Enquirer*, Feb. 3, 1896.

"Hanrihan Released." *Cincinnati Enquirer*, Feb. 5, 1896.

"He Had to Go, Sah." *Cincinnati Enquirer*, April 15, 1894.

"Damages for Broken Leg." *Cincinnati Enquirer*, May 8, 1903.

"Mrs. Hart Wept." *Cincinnati Enquirer*, Feb. 4, 1896.

"Special Dispatch to T.E.: You Dance!" *Cincinnati Enquirer*, Dec. 13, 1895.

"That Murder Mystery." *Louisville Courier-Journal*, Feb. 4, 1896.

Wayland, Francis, "Papers on Out-Door Relief and Tramps," Hoggson & Robinson, New Haven, 1877, http://quod.lib.umich.edu/cgi/t/text/text-idx?c=moa;idno=AAW7999.

Poock, L.D. (The Shoe Man), *"Headless, Yet Identified": A Story of the Solution of the Pearl Bryan or Fort Thomas Mystery Through the Shoes*, Hann & Adair, Printers, Columbus, Ohio, 1897.

Secondary Sources

Leonard, Frank, "'Helping' the Unemployed in the Nineteenth Century: The Case of the American Tramp," *Social Service Review*, 40, no. 4, Dec. 1966.

Katz, Michael B., *In the Shadow of the Poorhouse: A Social History of Welfare in America*, Basic Books, New York, 1986.

DePastino, Todd, *Citizen Hobo: How a Century of Homelessness Shaped America*, University of Chicago Press, 2003.

Harring, Sidney L., "Class Conflict and the Suppression of Tramps in Buffalo, 1892-1894," *Law & Society Review*, 11, no. 5, Summer 1977.

Cooper, Catherine, "Cincinnati's Super Sleuth," *Cincinnati Magazine*, August 1983.

The Mysterious Murder of Pearl Bryan or the Headless Horror, author unknown, Barclay and Company, 1896.

CHAPTER 5: MARRIAGE

Primary Sources

"United States Census, 1910," *FamilySearch* (https://familysearch .org/ark:/61903/1:1:MPX1-N7X: accessed July 26, 2015), John C. Kettner, Leola, McPherson, South Dakota, United States; citing enumeration district (ED) 303, sheet 3A, family 54, NARA microfilm publication.

"United States Census, 1900," *FamilySearch* (https://familysearch .org/ark:/61903/1:1:MSMY-KKP: accessed July 27, 2015), Conrad Kettner, Precinct 3 Grand Rapids City Ward 7, Kent, Michigan; citing sheet 4A, family 82, NARA microfilm publication T623.

"Michigan Marriages, 1868-1925," database with images, *FamilySearch* (https://familysearch.org/ark:/61903/1:1:N3V6- N8C: accessed July 29, 2015), Charles Wertsch and Frances Kettner, Aug. 31, 1908; citing Grand Rapids, Kent, Michigan, vol. 3, p. 173, rn 2866, Department of Vital Records, Lansing; FHL microfilm 2,342,681.

"United States Census, 1880," database with images, *FamilySearch* (https://familysearch.org/ark:/61903/1:1:MHSW-T1Z: accessed August 14, 2015), Mary Bryan in household of Alexander Bryan, Greencastle, Putnam, Indiana, United States; citing enumeration district 155, sheet 442C, Nara microfilm publication T9 (Washington DC: National Archives and Records Administration, n.d.), roll 0306; FHL microfilm 1,254,306.

"An Advertisement." *Cincinnati Enquirer*, May 21, 1894.

"Almost Positive." *Cincinnati Enquirer*, Feb. 5, 1896.

"Ballot Box Stuffer Attempts Murder." *New York Times*, March 9, 1895.

"Charged with Poisoning His Wife." *New York Times*, July 4, 1895.

"Death of a Good Woman." *Cincinnati Enquirer*, Feb. 3, 1896.

"He Had to Go, Sah." *Cincinnati Enquirer*, April 15, 1894.

"Husband Murder in India." *New York Times*, July 6, 1895.

"Mystery." *Cincinnati Enquirer*, Feb. 5, 1896.

"Murder in An Air Shaft." *New York Times*, Sept. 21, 1896.

"Some Passengers." *Cincinnati Enquirer*, Feb. 4, 1896.

"Special Dispatch to, T. E.: He Must Settle." *Cincinnati Enquirer*, May 20, 1894.

"Ties." *Cincinnati Enquirer*. Feb. 1, 1896.

"That Murder Case." *Daily Greencastle Banner and Times*, Feb. 3, 1896: https://newspapers.library.in.gov/cgi-bin/indiana?a=d&d=DGBT18960203-01&e=—en-20—1—txt-txIN————#.

The First Biennial Report of the State Board of Health and Medical Examiners, News Printing Company, Aberdeen, SD, 1914.

"Evangelical United Brethren Church 9th and Ann St—Newport," http://www.rootsweb.ancestry.com/~kycampbe/unitedbrethren.htm

Poock, L.D. (The Shoe Man), *"Headless, Yet Identified": A Story of the Solution of the Pearl Bryan or Fort Thomas Mystery Through the Shoes*, Hann & Adair, Printers, Columbus, Ohio, 1897.

Secondary Sources

Hartog, Hendrik, "Marital Exits and Marital Expectations in Nineteenth Century America," Georgetown University Law Center, 1991, http://scholarship.law.georgetown.edu/cgi/viewcontent.cgi?article=1016&context=hartlecture.

Schwartsberg, Beverly, "'Lots of Them Did That': Desertion, Bigamy, and Marital Fluidity in Late-Nineteenth-Century America," *Journal of Social History*, 37, no. 3, Spring 2004.

The Mysterious Murder of Pearl Bryan or the Headless Horror, author unknown, Barclay and Company, 1896.

CHAPTER 6: CHILDREN

Primary Sources

"The Cause." *Cincinnati Enquirer*, Feb. 4, 1896.

"Slaughtering Innocents." *Cincinnati Enquirer*, Aug. 13, 1882.

Burnett, J. Compton, MD, *Delicate, Backward, Puny, and Stunted Children: Their Developmental Defects, and Physical, Mental, and*

Moral Peculiarities Considered as Ailments Amendable by Treatment with Medicine, Homeopathic Publishing Company, 1895, London.

Riis, Jacob A., *The Children of the Poor*, Charles Scribner's Sons, New York, 1892.

Trumbull, Henry Clay, *Hints on Child-training*, John D. Wattles, Philadelphia, 1893.

Secondary Sources

The Mysterious Murder of Pearl Bryan or the Headless Horror, author unknown, Barclay and Company, 1896.

Cohen, Anne B., *Poor Pearl, Poor Girl!: The Murdered-Girl Stereotype in Ballad and Newspaper*, University of Texas Press, Austin, 1973.

Brodie, Janet Farrell, *Contraception and Abortion in 19th-Century America*, Cornell University Press, Ithaca, 1994.

Katz, Michael B., *In the Shadow of the Poorhouse: A Social History of Welfare in America*, Basic Books, New York, 1986.

Broder, Sherri, "Child Care or Child Neglect?: Baby Farming in Late-Nineteenth-Century Philadelphia," *Gender and Society*, 2, no. 2, Jun. 1988.

Hamlet, Barksdale, *History of Education in Kentucky*, Kentucky Department of Education, Frankfort, 1914.

Cayton, Andrew R. L., *Ohio: The History of a People*, Ohio State University Press, Columbus, 2002.

Lloyd, William J., "Understanding Late Nineteenth-Century American Cities," *Geographical Review*, 71, no. 4 (Oct. 1981).

Trachtenberg, Alan, *The Incorporation of America*, Hill and Wang, New York, 1982.

Institute of Medicine (US) Committee on the Future of Dental Education; Field MJ, editor. Dental Education at the Crossroads: Challenges and Change. Washington (DC): National Academies Press (US); 1995. 2, Evolution of Dental Education. Available from: http://www.ncbi.nlm.nih.gov/books/NBK232261.

Grace, Kevin, "Poor Pearl, Poor Girl! The Awful Story of the Murder of Pearl Bryan," http://libapps.libraries.uc.edu/liblog/2010/02/poor-pearl-poor-girl-the-awful-story-of-pearl-bryan%E2%80%99s-murder/, accessed Sept. 2015.

CHAPTER 7: SHOES

Primary Sources

Poock, L.D. (The Shoe Man), *"Headless, Yet Identified": A Story of the Solution of the Pearl Bryan or Fort Thomas Mystery Through the Shoes*, Hann & Adair, Printers, Columbus, Ohio, 1897.

"Wealthy Shoe Manufacturer Dies," http://old.minford.k12.oh.us/mhs/history/PortsmouthHistory/ShoeWorkers/GeorgeSelbyDies.htm, accessed Sept. 2015.

Secondary Sources

"The Portsmouth Shoe Industry," http://www.yourppl.org/history/items/show/268, accessed Sept. 2015.

"Reforming Fashion, 1850-1914: Politics, Health, and Art," http://costume.osu.edu/2000/04/14/reforming-fashion-1850-1914-politics-health-and-art/, accessed Sept. 2015.

Brodie, Janet Farrell, *Contraception and Abortion in 19th-Century America*, Cornell University Press, Ithaca and London, 1994.

Musto, David, "Opium, Cocaine and Marijuana in American History," *Scientific American* 1991, https://faculty.unlv.edu/mccorkle/www/Opium,%20Cocaine%20and%20Marijuana%20in%20American%20History.pdf.

"History of Cocaine," http://www-pub.naz.edu:9000/~jschmid2/templates/narrow_copy(1).htm, accessed Sept. 2015.

CHAPTER 8: GREENCASTLE

Primary Sources

"Nearer." *Cincinnati Enquirer*, Feb. 4, 1896.

"Poock's Discoveries." *Cincinnati Enquirer*, Feb. 5, 1896.

"Special Dispatch To, T.E.: Tragedy." *Cincinnati Enquirer*, June 10, 1897.

Jasper Weekly Courier, Aug. 2, 1872: https://newspapers.library.in.gov/cgi-bin/indiana?a=d&d=JWC18720802.1.6&srpos=1&e=————-en-20—1—txt-txIN-young+murder——-#.

Daily Greencastle Banner and Times, Feb. 4, 1896: https://newspapers.library.in.gov/cgi-bin/indiana?a=d&d=DGBT18960204-01&e=————-en-20—1—txt-txIN———.

Poock, L.D. (The Shoe Man), *"Headless, Yet Identified": A Story of the Solution of the Pearl Bryan or Fort Thomas Mystery Through the Shoes*, Hann & Adair, Printers, Columbus, Ohio, 1897.

Secondary Sources

"DePauw: History and Traditions," http://www.depauw.edu/about/history-traditions/, accessed Sept. 2015.

The Mysterious Murder of Pearl Bryan or the Headless Horror, author unknown, Barclay and Company, 1896.

"The Greencastle Fire of 1874," http://www.putnam.lib.in.us/lh/stories/fires.php, accessed Sept. 2015.

CHAPTER 9: AN ILLEGAL OPERATION

Primary Sources

"The Cause." *Cincinnati Enquirer*, Feb. 4, 1896.

Poock, L.D. (The Shoe Man), *"Headless, Yet Identified": A Story of the Solution of the Pearl Bryan or Fort Thomas Mystery Through the Shoes*, Hann & Adair, Printers, Columbus, Ohio, 1897.

Secondary Sources

Brodie, Janet Farrell, *Contraception and Abortion in Nineteenth-Century America*, Cornell University Press, Ithaca, 1994.

The Mysterious Murder of Pearl Bryan or the Headless Horror, author unknown, Barclay and Company, 1896.

Pollitt, Katha, "The Notorious Life of a Nineteenth Century Abortionist," *Nation*; http://www.thenation.com/article/notorious-life-nineteenth-century-abortionist/.

Kleinegger, Christine C., "Review: *The Wickedest Woman in New York: Madame Restell, The Abortionist* by Clifford Browder," *New York History*, 70, No. 3 (July 1989).

B.T.M, "Early Abortifacients," *Pharmacy in History*, 35, No. 2 (1993).

Peterson, Anna M., "From Commonplace to Controversial: The Different Histories of Abortion in Europe and the United States," *Origins*, 1, no. 2 (2012), http://origins.osu.edu/article/commonplace-controversial-different-histories-abortion-europe-and-united-states.

CHAPTER 10: PEARL AND SCOTT

Primary Sources

"United States Census, 1880," *FamilySearch* (https://familysearch.org/ark:/61903/1:1:MHSW-T1W: accessed October 5, 2015), Alexander Bryan, Greencastle, Putnam, Indiana, United

States; citingenumeration district 155, sheet 442C, NARA microfilm publication T9.

The United States Biographical Dictionary: Kansas Volume, S. Lewis & Co., 1879, Chicago and Kansas City.

"Pearl Bryan's Murder At Last Avenged." *Sacramento Daily Union*, March 21, 1897.

"Of The New Woman." *Indianapolis Journal*, Jan. 1, 1895.

Poock, L.D. (The Shoe Man), *"Headless, Yet Identified": A Story of the Solution of the Pearl Bryan or Fort Thomas Mystery Through the Shoes*, Hann & Adair, Printers, Columbus, Ohio, 1897.

Secondary Sources

The Mysterious Murder of Pearl Bryan or the Headless Horror, author unknown, Barclay and Company, 1896.

Coultrap-McQuin, Susan, "Gail Hamilton (1833-1896)," *Legacy*, 4, no. 2 (Fall 1987).

CHAPTER II: ARRESTED

Primary Sources

Appleton's Popular Science, Feb. 1896.

"At the Station." *Cincinnati Enquirer*, Feb. 6, 1896.

"Blood Spots." *Cincinnati Enquirer*, Feb. 6, 1896.

"Clothing Identified." *Louisville Courier-Journal*, Feb. 6, 1897.

"Identified." *Cincinnati Enquirer*, Feb. 6, 1896.

"Jackson Examined." *Cincinnati Enquirer*, Feb. 6, 1896.

"Lynching." *Cincinnati Enquirer*, Feb. 6, 1896.

"Special Dispatch to, T. E.: Tin Cup." *Cincinnati Enquirer*, Jan. 26, 1896.

Lunettes, Henry, *The American Gentleman's Guide to Politeness and Fashion*, Derby & Jackson, 1860, New York.

Poock, L.D. (The Shoe Man), *"Headless, Yet Identified": A Story of the Solution of the Pearl Bryan or Fort Thomas Mystery Through the Shoes*, Hann & Adair, Printers, Columbus, Ohio, 1897.

Secondary Sources

The Mysterious Murder of Pearl Bryan or the Headless Horror, author unknown, Barclay and Company, 1896.

Pillsbury, Samuel H., "Understanding Penal Reform: The Dynamic of Change," *Journal of Criminal Law and Criminology*,

Northwestern University, 1989; http://scholarlycommons.law.northwestern.edu/cgi/viewcontent.cgi?article=6631&context=jclc.

CHAPTER 12: THE ROOMMATE

Primary Sources

"Calendar of the Crime." *Cincinnati Enquirer*, May 15, 1896.

"Crime." *Cincinnati Enquirer*, Feb. 9, 1896.

"Wood Examined." *Cincinnati Enquirer*, Feb. 7, 1896.

"Walling Smiled." *Cincinnati Enquirer*, Feb. 7, 1896.

"Special Dispatch to T.E.: Another Suspect." *Cincinnati Enquirer*, Feb. 6, 1896.

"The Murder Mystery." *Wheeling Daily Intelligencer*, Feb. 6, 1896: http://Chroniclingamerica.Loc.Gov/Lccn/Sn84026844/1896-02-06/Ed-1/Seg-1/>.

"Jackson Gives Way" *Evening Star*, Washington, D.C., Feb. 4, 1896.

http://chroniclingamerica.loc.gov/ (Search of newspapers of the time that mention Pearl Bryan).

Secondary Sources

The Mysterious Murder of Pearl Bryan or the Headless Horror, author unknown, Barclay and Company, 1896.

Cohen, Anne B., *Poor Pearl, Poor Girl!: The Murdered-Girl Stereotype in Ballad and Newspaper*, University of Texas Press, Austin, 1973.

"Cincinnati's West End," Paul Tenkotte teacher, class at Northern Kentucky University, 2010.

Sasinoski, Megan, "Homicide Trends in America 1850-1950," Carnegie Mellon University, 2011, http://repository.cmu.edu/cgi/viewcontent.cgi?article=1137&context=hsshonors.

CHAPTER 13: METHODS

Primary Sources

"A In Words." *Cincinnati Enquirer*, Feb. 6, 1896.

"Disdain." *Cincinnati Enquirer*, April 19, 1896.

"Delving." *Cincinnati Enquirer*, June 13, 1896.

"In The World Of Science." *Louisville Courier-Journal*, Jan. 7, 1895.

"Special Dispatch to T. E.: A Checkered Career." *Cincinnati Enquirer*, Feb. 7, 1896.

"Psychological Notes," *Science*, 9, no. 216, March 1887.

Kellor, Frances Alice, "Criminal Anthropology in Its Relation to Criminal Jurisprudence," *American Journal of Sociology*, 4, no. 4, Jan., 1899.

Galton, Francis, "On the Causes Which Operate to Create Scientific Men," *Fortnightly Review*, 13 (1873).

Galton, Francis, "Three Generations of Lunatic Cats," *Spectator*, April 11, 1896.

For works by and about Sir Francis Galton: http://galton.org/.

Proceedings of the National Conference of Charities and Correction, ed. Isabel Barrows, Geo. H. Ellis, Boston, 1896.

Secondary Sources

The Mysterious Murder of Pearl Bryan or the Headless Horror, author unknown, Barclay and Company, 1896.

"What is Phrenology," Phrenology Lab, Stanford Medicine Web Training; accessed Oct. 2015; http://med.stanford.edu/medweb-training/shc-class/student5/treatments/phrenology-lab.html.

"Forensic Timeline," http://plaza.ufl.edu/jhefner/forensic_Time line.pdf.

Mitchell, Henry, "Maria Mitchell," *Proceedings of American Academy of Arts and Sciences*, Vol. 25 (May 1889–May 1890).

Pearson, Karl, *The Life, Letters and Labours of Francis Galton*, Cambridge University Press, London, 1914, 1924, 1930.

CHAPTER 14: BLAME

Primary Sources

"Face to." *Cincinnati Enquirer*, Feb. 7, 1896.

"Chief Deitsch and Mayor Caldwell Cross-Examining Jackson and Walling in the Chief's Private Office." *Cincinnati Enquirer*, Feb. 7, 1896.

"Jackson's Story." *Cincinnati Enquirer*, Feb. 7, 1896.

"Important Part." *Cincinnati Enquirer*, Feb. 7, 1896.

"Newport." *Cincinnati Enquirer*, Feb. 7, 1896.

"Poison." *Cincinnati Enquirer*, Feb. 7, 1896.

Secondary Sources

The Mysterious Murder of Pearl Bryan or the Headless Horror, author unknown, Barclay and Company, 1896.

CHAPTER 15: THE VALISE

Primary Sources

"The Police Court." *Cincinnati Enquirer*, Feb. 8, 1896.

"A Bloody Valise." *Cincinnati Enquirer*, Feb. 7, 1896.

"Head Not Buried." *Cincinnati Enquirer*, Feb. 9, 1896.

"Jackson Has A Theory." *Cincinnati Enquirer*, Feb. 9, 1896.

"Mrs. M'nevin." *Cincinnati Enquirer*, Feb. 8, 1896.

"All Day." *Cincinnati Enquirer*, Feb. 8, 1896.

"Where Was Walling?" *Cincinnati Enquirer*, Feb. 7, 1896.

"Secretary Tibbits." *Cincinnati Enquirer*, Feb. 8, 1896.

"Compendium of Eleventh Census," https://www.census.gov/prod/www/decennial.html.

Secondary Sources

The Mysterious Murder of Pearl Bryan or the Headless Horror, author unknown, Barclay and Company, 1896.

Trachtenberg, Alan, *The Incorporation of America*, Hill and Wang, New York, 1982.

Spargo, John, "Christian Socialism in America," *American Journal of Sociology*, 15, no. 1 (July 1909).

CHAPTER 16: FUNERAL

Primary Sources

"An Awful Scene." *Cincinnati Enquirer*, Feb. 9, 1896.

"Face To Face." *Cincinnati Enquirer*, Feb. 8, 1896.

"What Weapon." *Cincinnati Enquirer*, Feb. 3, 1896.

"Jackson's Razor." *Cincinnati Enquirer*, Feb. 9, 1896.

"Special Dispatch to T.E.: Beheaded." *Cincinnati Enquirer*, June 20, 1895.

"Missing." *Cincinnati Enquirer*, Feb. 12, 1896.

"Wholesale Removal of Federal Officers." *Cincinnati Enquirer*, Aug. 19, 1895.

Cunningham, John Daniel, *Manual of Practical Anatomy: Thorax, head and neck*, Young J. Pentland, Edinburgh, 1896.

Secondary Sources

The Mysterious Murder of Pearl Bryan or the Headless Horror, author unknown, Barclay and Company, 1896.

"The Kingsbury Run Murders," http://www.clevelandpolicemuseum.org/collections/kingsburyrun.html, accessed Nov. 2015.

CHAPTER 17: GEORGE JACKSON'S STORY

Primary Sources

"A Good Test." *Cincinnati Enquirer*, Feb. 17, 1896.

"Clinched." *Cincinnati Enquirer*, Feb. 16, 1896.

"The Inquest." *Cincinnati Enquirer*, Feb. 12, 1896.

"Another Link." *Kentucky Post*, Microfilm at Kenton County Public Library, Feb. 17, 1896.

"Sheriff Plummer." *Cincinnati Enquirer*, Feb. 13, 1896.

"Will Wood." *Kentucky Post*, Feb. 25, 1896.

CHAPTER 18: COMPLICATIONS

Primary Sources

"She Gave Her Drugs." *Indianapolis Journal*, Feb. 1, 1896.

"Special Dispatch to T.E.: An Awful Confession." *Cincinnati Enquirer*, Feb. 11, 1896.

"Don't Know Her." *Cincinnati Enquirer*, Feb. 14, 1896.

"Wood's Say." *Cincinnati Enquirer*, Feb. 21, 1896.

"Dismissed." *Cincinnati Enquirer*, Apr. 16, 1896.

"Special Dispatch to T.E.: Pearl's Father." *Cincinnati Enquirer*, Feb. 29, 1896.

"Many Visitors." *Cincinnati Enquirer*, Feb. 15, 1896.

"The Prisoners." *Cincinnati Enquirer*, Feb. 16, 1896.

"Special Dispatch to T.E.: Baptized." *Cincinnati Enquirer*, Feb. 16, 1896.

"Conflicting." *Cincinnati Enquirer*, Feb. 16, 1896.

"Special Dispatch to T.E.: Bob!" *Cincinnati Enquirer*, Feb. 17, 1896.

"Special Dispatch to T.E.: Ready." *Cincinnati Enquirer*, Feb. 19, 1896.

"Special Dispatch to T.E.: Bent." *Cincinnati Enquirer*, Jan. 10, 1897.

"Laws of the State of Indiana Passed at the Sixtieth Regular Session of the General Assembly, Wm. B. Surford, Indianapolis, 1897.

Secondary Sources

Reis, Jim, "Pearl Bryan Murder," printed from his book *Pieces of the Past:* Volume One; http://www.rootsweb.ancestry.com/~ky campbe/piecespearlbryan.htm.

"Pearl Bryan," http://www.findagrave.com/cgi-bin/fg.cgi?page= gr&GRid=30686832.

CHAPTER 19: MISTAKES

Primary Sources

"Letters." *Cincinnati Enquirer*, Feb. 20, 1896.

"Special Dispatch to T.E: Coachman Jackson." *Cincinnati Enquirer*, Feb. 20, 1896.

"A Report." *Cincinnati Enquirer*, Feb. 21, 1896.

"Mistakes of the Police in Handling the Pearl Bryan Case." *Kentucky Post*, March 13, 1896.

"Detectives." *Kentucky Post*, March 14, 1896.

"Cox." *Cincinnati Enquirer*, March 6, 1896.

"Influence." *Cincinnati Enquirer*, Feb. 23, 1896.

"Special Dispatch to T.E: Doubled," *Cincinnati Enquirer*, March 8, 1896.

"Why Women Want the Ballot." *Cincinnati Enquirer*, March 20, 1896.

"Sustained." *Cincinnati Enquirer*, March 17, 1896.

"In Newport." *Cincinnati Enquirer*, March 2, 1896.

"Nathoo." *Cincinnati Enquirer*, March 5, 1896.

"A Fair Trial." *Cincinnati Enquirer*, March 11, 1896.

Secondary Sources

Beall, Joel, "George 'Boss' Cox," http://www.cincinnati.com/story/ news/history/2015/02/26/george-cox-boss-cincinnati/24057179/.

"William Taft," http://millercenter.org/president/taft, accessed Nov 2015.

Trachtenberg, Alan, *The Incorporation of America*, Hill and Wang, New York, 1982.

CHAPTER 20: SUPPORTERS

Primary Sources

"At Last." *Cincinnati Enquirer*, March 13, 1896.

"In Eight Minutes." *Cincinnati Enquirer*, March 18, 1896.

"Now in Kentucky." *Louisville Courier-Journal*, March 18, 1896.

"In Their Cells." *Cincinnati Enquirer*, March 18, 1896.

"C. M. M. L.: Letter Writers." *Cincinnati Enquirer*, Feb. 22, 1896.

"Jackson." *Cincinnati Enquirer*, Feb. 18, 1896.

"No Row." *Cincinnati Enquirer*, March 27, 1896.

"Colonel Washington." *Cincinnati Enquirer*, March 24, 1896.

"Disappointed." *Cincinnati Enquirer*, March 20, 1896.

"Many Visitors." *Cincinnati Enquirer*, Feb. 20, 1896.

"Standing Room Only." *Cincinnati Enquirer*, Feb. 22, 1896.

"Cynical Views." *Cincinnati Enquirer*, March 2, 1896.

"Separately." *Cincinnati Enquirer*, March 24, 1896.

"Callers." *Cincinnati Enquirer*, March 21, 1896.

"Setting Traps for the Prisoners." *Louisville Courier-Journal*, March 20, 1896.

"Unsolved." *Cincinnati Enquirer*, August 31, 1895.

The History of the National Republican League of the United States, ed. John F. Hogan, Detroit, 1898.

Poock, L. D. (The Shoe Man), *"Headless, Yet Identified": A Story of the Solution of the Pearl Bryan or Fort Thomas Mystery Through the Shoes*, Hann & Adair, Printers, Columbus, Ohio, 1897.

Secondary Sources

The Mysterious Murder of Pearl Bryan or the Headless Horror, author unknown, Barclay and Company, 1897.

Griffiths, Mark D., "Passion Victim," *Psychology Today*, Oct. 2013, https://www.psychologytoday.com/blog/in-excess/201310/passion-victim.

"Crimes, Confessions, Culprits, and Convicts—19th Century Tales of Murder," http://blogs.law.harvard.edu/preserving/2013/01/17/crimes-confessions-culprits-and-convicts-19th-century-tales-of-murder/.

CHAPTER 21: SCOTT JACKSON'S TRIAL

Primary Sources

"Weather 1—no title." *Cincinnati Enquirer*, April 7, 1896.

"Whole Town." *Cincinnati Enquirer*, April 8, 1896.

"The Audience." *Cincinnati Enquirer*, April 8, 1896.

"Two Weeks Only." *Cincinnati Enquirer*, April 8, 1896.

"For Woman's Eyes." *Cincinnati Enquirer*, April 10, 1896.

"Holmes." *Cincinnati Enquirer*, April 10, 1896.

"Weather Forecast." *Cincinnati Enquirer*, April 22, 1896.

"Coroner Tingley." *Cincinnati Enquirer*, April 22, 1896.

"Face To Face." *Cincinnati Enquirer*, April 22, 1896.

"A Day." *Cincinnati Enquirer*, April 23, 1896.

"Damaging Evidence." *Louisville Courier-Journal*, April 24, 1896.

"Error." *Cincinnati Enquirer*, April 25, 1896.

"A Day." *Cincinnati Enquirer*, April 28, 1896.

"A Resume." *Cincinnati Enquirer*, May 3, 1896.

"Mass Of Contradiction." *Cincinnati Enquirer*, May 2, 1896.

"Jackson." *Cincinnati Enquirer*, May 1, 1896.

"Trusty." *Cincinnati Enquirer*, May 7, 1896.

"Trapped." *Cincinnati Enquirer*, May 5, 1896.

"Day In Detail." *Cincinnati Enquirer*, May 5, 1896.

"Closing Scene." *Cincinnati Enquirer*, May 15, 1896.

"Must Die." *Louisville Courier-Journal*, May 16, 1896.

"Jackson Is Guilty." *Maysville Evening Bulletin*, May 15, 1896.

"Murder In The First Degree." *Roanoke Daily Times*, May 15, 1896.

"He Was Found Guilty." *Arizona Republican*, May 15, 1896.

"Jackson Is Guilty." *Anaconda Standard*, May 15, 1896.

CHAPTER 22: STORIES

Primary Sources

"Liberty." *Cincinnati Enquirer*, May 17, 1896.

"Courts." *Cincinnati Enquirer*, May 13, 1896.

"Death." *Cincinnati Enquirer*, June 19, 1896.

"Miss Marre Dead." *Cincinnati Enquirer*, July 26, 1896.

"Complicated." *Cincinnati Enquirer*, July 29, 1896.

"Applications For Pardons." *Louisville Courier-Journal*, July 30, 1896.

"Jackson And Walling." *Louisville Courier-Journal*, Dec. 10, 1896.

"The Confession." *Louisville Courier-Journal*, March 19, 1896.

Poock, L.D. (The Shoe Man), *"Headless, Yet Identified": A Story of the Solution of the Pearl Bryan or Fort Thomas Mystery Through the Shoes*, Hann & Adair, Printers, Columbus, Ohio, 1897.

CHAPTER 23. PENALTIES

Primary Sources

"The Ropes Made." *Cincinnati Enquirer*, March 16, 1897.

"Ended." *Cincinnati Enquirer*, March 18, 1897.

"From Dawn to Death." *Cincinnati Enquirer*, March 21, 1897.

"Their Last Meal." *Cincinnati Enquirer*, March 21, 1897.

"Slowly." *Cincinnati Enquirer*, March 21, 1897.

"Where Pearl Bryan's Body Was Found." *Cincinnati Enquirer*, June 16, 1901.

"Cremated." *Cincinnati Enquirer*, March 21, 1897.

"Special Dispatch to T.E: Inclosed." *Cincinnati Enquirer*, March 26, 1897.

"Special Dispatch to T.E.: Spirit." *Cincinnati Enquirer*, Aug. 2, 1897.

"Verdicts." *Cincinnati Enquirer*, April 11, 1897.

"Rev. J.A. Lee's Case." *Louisville Courier-Journal*, April 4, 1897.

"Classified Ad 1—No Title." *Louisville Courier-Journal*, April 10, 1897.

"Harper." *Cincinnati Enquirer*, Feb. 6, 1898.

"Special Dispatch to T.E.: Will Wood." *Cincinnati Enquirer*, March 2, 1898.

"Special Dispatch to T.E: Hunted." *Cincinnati Enquirer*, Jan. 2, 1901.

"Enlisting." *Cincinnati Enquirer*, Sept. 20, 1899.

"George Jackson Again Arrested." *Cincinnati Enquirer*, June 9, 1900.

"Inherited." *Cincinnati Enquirer*, Jan. 6, 1902.

"Special Dispatch to T.E.: Two Charges." *Cincinnati Enquirer*, May 9, 1896.

"United States Census, 1910," *FamilySearch* (https://family search.org/ark:/61903/1:1:MK52-B26: accessed December 1, 2015), William F. Wood, South Bend Ward 4, St. Joseph, Indiana, United States citing enumeration district (ED) ED 174, sheet 1A, NARA microfilm publication T624.

Secondary Sources

Cooper, Catherine, "Cincinnati's Super Sleuth," *Cincinnati Magazine*, August 1983.

"Campbell County's 'Crime of the Century,'" image, accessed Nov.

2014; http://www.jacksonsun.com/apps/pbcs.dll/gallery?Site=A B &Date=20130321&Category=NEWS01&ArtNo=303210147& Ref=PH.

The Mysterious Murder of Pearl Bryan or the Headless Horror, author unknown, Barclay and Company, 1897.

"USS *Iowa* (BB 4)," accessed Nov. 2015, http://www.navy.mil/navy data/ships/battleships/iowa/bb4-iowa.html.

"Pearl Bryan's Shoes," accessed Dec. 2015, http://hauntedohio-books.com/news/pearl-bryans-shoes-mr-poock-and-the-clew-that-solved-her-murder/.

Epilogue

Primary Sources

"Thief's." *Cincinnati Enquirer*, Oct. 22, 1901.

"Encouraging." *Cincinnati Enquirer*, Oct. 28, 1901.

"Hopeless." *Cincinnati Enquirer*, Nov. 12, 1901.

"Crim is Better." *Cincinnati Enquirer*, Dec. 27, 1901.

"Slurred." *Cincinnati Enquirer*, Jan. 15, 1902.

Secondary Sources

Cooper, Catherine, "Cincinnati's Super Sleuth," *Cincinnati Magazine*, August 1983.

"The Murder of Pearl Bryan," http://www.prairieghosts.com/bobby.html.

Baker, Ronald L., *Hoosier Folk Legends*, Indiana University Press, Bloomington, 1982.

ACKNOWLEDGMENTS

THANKS AS ALWAYS TO MY EVER-PATIENT WIFE, WHOSE SELF-sacrificing nature makes it possible for me to do this sort of thing. Thanks to Bruce H. Franklin and everyone at Westholme Publishing for being so encouraging and helpful. My appreciation also goes to Dr. Paul Tenkotte who helped get me to many of the resources I needed for this book and introduced me to the story years ago. Also, I would like to thank Boone County Public Library, Kenton County Public Library, and Campbell County Public Library for their resources and help. I am indebted to the kind people at the Campbell County Historical Society, who are truly the custodians of the Pearl Bryan story. I would also like to thank my father, who has been so encouraging in my writing and my life. My wonderful children don't understand why I am so often hunched over the laptop or making trips to various libraries, but put up with it as best they can and sometimes pull me away for a much needed break. Also it wouldn't be right if I didn't thank Shirley and Bill Robinson for the kind support and interest.

INDEX